What They're Saying

MW00770964

"Brilliant – an instant classic! *Playing Well V* conscious kink for years to come. This en indispensable wisdom for newcomers and experienced players alike. I love this book!" – Barbara Carrellas, Author, *Urban Tantra, Ecstasy is Necessary*

"Mollena Williams and Lee Harrington are a much-needed team of sex ed bandits on the loose, spreading their gospel of stigma-free power exchange in everyday life. This lifestyle advice and community guide's 'choose your own adventure' approach will be helpful to all readers from curious closeted freaks to experienced public pervs." – Abiola Abrams, *Official Bombshell Handbook,* Curator of Passionate Living at AbiolaTV.com

"A reader-friendly, upbeat, one-stop guide to everything you need to know to play safely and joyfully in the BDSM community, from defining your own journey to playing well with others. Authors Harrington and Williams bring their own special brand of intelligence, warmth, fun and wisdom to dispelling myths and promoting blissful BDSM in a book that is an instant classic in BDSM education." – Dr. Gloria G. Brame, *Different Loving, Come Hither: The Truth About Sex*

"If you've wondered about venturing into that strange and mythical bunch of people who supposedly have those dangerous whips-and-handcuffs parties in sleazy clubs or dim basements, but the stereotype has scared you off, take heart: Lee and Mollena have blown away those fictional bogeymen and given you an easy step-by-step guide to safely entering this domain, and in the process they've shown that it isn't nearly as scary or sleazy as you think. *Playing Well With Others* lets you know what you can expect, what will be expected of you, and how you can get the most out of your visits into this realm. While it doesn't guarantee to get you kinky sex, it will make the process of trying look a lot easier, and it ought to have "Don't Panic" written on in the cover in large, comforting chains." – Raven Kaldera, *Dark Moon Rising*

"An insightful and thoroughly entertaining book. Full of humor, playfully presented insights, and profound truths. Whether you're a seasoned player or new to the kink community, this book is a must read. Quite honestly, it's the most complete and accurate presentation of kink community dynamics I have ever read!" – JD of Two Knotty Boys, *Showing You the Ropes*

"If you are a newcomer to the world of BDSM, you could have no friendlier or more supportive guides than Lee Harrington and Mollena Williams. In *Playing Well with Others,* you will find everything you need to know about how to find the kink communities, connect with fellow kinksters, and negotiate with honesty, practicality, and courtesy to make your wildest dreams come true: this book is the roadmap you've been looking for." – Dossie Easton, MFT, *The Ethical Slut, The New Bottoming Book, The New Topping Book* and more

"Lee Harrington and Mollena Williams have written a 'Welcome to BDSM' guidebook that tackles the who, what, when, where and why of kink. They break down everything from cons to collars and munches to masochism with an easygoing, informative style that tells it like it is. Newbies and seasoned kinksters alike will appreciate their wisdom."
– Rachel Kramer Bussel, editor, *Cheeky Spanking Stories* and the *Best Bondage Erotica* series

"These two educators have really hit it out of the park with *Playing Well With Others*. From newly minted kinksters to experienced edgeplayers, fabulous fetishists to savvy swingers, this book provides a wealth of useable information and incredible resources on how to optimize your experiences in the kink, leather and even swinging communities. A must have!" – Shanna Katz, M.Ed, ACS, Sexuality and Board Certified Sexologist

"Consider this book a safe haven for perverts. Wrap yourself in the reassuring language of Lee and Mollena's thorough overview of the myriad kink communities. Know that you will be well-equipped with an easy-to-navigate map that will take you from Vanilla Town to Rocky Road in style. Really, this book is an excellent primer for learning how to be a decent human being. The kink element is just an added bonus." – Kendra Holliday, writer and editor of *The Beautiful Kind*

"Congratulations! What you hold in your hands may just be the most thorough and up-to-date book illuminating the multifaceted world of BDSM and Kink. Mollena and Lee take you on a step- by-step journey where nothing is taboo! If you are just starting out or have been playing for years, you'll find the latest on everything from power dynamics to human pups! Embrace your desires. Let your erotic archetypes out to play; pleasure, intimacy, healing and fulfillment await you! – Cléo Dubois, Academy Of SM Arts

"Two words, Dear Reader: Sustainable. Community. Though packaged in a pervy panoply of passion and possibility, this island in the sea of kink is home to the treasures of truth necessary to create and foster any type of affinity-based sustainable community. This field guide to kink communities, with a consent-based model featuring personal empowerment, is a tool I wish I'd had thirty years ago when I first came out into kink. From the absolute noob we've all been to the credentialed members of an Old Guard that has never existed, there's something for all. This book might wear a leather jacket, but beneath its cover lies the naked truth of how to be completely, authentically human in appropriate community." – Rev. Deborah Addington, author, *A Hand in the Bush: The Fine Art of Vaginal Fisting*, *Fantasy Made Flesh: The Essential Guide to Erotic Roleplay*, *Play Piercing*

"Feeling like Cinderella going to your first kinky ball? This book is your Fairy Godmother! *Playing Well With Others* is a must-read guide to your foray into the kinky realms. Practical, hilarious, helpful, smart and generous." – Midori, Sexuality educator, author, founder of Rope Bondage Dojo & ForteFemme, www.FHP-inc.com

Playing Well With Others

Your Field Guide to Discovering, Navigating and Exploring the Kink, Leather and BDSM Communities

Lee Harrington

&

Mollena Williams

greenery press

© 2012 by Greenery Press, Inc.

All rights reserved. Except for brief passages quoted in newspaper, magazine, radio, television or Internet reviews, no part of this book may be reproduced in any form or by any means, electronic or mechanical, including photocopying or recording or by information storage or retrieval system, without permission in writing from the Publisher.

Cover design by Johnny Ink, *www.johnnyink.com.*

Interior art by kd, *www.katiediamond.com.*

Published in the United States by Greenery Press. Distributed by SCB Distributors, Gardena, CA.

Readers should be aware that the activities and behaviors described in this book carry an inherent risk of physical and/or emotional injury. While we believe that following the guidelines set forth in this book will minimize that potential, the writers and publisher encourage you to be aware that you are taking some risk when you decide to engage in these activities, and to accept personal responsibility for that risk. In acting on the information in this book, you agree to accept that information as is and with all faults. Neither the authors, the publisher, nor anyone else associated with the creation or sale of this book is responsible for any damage sustained.

Introduction

DARK DUNGEONS WHERE CHAINS RATTLE, bodies writhing in the shadows. Latex clad mistresses who entertain the most select clients who have found the one true way into their domains. Ancient traditions of leathermen passed down from man to man, available only to those willing to endure the trials of indoctrination...

It's hot porn.

If you want to keep dreaming that the world of BDSM, fetishism and kink is a scary place full of depraved taboos and grinning demons who will force you to do their bidding –

PUT THIS BOOK DOWN NOW.

Do you, instead, long to traverse and explore the many and varied gatherings within the alternative sexuality communities from a place of emotional, social, psychological and physical well-being? Then this book will help you discover the diversity of possibilities available, and make them a part of your life should you so choose. From munches to fetish balls, shopping excursions to public dungeons, fantasy retreats to intensive educational opportunities, there are many options nowadays. In your hands is a survival guide, complete with helpful tips and tricks, to support you as you explore, navigate and integrate yourself into this community, and make it your own.

Curious about kink? Or perhaps highly experienced and looking for some tips to take your journey even deeper? Ready to dive in fully, or perhaps just take a peek?

Here is a map to the terrain you hope to explore, and we are here to be your guiltless guides, your erotic assistants, your sexual Sherpas.

This is the book we wish had been around when we began our own forays from private kinky sex to public, playful and profound perversion. With so much reference material, so many websites and resources detailing how to be kinky and enjoy diverse sexualities, how exactly do we meet others of our kind? It's about time we branched out and discussed how to play well with one another, how we build community, and how to have the best chance of success in our explorations.

We'll explore a wide variety of topics relevant to getting involved with kink communities, including:

- **Questioning** your own motivations, needs, wants and desires.

- **Easing** your way into established communities.

- **Understanding** etiquette in different adventurous sex communities.

- **Familiarizing** yourself with the many types of events available to explore.

- **Caring** for your relationships as you explore new territory.

- **Negotiating** for play and aftercare.

- **Learning** to operate back in the "world at large"

- **...and of course** the all-important question: What do you wear?!

Come along with us, and know you are not alone.

Your Sexual Sherpas,

Lee Harrington and Mollena Williams
New York City 2012
PassionAndSoul.com **and** Mollena.com

1

Welcome to the Jungle: Your First Steps Into Adventure

Kink? What Is This Kink Thing?

THE KINK COMMUNITY is known by many different terms...

... and many others.

For the case of our discussion in this book, we will be using "kink" as shorthand for:

The great big world of sexual adventure, including, but not limited to, voyeurism, exhibitionism, fetishism, fantasy role-playing, cross-dressing, power exchange, swinging, leather identity, erotic restraint, consensual non-monogamy, 'naughty sex' and BDSM between consenting adults. In short, the realm of sexuality perceived to be outside the mainstream.

Our definitions may or may not match yours, and your definitions can and will shift with time and experience. If you don't see your thoughts, ideas and feelings precisely mirrored here, feel free to use your own. This book is geared toward helping you traverse the communities out there, figure out where to invest your energy, and decide where you will have the best time, as well as to learn more, network, make friends, and go to events. We hope that it will also help you avoid many of the challenges others have faced — thereby improving your interactions with these cultures, and improving the communities with your energy and presence.

Being kinky or becoming a part of the kink community is not an express ticket to sexual enlightenment, erotic godhood, or having hotties swooning at your feet. You may, however, have all kinds of fun, learn a lot, and connect with new people. Or you may find it's not for you, or that a particular facet of the community or type of event is not your cup of tea. If you're already part of one or more of these communities, we hope to share with you ways to have a better time, increase awareness of the many avenues of exploration available to you, and be more successful within this place we call home.

As we explore this world, you will run into a lot of words you may not have encountered before, or have encountered in another context. Don't worry if you don't know what a "munch" is and have no clue what a "dungeon monitor" does: Appendix 1, Kink Lingo, is your friend.

There is wide spectrum of opinion of what it means to be "into kink." Thus, this book is intended to be a tool for folks from a wide variety of backgrounds, and into a wide variety of kinks or interests. Not everything in this text will apply to you, but you can find your own way to adapt the information to your needs. You may well read about stuff you're not into, and you may well be intrigued by something you never even dreamed possible. Take what you need, what feeds you, what titillates you, what intrigues you... and leave the rest.

Who Is Into Kink?

The variety of humans interested in kink is mind-boggling. The kink community includes...

Single parents	College students	Grandparents
CEOs	Tech geeks	Teachers
PTA members	Politicians	Clergy
Retirees	Mechanics	Plumbers
Lawyers	Musicians	Homemakers
Doctors	Activists	Photographers
Tattoo artists	Porn stars	Small business owners...

Though commonly referred to as an "alternative community," the world of kink is a microcosm of the world at large. It is a slice of the mainstream population; folks from all walks of life are drawn to kink gatherings and events. This diverse population includes individuals from different backgrounds, faiths, politics, cultures, ethnicities, education levels, sexualities, genders and gender presentations, approaches to life, outlooks, and philosophies. Straight, gay, lesbian, bisexual, queer, pansexual, omnisexual, asexual, and sexual-identity-flexible folks are all part of the kink communities. One of the amazing things about people exploring this world is that it offers an opportunity to folks to meet who might not cross paths in any other context.

Thus, the kink communities are not only for "alternative" individuals. Not everyone is covered in tattoos and wears only gothic or punk clothing — though the kink community has a place for these folks as well. Some folks come to kink as a way to spice up their sex life, and others have taken it on as a full-time lifestyle choice. Kink is made up of individuals, all on their own path, who share space and create a way to explore their world together.

Not so long ago, the only way to find any community among like-minded kinksters was through careful and very discreet networking. People who were looking for "something different" found one another through coded advertisements in newspapers, secret signals and sartorial clues. These days, your local dungeon and fetish clothing companies are only a few clicks away. The thing that has not changed is the desire for connection, for energy, for adventure. The scenarios might change, the play might shift, but at the core of our communities are the hearts, souls and spirits of the adventurers who comprise them.

Why Are People Into Kink?

Before we unpack the nuts and bolts of getting involved with alternative lifestyle communities, it's important to know why you think you are into kink. This will allow you to set realistic expectations and goals as you explore. If what you get out of kink is a deep sense of intimacy and the thrill of taboo exploration with only yourself or your partner, you may be satisfied by leveraging the kink community to gain access to those specific resources. If what you are drawn to is the opportunity to make new connections, relax with friends, or become an activist... you may be drawn to different types of events and gatherings, or you may approach the same events with a different intent.

Are you here to keep a partner happy? Or have you been waiting your whole life to find just this type of connection? Is being kinky a way to cope with desires that you haven't ever had words for? Do you see this as an occasional escapist retreat? A coping mechanism? Or is this a wholesale shift in the paradigm of your life? Is it all about sex, or is it something beyond the carnality of a sexual liaison? Spiritual? Secular? All these in turn? You may not have the answers to any or all of these questions, but keeping them in mind will help to ground you as you further your explorations and delve into the wealth of information and sensations becoming available to you.

So, what are some of the reasons people are into kink? Everyone has their own answers. We have interacted with many thousands of folks about their reasons for enjoying kink, kinky sex, fetishism, voyeurism, exhibitionism, erotic power exchange, swinging, fantasy role-playing, leather, cross-dressing, BDSM, swinging or consensual non-monogamy, so we can share with you some of the myriad reasons that people enjoy these explorations.

Because it's sexy!

That's right, kink can be flat-out sexy. It is a chance to make noise, moan, experience adrenaline highs, and get turned on. For those of us that are thrill-seekers, the physical rush is an opportunity to dive into the intensity of experience, to explore strong sensations, and to enjoy the tactile "realness" of it all. Kink is an opportunity to sample everything on the buffet of erotic life, to manifest joy with our bodies.

Some are sexually aroused by the beauty and aesthetics of their erotic explorations – the curve of a heeled foot, the sounds of clanking chains or cracking whips, the pungent scent of leather. Others have a specific fetish or paraphilia, and the kink community is a safe place in which to explore that desire. Some folks want the sexual arousal that comes from trying something new, or with someone new, or in a new place – an opportunity to "walk on the wild side," be naughty, and be the delightfully depraved sexual human beings that we read about in porn stories.

Being into kink gives us permission to embrace what gets us wet, hard or riled up. Whether that is being turned on by aggression, aroused by surrender, titillated by the sensual touch of a thousand hands or deeply connected as two bodies unite in a single breath... we are granted permission to embrace, not just accept or cope with, our desires. It's one thing to secretly contemplate your innermost sexual fantasies, and another thing to celebrate them with others who will celebrate right alongside you. The heat of desire can fuel the engine of your

> ### Para-what?
> A paraphilia refers to a sexual arousal towards a specific object, situation or individual that is not considered "normal" in culture. A paraphilia becomes debilitating if these arousals and interests become obsessions, or cause serious problems for the person or their friends, partners and random strangers. The word "fetish" is technically synonymous with a paraphilia, but in modern times mass media and the kink community alike have come to conflate "fetish wear" with "anything black, shiny and high-heeled" instead of "a clothing item that specifically arouses the wearer or viewer of that individual" as it used to. Note the "normal in mainstream culture" point. "Tit men" or "ass men" are considered normal because mainstream culture says attraction to tits and asses is "normal," while attraction to feet, leather or balloons is considered "kinky."

When I asked students and readers of my work why they were into kink, a fairly large number mentioned childhood memories or early obsessions. They had, in some way, always been "like this." Whether mesmerized by Houdini, turned on by bound women in cartoons, transfixed by extreme practices featured in *National Geographic,* or fascinated seeing Captain Kirk wearing a collar on *Star Trek,* many of us  have had concepts of power and passion in the media spark our interests. Or perhaps they were the kids who, when playing Truth or Dare, always chose "dare." ~ Lee

imagination; becoming a part of this community can, in and of itself, be an adventure in arousal.

Because it is an adventure.

Exploring kink can be a great way to try out novel things, make new friends, stretch your boundaries, and have a good time. Some people discover a chance to identify and meet their core desires, while others wish to splash around in an erotic playground. The adventure can also lead to the creation of vivid memories, maybe only a few fleeting moments, that may stay with us for a lifetime.

For others, the adventure was proposed by a lover or friend. By exploring the shadows of their own psyche and facing the unknown, these individuals can make the unknown known, and shine a light onto parts of them they might not know otherwise. The adventure need not always be profound – it may just be a chance to try something that feels good, is new, shiny, exciting, fascinating. It may be a chance to feel more alive.

Because we are wired this way.

There are those who have longed for alternative sexual practices for most of their lives; for such people, kink comes naturally. Engaging in kink activities is their "normal" sexuality, not a form of fringe sex. To deny their organic longings would harm their own emotional and psychological health, because they are hard-wired this way. They may have been deeply kinky without any instruction, direction or guidance, and they may not have formal names for their desires for SM and power plays: "rough sex" may be as far as descriptors go for some who have had an organic lifelong attraction to kink.

Sometimes the desires for kink and adventurous sexual practices come later in life. A hot porn story or image on the internet can get the fantasies working overtime, unleashing heretofore unknown desire.

A book, music video, movie, television series, magazine advertisement, or theatrical production can awaken us to a world of possibilities. Something as innocuous as seeing someone wearing a collar at the mall or science-fiction conference can trigger for some long-held desires that have no specific source... they just *are*.

Because we need decompression and touch.

Whether decompressing after a hard day at the office, or grounding back into a touch- and sensation-deprived body, many people report that kink activities help them reach emotional or energetic equilibrium. Relaxing, letting go, or succumbing to sensory experiences like ice cubes melting on skin or leather caressing our flesh might be a powerful reason to embrace kink.

Role-playing can be an excellent way to hit your "reset" button. By getting out of our heads and away from our day-to-day worries for a few hours, becoming naughty nurses or surrendering slaves can give us the opportunity to return to our daily lives with new eyes and refreshed hearts. Others report that the intensity of play gives them room to abandon "rational thought" and the minutiae of daily life. This physical approach to clearing the mind can create sensations of cleansing the spirit – removing the debris from our lives so that we may return refreshed, shaking up our brains like an Etch-A-Sketch. Kink, in its myriad forms, can provide a chance to recharge our emotional and intellectual batteries and boost our overall quality of life.

There are also people for whom kink is an opportunity to get more physical contact in their lives. We live in a touch-starved culture where we have to ask for hugs... and even then, social situations do not always allow us the amount and quality of physical contact that we need. For those hungry for human contact, the ability to receive sensual massage, cuddling after intense experiences, or an erotic spanking can feel incredibly nurturing. Loving touch comes in a variety of intensities, and being able to ask for the type of touch we long for can be fulfilling and empowering.

Because it is a challenge.

Screaming, moaning, and tears are not always a negative thing. They can be a tool for pushing through our fears, purging our personal demons, and therapeutically releasing pain from the past. For those who long for catharsis, kink practices may help them face their fears and sorrows, embrace them, and reclaim their bodies or personal power. In some parts of the kink community, this sort of BDSM practice is often referred to as "work" rather than "play," because work can be required to dive into the underworld of our spirit and come back again. By creating scenarios or "scenes" where our challenges can be faced in the form of ordeals, we can reprogram ourselves, find personal strength, and discover new frontiers of our being. For others it is not about pushing past our limits or demons, but finding power in acknowledging our limits and embracing our ability to stand up and say "no."

Many individuals come across these transformations during their journeys, even when such experiences were not planned. The opportunity to overcome shame, explore boundaries, and reach into the shadows of ourselves can leave us profoundly altered. Not all of these revelations are easy to accept, but sometimes we do not want or need the easy path in our lives – whether facing our own strength and suffering, or discovering some new part of our true selves hiding behind the masks they wear in their daily lives.

Because we want to connect with others.

For some individuals, kink activities are a way to express love, passion, desire, devotion and connection. When we feel our power or pleasure reflected in a lover's eyes, we have the opportunity to connect with them on a whole new level. Exploring erotic trust games can deepen and intensify the levels of intimacy between partners, even long-time companions. Using kink as a way to get into our significant other's heads can also create a deep sense of oneness or attachment.

Romance, love and affection for a partner (or partners) is another reason some individuals explore kink. It can feel great, and be a means toward closer bonding, when someone helps their lover fulfill a fantasy. Some do kink out of a sense of obligation, to a partner to whom they are profoundly bonded – and even there, many find satisfaction in giving pleasure, pain, or other blissful and desired sensations to those we cherish. There are those who fall in love as a result of these deep glimpses into the hearts and minds of another.

Participation in these communities can be the gateway through which some individuals pass in order to build families of choice, tribes of the heart, places they feel they belong. For those who feel that power exchange or non-egalitarian relationships feel more fitting than an association between "equals," exploring kink can be a wonderful way to find those who understand their desires.

Because it is personal and profound exploration.

Though many people engage in kink for fun and to indulge hedonistic desires, there are others who are called to their erotic exploration as a tool for spiritual, energetic or personal exploration. For these individuals, kink is a tool for altered states of consciousness, and sensation is a quest for transcendence.

By playing with taboos, breath, rhythm and ritual, some individuals can fulfill a spiritual calling, connect to divinity, or embrace their faith. History has a rich collection of energetic psychonauts who used sexual or bodily practice to connect with the universe or specific spiritual traditions. Others use similar techniques to embrace their personal identities or gender, re-claim their own unique journey, or find profound self-awareness. This can include finding clarity of thought that strips away ego and leaves the journeyer aware of their pure instincts.

Some are called to harnessing and channeling power, some to consciously relinquishing power to another, others to expressing vulnerability, still others to finding acceptance for themselves and their dreams. Some may see themselves on a pilgrimage with kink and sacredness entwined, the path and the journey and the destination flowing seamlessly into one another. Some folks seek this quest specifically; still others find themselves wide-eyed with wonder at a newly discovered spirituality within the realm of the kink.

Why are YOU into kink?

Reflecting on what draws you to the wide varieties of sexual adventure out there will help you understand why you might want to be part of a kink community. It will also help you determine what kinds of kink gatherings are right for you, and what intent might serve you best for making this adventure be the best it possibly can be for you.

If you are embarking on this adventure into the community

I believe that all spiritual practices have, at some point in their development, looked to the mortification of the flesh, to service, to slavery and submission as vital pillars of their foundation. Whether the mortification of the flesh is actual flogging, or the deprivations of fasting, pilgrimages or rigorous meditation, this is a universal theme. Whether the submission, service or slavery is to god, to a spouse, to the church, or to the spiritual practice, all of these activities have been nestled within spiritual and religious rituals since they first took root.
~Mollena

with a lover, a partner, a friend, or an entire tribe diving in together as a group, discussions about why you are exploring this lifestyle can help you learn more about each other. If you dig kink because of the profound intimacy, and your sweetie loves the risk and adrenaline rush, it can be helpful to understand the difference before jumping on that ride together.

It can take a profound act of bravery to embrace all aspects of ourselves, and it takes gumption to put trust in yourself enough to seek your joy, even if it is the road less traveled. Taking responsibility for our desires and our actions is a big deal. Deciding to explore kink, regardless of whether you bask in it occasionally or immerse yourself in the murkiest depths, is a testament to your personal responsibility and commitment to living a deeply authentic life.

Why Join the Community?

Before we go any further let us state clearly — *you do not have to be part of a public community to be kinky.*

Seriously.

Lots of folks engage in kinky behaviors every day and they are not a part of any public group, have never attended play parties and are very happy staying at home on their own, with lovers, or with close friends. Some private players might dip occasionally into the wider world to gather inspiration, to socialize, even to meet new partners — and then quietly exit stage left, going about their lives. Even if the thought of diving in to a huge kinky jamboree holds zero interest for you, there is plenty of helpful information in the following pages that may help to illuminate your very individual, personal explorations.

As we go through this book, though, you will find many excellent reasons why people choose to get involved with the community, such as creating support networks, checking a potential partner's references, finding places to learn or play, gathering allies for creating fantasies, and more. When we talked with a bunch of kinksters about why they are into kink, these were their responses. The answers are as varied as the individuals who offered them. We hope they can help you decide what aspects of the kink community appeal to you, what degree of involvement is right for you, and what you might hope to gain from your journey.

"I like to look!"

Going to kink gatherings can provide you with a veritable smörgåsbord of eye candy. The diversity of bodies, stunning wardrobe selections, and beautiful beings of all genders, sizes, shapes and orientations provide a great chance for voyeurs to get their peep on and for all of us to be inspired into our own magnificence. And then there's what those bodies get up to! Hot scenes, sensual connections, humbled men kneeling in corners, women straining against their cuffs, genderqueer switches turning the tables on their partners, human-animal creatures prowling on all fours...the chance to see our porn, our fantasies, take life before our eyes can be incredibly titillating.

"I like being with peers and making friends."

It is human nature to want to connect with like-minded individuals, and the desire to find peers who understand our sexual journeys is no different. Those who can acknowledge and accept our desires freely, and embrace our journeys as valid and worthwhile, may feel like family. The kink communities can provide opportunities to meet those who "get it."

To get to be a freak amongst other freaks, to dance with others on the fringe of society, or to simply share our different-ness (even if the next guy's different-ness is different from yours) can be a profound experience for those who have been seeking tribal connections. When we have had to hide or explain ourselves to death, having those around whom we can "let it all hang out" can be fulfilling indeed.

These communities can present an unparalleled opportunity to network, bond, and connect with people who you know already have a particular bent. It can be heart-warming to find a circle of friends with whom you can talk about your kinky desires without fear of them balking. The validation one feels when entering this circle can feel very much like home.

The world moves with increasing speed with every new innovation in communication. Though these advances are indispensable when it comes to our daily lives, sometimes it can feel like they leave us increasingly isolated. The beauty of finding a safe social space, a tribe, a clan, chosen family, friends, lovers, mentors, and, yes, even foils and foes can provide us with a richness that technology simply cannot match — a place where we can look people in the eyes and get a flesh-and-blood hug.

"I want to learn."

One of the many benefits of participation in the kink communities is your access to what seems like an endless stream of information, input, advice and educational opportunities. Whether it is a peer-sharing group hanging

When I first started picking up books about kink, about leather, about BDSM, I was hesitant. This seemed like such an impenetrable, secret society. It was so complicated, with so many rules and protocols... I would never have a chance of understanding all of it. Once I finally went from books, articles, websites and chat rooms to real time, the light bulb went on for me. These are people, I realized... and not just people, these are people who are like me. I had found a place where I could be more fully "me." It was a huge step in loving myself once I met others who accepted themselves, and accepted me as a freaky, kinky human being.

out in someone's living room or a full-tilt week-long kinky camp, there are many ways to avail yourself of the expertise of those who have gone before you and who are happy to share their knowledge and experience.

Education might cover techniques, hard science, physiology, the psychology of why we do what we do, the history of our communities, spirituality, toy and cloth-ing maintenance...the topics are endless, and educators are always pushing themselves to come up with new and interesting subjects. Availing yourself of the broad variety of educational opportunities and interaction available is a great way to keep it "fresh."

Attending a class hosted by your local group will give you access to expe-rienced players as well as a chance to meet and talk to new folks. You may dis-cover new playstyles, even if you are a grizzled, jaded veteran of the dungeon. The act of learning, sharing, and growing can help bond you with your fellow kinksters, and you may surprise yourself with the realization that you, too, have things to share! Perhaps you are an experienced event planner, rock climber, law-enforcement officer, nurse, massage therapist or carpenter. These skills and many others have utility in our communities, and you may well soon find yourself tapped to step up and teach a thing or two to the long-time players. And the folks who have been around for decades have much to teach us about the history of our communities, our origins, our traditions and that which will eventually be our legacies.

"It's easier to find compatible, like-minded partners."

You may already have a partner who is also interested in taking that step with you, but this is not the case for many people who come into the kink communities. Sure, there's a chance you could find the dominant partner of your dreams, the submissive slut of your fantasies or that seductive switch while in line at the grocery store, but being a part of a self-selecting social group certainly ups your chances of meeting that special someone. If you are looking for a new connection, having a vibrant community of self-identified kinksters is a great way to increase your chances of finding someone who likes the same kinky stuff you like.

"I get to access so many amazing resources!"

Sure, some of us have dungeons in the basement, soundproof rooms where we can get up to our kinkiest play without fear of neighbors calling the cops because of the strange sounds emanating from our homes. For the rest of us, being a part of a broader kinky community gives us access to dungeons, play-spaces, other people, places and kink-specific props and items that you may never have believed existed until you saw them. For those of us who love sharing in the energy of other folks playing, or who enjoy specialized play, the dungeon is the place to be. You might not be able to maintain two hundred acres on a clothing-optional resort where you can roam freely while riding your very own human pony, but get a few dedicated kinky folks together and voila! You can create just that. There are at least five or six such events every summer in the US alone.

And beyond the playtime benefits to moving within the community, there are very real benefits to accessing resources designed specifically for alternative lifestyle people. Need a doctor or acupuncturist who will understand that your bruised butt is the result of sexy, consensual fun? We've sought them out. Perhaps you need legal help, and a kink-friendly lawyer would be indispensable? Being a part of our community means you won't be alone should you need to reach out for help. And you may well find yourself in a position to help others, too. Fewer things are more satisfying than being able to provide advice, moral support or just a sympathetic ear. The community is a resource limited only by what you put into it and your fertile imagination.

"I feel safer exploring my kink within the community."

Your initial entry into public kink, when all you've had is fantasy, can feel very scary. The community can provide a measure of safety to help ease the transition. Yes, we are a community of people, and as such are subject to the failings and foibles of any social group. However, most kinksters endeavor to provide safe emotional space for exploration, learning, and many different types of loving, sensual interactions. We strive for open, clear communications so we can minimize mismatched expectations.

Many of us who felt like misfits in the "default world" breathe easier in kink and alternative communities. We have banded together to create an environment where there is an acceptance of folks of all backgrounds, genders, races, body types, abilities, social backgrounds, and more, to come together and get their freak on.

Which one are you?

All, some or none of these explanations might resonate for you. Fantastic! We hope that folks approach our community in a way that helps them to seek their own bliss.

Please keep in mind that any of the above reasons could have a darker and less positive bent. It is wonderful if you venture into these waters because your sweetie thinks spanking is the bee's knees and you say "well, hell, why not!" It is less wonderful if your partner uses coercion, guilt or emotional blackmail to drag you into this realm. Take a close, critical look at your motives, and consider whether they are coming from a place of joy or fear, of guilt or relief, of desire or apprehension, and make sure you are comfortable and that you are taking care of yourself. Our hope for you is that you enjoy the explorations and thrill to this amazing journey.

Choose Your Own Adventure

Different kinky individuals get involved in the community in different ways. For some folks, life circumstances dictate a limited extent to their involvement: family life, chronic ailment, holding public office, a high-profile career or just a really full calendar might restrict them from being regular participants. You may live in a jurisdiction where legal restrictions make in-person involvement too risky for you. You may realize that your personal needs dictate that one big event every few years is plenty for you. Or you may find that your personal desires and unique authenticity mean that you need to be constantly involved in this world.

Others come and go, ebb and flow, oscillating from high-profile movers and shakers to being only involved online, or fading away entirely, only to re-emerge years later to take on leadership responsibilities. The wonderful thing is that kink will still be here. You can move at your own pace, come and go, dance with us or solo for a while, and come back to find us when you need and desire us.

How involved we are doesn't always reflect how kinky we are, or how committed we are to our kink identities. There are folks who get their freak on every day and yet are not a part of the community, and there are people who are profoundly involved with the community who very rarely engage in scenes or "play." Just because someone is an event organizer or presents a class on a particular topic does not mean they have the highest level of skill in an activity. Conversely, someone you've never seen at the local play party or who only comes out for special events can't be assumed to be a clueless "newbie."

Our degree of involvement is just that – how involved we choose to get. It does not express our level of passion, commitment, expertise, desire, or how much pleasure we derive from these activities. Being clear enough to be able to say "I like coming out to big events once in a while, but I have little interest in ever taking dungeon monitor training or hosting a munch," can help others understand your journey.

Internet only

The explosion of the Internet in the early '90s ushered in a new era for alternative communities. Many people who had felt isolated and alone found that they were far from alone, and those first bulletin boards were quickly populated with kinksters comparing notes, swapping stories and sharing fantasies. And it has only grown from there, with kink-specific dating sites quickly cropping up all over.

After creating a profile on a kink message board, social networking site or chat system, many are happy to contribute to the discussions, read the occasional article or find delicious kinky porn, but never come out to a party or event. In fact, some "online-only" folk are incredibly involved – online. They host websites, run podcasts, post images, or are immersed every day in debates and dialogues, while seldom if ever attending an in-person event. Others might choose to check their accounts very rarely, and engage only in those discussions that catch their eye. Ever-evolving innovations in online communities, social networking, gaming and virtual life systems make immersion in virtual kink an enticing choice for some who might otherwise have no outlet. "Online only" is for some a gateway; for others, it is where they live and breathe their kinky desires.

"OK, maybe just this once..."

Going out to a fetish club night, making a vacation of attending a week-long fantasy retreat, or visiting your friendly neighborhood kinky sex club can be an amazing once-in-a-lifetime experience. Whether or not you ever attend another event, bearing witness to the wide diversity of wardrobe, fetishes and fantasies, and being titillated by the possibilities out there, can fuel a lifetime of bedroom electricity. For others interested in a specific sub-category of kink, going to a class on that topic might be just enough to feel confident in progressing forward with their desires behind closed doors. There are so many types of events to choose from (see Chapter 3) that you can be sure to find something meeting your comfort level and fulfilling that one-off itch.

Once a year

Some events have an annual life cycle. And some kinksters thrive within a kink life that embraces that yearly return: a way to get a regular jolt of fun or taboo into their lives, connect with old friends, or refresh kinky batteries. Such folks might like to dress up for a yearly major event such as a fetish ball, kinky convention or street festival. They might like to attend or participate in a pride parade, or come out to a holiday play party – a great option for those who lead very busy lives but who love to have that one outlet to which they may look forward and recall fondly year after year.

Attending munches

A munch is a low-pressure social gathering for people involved in or interested in kink. They are usually at a restaurant, coffee house, or similar venue: in Europe, for example, munches are often held in pubs. Coming out to a munch is a great way to network with others in a local area, meet new play partners, learn about events and resources, and in general not be isolated in our desires. The relaxed environment is great for newcomers as well as long-term kinksters looking to socialize. Munches can provide a comfortable degree of involvement for individuals whose kink lives are highly personal, and those who are not exhibitionists or voyeurs. Some people go to their local munch faithfully every month/week (depending on the frequency); others just drop in from time to time to touch base and feel connected.

Attending play parties and events

For those who love the energy of playing in front of others, are looking to get new ideas for playing at home, don't have equipment in their own home, or who live in apartments with thin walls, attending a local play party can be a fantastic choice. Kink-themed special events and conventions take this idea further, with classes, workshops, and shopping combined with play. In many places around the world, these events occur with such regularity as to allow the discerning adventurer to pick and choose from a veritable kinky cornucopia. Some people who may not identify specifically as kinky might still come out once in a while to play parties or events, thus getting a little spice in their sex. However, you might live in a city or town where the pickings are slim, and the available venues tough to find. In that case, you may well want to consider...

Starting a munch, hosting a party

Every recurring or ongoing event or group needs people who believe enough in the event to get it off of the ground and to keeping it running. Sure, a handful of events run themselves through tradition or habit, but even these groups once needed someone or a group of someones who came up with the brilliant idea, ignited the spark, and got it burning.

Often, a group of friends, an affiliation of like-minded kinksters, or a strong individual will take the leadership position within an event – hey, someone's gotta send out announcements about upcoming happenings, make sure that the venue is available on a given night, arrange food or drinks, set up furniture, clean up after everyone leaves, and administer the many details needed to make the event happen. Giving back to your local community through doing the day-to-day work of keeping meeting spaces available to attendees can be incredibly fulfilling. This level of involvement is an excellent way to meet people if you are new to the community, and a fantastic way to keep in the thick of things if you are a long-time community member.

Getting on board!

Some groups are ad-hoc, casual, seat-of-the-pants ventures. For others, though, Robert's Rules of Order is a fetish. If you have a deeply organizational streak, and love the idea of helping an organization get off the ground or keep flying, a position on a board of directors might be right up your alley.

Registered nonprofit organizations and for-profit businesses often work under a board structure, with attendant bylaws and regulations, in kink as in the bigger world. In major metropolitan areas, kink-focused organizations are often the ones who produce the large or recurring events – and being a trustee means helping shape the future of far-reaching community activities. Sometimes just running for a board position, even if you are not elected, can let your peers know you are passionate about being active and want to be deeply involved.

Producing events

Scouting and booking exciting presenters, arranging large-scale venues, financially backing events, scheduling saucy entertainment and intriguing classes, dreaming up fantastic, innovative ideas to entertain and educate the pervy masses — all these things and more appeal to the hardy souls who are our kink event producers. Running the show is a great way to bring your dedication and energy to your local, national and even international kink communities.

Some produce events as a professional calling, taking their expertise from a career in event production, project management or entertainment and lending it to kinkier exploits. Others learn as they go, freely giving of their time and sometimes funds to materialize their own unique vision for the world. Still others choose to become visible or active through becoming financial or product sponsors of events and groups. It isn't unusual to see a kinky real-estate agent or bondage gear supplier supporting a leather event with an advertisement or financial backing, because they believe in what the event has to offer to the broader alternative communities. Sometimes, writing a check is the kinkiest thing you'll ever do!

Sharing your skills

Every single human on this planet has something to share. In the case of the kink community, deepening your involvement by sharing information is one of the pillars that make our community a community. Be it one-on-one mentorship, sharing ideas online, leading discussion groups, teaching classes, running workshops, writing a kinky blog, exchanging ideas online, creating videos or photos, or doing educational scenes at local clubs and parties, different individuals share their passions and expertise in many different ways.

Working in the community

There are those for whom the kink community is also a career. Professional dominants and submissives (aka dominatrixes, pro-doms, pro-dommes or pro-subs), event producers, promoters, makers of kink gear and furniture, sex shop owners, fetish models, adult film actors, sexuality educators, photographers/videographers, website designers, bar owners, tantrikas, dakas and dakinis (aka sacred sex guides), caterers, clothing designers, DJs, performance artists, body modification professionals, escorts, authors and publishers are but some of the careers that have manifested within the kink population.

There are also "classical professionals," who choose to specialize in catering to the needs of our community, or will speak on behalf of our community in professional contexts. People who are massage or physical therapists, psychiatric professionals, kink-friendly doctors, activists, lawyers, university academics, and medical researchers can be powerful voices in advocating for our communities.

Titleholding

An outgrowth of contests held in leather bars to entice hot leathermen to admire the physiques and attire of other hot leathermen, title contests have expanded into the wider kink communities. Like beauty pageants with attitude, title competitions in the kink community range from folks dressing up (or down) for fun, to people who fiercely compete against many dozens of competitors for a coveted national or international sash, leathers, or patch.

Some competitors are truly moved to represent their community as a form of visibility and activism. Others are just excited by getting sexy on stage and raising funds as well as temperatures. Leathermen, leatherwomen, leather transfolk, bootblacks, age players, human ponies, and many other varieties of title holders may well become a voice for the local, national or international kink community, host fundraisers for charity, and perform other forms of outreach and community service. For some people, their leather title becomes a cornerstone of their sexual and emotional identity for the rest of their lives; for others, it was a fun thing they did and look back on fondly.

Should you run? Having held titles ourselves, we encourage those considering running to be rigorously honest with themselves about their motives. Altruistic ideals are great, and it's also actually fine to run because you feel like it will improve your standing in the community, or because you're curious about the titleholder system. Once you know your answer, make sure to ask a few questions about the title and competition:

- **What is the nature of the title?** Research the history of the event, talk to event producers, check their website or material, find out if it is a political title or beauty parade... and if in doubt, ask someone who has held the title themselves!

- **Who is eligible?** Are there any gender, sexual orientation or age restrictions on the title?

- **What are the commitments and responsibilities of the winner?** Will there be specific events at which you will be required to "represent" your title? By winning, are you committing to compete at the next event in the chain? Who pays for all that travel? Do winners have to run fundraisers or produce events?

Making the scene your home

For folks who consider the community their home, it is where they create chosen families of all shapes and sizes, construct tribes of the heart, and in other ways invest emotionally. Kink, or their corner of the kink world, is where they are free to be themselves, express their personal truth, and be who they know themselves to be. It might be a hierarchical leather household, or it might be a loose-knit far-flung family with complex relationships and challenges, but it is family. Kink is their world, and they embrace it wholeheartedly.

And then of course, there is you, in your special unique you-ness. Remember, these categories are simply keys to thinking about how invested you want to be. Consider what best suits you... today. You will change and grow, and the community can change and grow with you. Listen attentively to your gut as you explore, surging forward and holding back as you feel is best. Your journey will be different than ours, and that difference is part of what makes being in this community so rich and fulfilling.

Take what you need, and leave the rest!

Chapter 2.

Does This Flogger Make My Ass Look Fat?: Kink Etiquette, Kink Culture

WHEN WE ASKED seventy kinksters "What do you wish you had known before going to your first kink event?" the most common response was that they wished they'd had more information on community etiquette, on how not to step on people's toes. Through dispelling myths, and creating some basic guidelines, we hope to encourage an atmosphere of civility throughout the kink communities. Think of it as Miss Manners... for perverts.

A Gathering of Tribes vs. a Monolithic "Community"

We use the word "community" loosely. Many kinky folks eschew that word entirely, being the rogue lone wolves that they are. For the purposes of our discussion, we use "community" as a handy way to discuss people who choose to identify as kinky, and/or to incorporate kink into their social, sexual, emotional and physical lives. This "community" is actually a somewhat anarchic confederation of many city-states, realms, fiefdoms, tribes, factions, unions, guilds, associations and travelers. A sampling of the many, many loose-knit groups that may be included under the umbrella of the "kink community" includes folks who are attracted to:

> **Hey, Pervert.**
> ...a note on the use of the term "pervert." Yeah, it has some pretty shady connotations. But like other culturally difficult terms, like "faggot" and "dyke," many kinky folks have taken this previously purely disparaging term, embraced it, and made it our own. When we refer to ourselves and others as perverts, it certainly is not with a shameful criminal connotation. We defy many of the so-called norms of broader society in favor of finding our own bliss in consensual acts of, well, perversion.

Fetishism · Latex/Rubber · Gorean Philosophies · Master/Slave · Fursuits · Spanking · Rope Bondage · Cross Dressing · Power Exchange · Leather · Female Supremacy · Erotic Wrestling · Human Animal · Bondage · Age Play · Swinging · BDSM

...and much much more! In fact, there are kinky people who don't do any of these things, but instead consider kinkiness their identity, something that transcends activities and desires.

You will find that different etiquettes and protocols apply throughout the different offshoots and sub-sections of these communities. The specific rules for a swinger gathering may look dramatically different from a leather bar, a bathhouse, a fetish gathering, or an educational weekend.

Don't freak out. It will be OK! And when in doubt, a polite question will often carry the day.

Dispelling a Few Myths

Most folks have a few ideas about "those kinky folks" based on a narrow glimpse into the kink world. There's a vague notion of "dungeons and pain and whips and chains" (oh my!) when thinking of our communities. You have undoubtedly encountered myths about the kink community that may have stuck with you. Most of them are not true, but they may have a kernel of truth within them.

Let's take a look at a few of some common myths that swirl around concerning the kink community, see how they might have evolved, and dispel some of the mystery.

Myth #1: "Everyone has sex with everyone else."

BZZT!

The kink community does attract a high percentage of people who identify as "sex-positive": people who openly acknowledge, discuss and celebrate sexuality in its many and varied forms. And this is awesome. However, our communities include relatively few omnivorous, prowling sex sharks on a never-ending quest for fresh meat. Some folks are asexually kinky, separating their kink from explicit sexual congress. Others are monogamous, partnering and playing only with their lover, husband, wife, or partner. Some are involved in closed polyamorous groups, only doing kink activity with those in their circle. Some are serially monogamous, or only play within a small group of lovers and friends. Some have open, far-flung networks of play-partners, lovers, fuckbuddies, and more, with whom they form various degrees of intimacy. And of course, there are the prowling omnivorous sex sharks. You, and only you, get to choose who you engage with and to what degree.

Myth #2: "Kinky parties are one big orgy and erotic free-for-all."

NO DICE.

Some parties are organized around the idea of free sex and free love, often with strict codes of safer sex behavior. Others explicitly forbid sexual intercourse. The rules will vary according to the needs and desires of the people hosting the party, the laws in the area where the party is being held, and the style of event. Some people have no desire to combine explicit sexual contact and kink, some people use kinky play as foreplay, and still others just want to gaze upon the wonders of the perverted playground before them. Reading the descriptions, rules and guidelines for an event before you buy that ticket or get gussied up and head down to that play space will help you know what you're signing up for and make sure your expectations meet what's on offer.

Myth #3: "If you are into kinky sex, you are into all forms of kinky sex."

TO QUOTE THE MAGIC 8-BALL, "MY SOURCES SAY 'NO'."

You may well have a very specific kinky fantasy, and zero interest in anything else. Fantastic. Get your highly focused freak on. Being a part of the community doesn't mean you must embark on a race to earn erotic merit badges; it is about you exploring your desires and fantasies. Some people find that their desires expand as they explore, and others, who thought they wanted to perform every kink under the sun, find themselves narrowing their focus as time goes on.

Engaging in baroque and highly technical scenes right out of the gate is OK — if that is what you want to do, and if you know what you're doing. Go earn those badges! Taking things at your own pace and in your own time, though, is always a good bet.

Some people enjoy what is sometimes referred to as "edge play": scenes that push the "edge" of comfort for the people involved or the kink community at large. However, the funny thing about "edgy" stuff is that everyone has their own edge. You might walk into a party and see someone playing in a way that draws blood; for some people, that's quite edgy. Right next to that scene, though, you might see a scene involving someone being required to sing *I'm A Little Teapot* to a group of laughing bystanders. Which is the edgier scene? For a painfully shy person, the latter might be incredibly difficult, while the former is no big deal. Take your cues from your own comfort level; the only real "edge" is yours and your partner's.

Myth #4: "Dungeons are gross and scary."

CLOSE BUT NO CIGAR—! ER, WELL, ACTUALLY...

OK, all right, yes. Some dungeons are gross and scary and... dungeon-esque. And do you know why? Because some perverts enjoy the down-'n'-dirty, hot and taboo energy they experience in such a space.

Most dungeons, though (also known as play spaces, kink clubs, erotic arenas, bondage dojos, sex temples and many other terms), are well kept. They are sometimes darkly lit for mood, and sometimes brightly illuminated so you can see what you are doing. Usually, play spaces are cleaned regularly, and exist within well-maintained venues. You will encounter the occasional venue that is not kept up, is rarely (if ever) cleaned, and really is downright creepy. Vote with your feet and your dollars. Try out the various venues available to you. When you find what works for you, enjoy what that venue has to offer.

I met a guy who, upon eagerly arriving at a dungeon, seemed to become more and more deflated as he took in what was happening around him. When I asked him what was up, he said he was really disappointed. The dungeon wasn't very... dungeony. It was clean, and comfortable. Apparently, his perception of the scene was that he would, upon arriving at the venue, find himself beset by erotic ninjas who would overpower him and "force" him to play with everyone. While you can probably find events where one can pre-negotiate to be abducted by sexy ninjas, such activities will require a lot of advance legwork.

Myth #5: "Walking into a kink event makes you an available target for any type of perversion."

DENIED!

First of all, we are all about consent. Permission must be requested and granted before any of this freaky deliciousness takes place. Period. Second, not everyone enjoys the same activities. Third, you don't have to play in public. You can be kinky and a wholly private player. If you occasionally wish to share in the energy of an open dungeon, that is fine. If you thrive under the admiring glances of fellow kinksters, public play is your happy place. And if you never want to be seen in public playing, that is absolutely fine too. You get to make that call, and you get to change your mind if you want, down the road.

Myths Within the Community

As you discover the community, you will also discover that we have a few myths and fairy tales of our own — ideas that might not serve us so well and that can seem like hard-and-fast rules when they are actually subject to your experience, your intuition, and your interpretation. Let's explore a few of the common ones...

Myth #6: "The kink community is a perfect utopia."

DO NOT PASS GO, DO NOT COLLECT $200.

Like Soylent Green, the kink community is made of people. We are a microcosm of the world at large. We are not a utopian society in which everyone is more evolved, sexier, cooler, smarter, better, faster, stronger, or floating on an ethereal cloud of spiritual and sexual enlightenment. You will run into people who rub you the wrong way, and you will eventually ruffle a few feathers, too. You will meet some jerks, closed-minded people, folks with personal beliefs and politics that are abhorrent to you, racists, misogynists, homo/hetero/transphobic individuals, left-and-right-wingnuts, and people who act as though they fart rainbows and poop cupcakes. Endeavor to keep a sense of humor, tolerance, understanding, supportiveness, acceptance, and willingness to listen, as well as share ideas and resources. And always remember: nobody – not you, not anyone else – is right all the time. Keep hold of your own ethics, your values; follow your gut and your heart.

Myth #7: "There is 'One True Way' to do kink right."

NICE TRY, KID.

There are many schools of thought on how to do kink, and each of them is exactly right – for the people who do it that way. Some things, though, are usually done in specific ways in order to mitigate the chances of potential harm to ourselves and our partners; in such cases, reinventing the wheel may not be the best approach. Sanitizing toys and practicing safer sex, for example, might be "rules" that are ignored at your peril.

Individuals who are passionate about their life path and deeply invested in their approach to kink and sexuality may believe deeply that their choices are superior. This is a human thing: we come to this world with so much energy, and once we find a way that works for us it can sometimes feel like we are compelled to share our discovery with everyone – and sometimes that sharing can become a bit dogmatic. Such dogmas do not have to be shunned wholesale. Perhaps these disciples of deviance have a few ideas or methods you might incorporate into your approach, picking up just the bits that work for you. Or perhaps they do not. There is a right way to do kink for you – your way.

Myth #8: "Collars mean the same thing to everyone."

JUMP BACK, JACK!

For some, collars are a fashion statement. Others use them as an indicator of identity. There are people who believe collars should only be worn as a statement of serious commitment to a relationship. Some dominants might wear a collar, and a collared, owned slave might not wear a collar at all. As you navigate the kink community, know that the beliefs around what these symbols of erotic expression mean will vary.

Just because someone is wearing a collar, do not assume they are free to boss around. And even if they are slave-identified, this does not mean they are *your* slave. If you see someone wearing a collar, politely ask them what the collar symbolizes, if anything, to them – it's the only way you'll find out.

Myth #9: "Everyone is OK with everyone else's kink."

IF ONLY!

There is an almost ubiquitous mantra in the kink community: "Your kink is not my kink, but your kink is OK." It's a great romantic ideal, and a wonderful goal. Someday, our community may achieve that level of full inclusion, tolerance, and openness. Until that day comes? Be aware that some people may not "get" what you are into, and that there may be clashes between subcommunities based on ethical framework, personal values, discomfort, life history, and more.

As people, we make judgments about what does and doesn't work for us. But keep in mind: we are sharing the playground with people who will love differently. Vociferous and pointed attacks on others based on our own limits and belief systems is not a pathway to community, tolerance and understanding. It helps to keep in mind that, regardless of whether or not others accept your kink, you will find fellow travelers who do understand, embrace and celebrate your diversity. And you can celebrate them in turn.

Myth #10: "The past was the golden age of BDSM."

NOT SO MUCH.

Our various origin myths are often rather romantic – that long ago there was some secret, powerful cabal of gay leather men/enlightened heterosexual swingers/wealthy European and Asian fetishists who had a single unified vision hidden away from the world at large. They were sexual masters and held the key for all wisdom and erotic evolution. There was only one way to do things "back then" and that way was the right way — and lo, we have since fallen from grace and sullied the traditions.

Of course, hindsight is not only 20-20, but often tinted with foggy, rosy, nostalgic sunglasses. Thirty years from now, folks will likely look back and laud this as the golden age.

The roots of our communities are rich, fertile grounds for research and study. However, it was not a golden age. In fact, large parts of it sucked. We are forever indebted to those who came before us as sexual explorers, who fought imprisonment, experienced abuse at the hands of police, had their children taken from them, and were murdered for their non-conformist sexual identities. The freedoms we experience today are a direct result of their struggles. Enshrining those experiences in the amber of some glowing, utopian ideal diminishes the reality of their sacrifices.

Myth #11: "Real kinksters follow formal dominant/submissive (D/S) protocols."

THAT'S A GOOD ONE, TELL ME ANOTHER!

If anyone says they are a "real" anything in the community, or exhort you that "real" players do so-and-so, consider taking it with a grain of salt. Whether they are a "real" master, "real" slave, "real" fetishist, "real"... well, you get the idea... they have an agenda. Their agenda may be a valid one for them and their circle of friends, chosen family and partners. And it may or may not have any relation to your journey.

Some events will request, or require, that attendees follow specific behavior patterns, manners and types of etiquette. This is what many folks mean when they say a newcomer should learn "protocols"; they are encouraging the new person to learn what manners, etiquette and behavior patterns will help them integrate into their chosen community. This is good advice (especially if you are attending events with specific/formal protocol systems, where attendance is based on the willingness to follow such protocols), but knowing protocols does not make you better at being kinky, and some groups of kinky people have very casual approaches to protocol.

Myth #12: "All kinksters play SSC ('Safe, Sane and Consensual')."

OOOOO... THAT ONE IS A BIT TRICKIER...

Safe, Sane and Consensual (SSC) has become an almost universal kinky catchphrase. It is a great place to start the conversation for many folks new to kink. The acronym originates from a "Statement of Purpose" released by the Gay Male SM Activists (GMSMA) of New York in 1983, and was written by slave david stein, along with board members Martin Berkenwald and Bob Gillespie. These three words proceeded to spread as an easy way to demystify kinky sex for a broader audience, and to demarcate the difference between consensual kink and predatory, abusive, antisocial behavior. Over the years, other acronyms have evolved as well. Gary Switch proposed Risk-Aware Consensual Kink (RACK) in 1999, in order to acknowledge the risks inherent in any kink activities.

At the end of the day, though, they are all acronyms — simplifications of the real desires and approaches many kinky people take to their journeys. For additional information on differentiating kink from abuse, please see Appendix 4H: SM vs. Abuse.

As you can see, these myths often have an origin in some truth, and may have lessons for us. They are not the be-all-end-all truth. When someone shares their truths with you, understand that their story hails from a specific voice, history, and perspective. See what resonates for you, and never stop questioning and exploring.

Courtesy and Respect

When discussing respect, we are not encouraging you to reflexively defer to people simply because of their given or assumed title, their position within their community, or their experience. We are talking about treating people courteously, about respecting their boundaries and their humanity.

We believe that individuals earn honor, esteem and high regard based on their values and behaviors. Respect and courtesy, though, belong to all of us. Here are some fundamental pillars of respectful behavior that we firmly believe will help facilitate your journey, within the kink world and beyond.

Respect yourself.

That's right: respect starts with that person in the mirror. It is absolutely critical that you maintain a solid level of self-esteem and respect for your humanity, your needs, wants, passions, limits and boundaries. Whether you are brand new to the community or have been around the block more times than you'd like to count, you can't have a sound foundation for your journey unless you have a healthy respect for yourself. Lack of self-respect can lead you to sublimate your own needs, be vulnerable to those who might take advantage of you, and experience unnecessary ennui. And we don't want that. You are the one living in your body: treat that individual with the utmost respect, and you will find that others are more likely to do so too.

Be honest and maintain personal integrity.

Sometimes, we can get caught up in a wave of new experiences and sensations, or after a time lose sight of our own internal compass. Examining your motives and acknowledging internal conflicts can facilitate a healthy level of self-respect. Keeping your truth at the forefront can help you to take the course that will be in your best interest. Respecting yourself enough to embrace your truth will serve as a blueprint for how others can respect you as well.

Respect your gut instincts.

The gut instinct, or "that little voice in your head," is a helpful ally in your erotic explorations. People, places and things can seem irresistible, seductive and highly alluring, and yet that little voice in the back of your head will some-times pipe up with a "Hold your horses there, cowboy..." that may well make the difference between an excellent adventure and a fast ride into a brick wall. Your body has amazing wisdom within it. It may be picking up on subtle cues, information that is not processed by your conscious mind. Respect yourself; do not suppress your gut-level intuition.

Respect your process by entering the community at your own pace.

Some folks are Deep-End-Plunging-Full-Immersion types. Others wish to take a far more conservative, one-toe-in-the-water-at-a-time approach. We very strongly advocate the pace that feels the most authentic to your personal truths. Pushing yourself forward or reining yourself in when it goes against your grain will not serve you well in the long run.

Some people will cast a jaundiced eye because they feel like you are moving too fast/slow, or that you take too many risks/are overly cautious. Their opinions may be useful to hear, but at the end of the day you are living your own life. So long as you take full responsibility for yourself and your choices, and avoid negatively affecting other people's lives, these decisions are best made from your own heart and mind. You can take as much time, or as little, as you need. The perverts will still be there, perving.

Dress (or undress) to a level that respects your comfort level.

Some folks are natural-born nudists, free with their bodies and naked at the drop of a flogger. Other individuals chose to remain fully clothed. Fetishwear can be a huge turn-on for some; others are great strolling into the dungeon in a pair of sneakers and a t-shirt. You absolutely do not have to run out and buy thousands of dollars in kinky clothes to have fun in the dungeon, though putting together a few outfits in basic black doesn't hurt. If fetish attire doesn't turn you on or those $600 boots are a bit out of your budgetary reach, that's fine. Many events and parties will have dress codes (as indicated in Chapter 3), but with a little imagination, you can look fabulous regardless.

Try on different hats!

As a sexual adventurer, you can feel free to explore a myriad of self-identifications, labels and identities. Some of us come into the scene just knowing that we are hardwired hardcore dominant sadists, only to discover that receiving a nice over-the-knee spanking is highly titillating. In fact, who says you can't be a dominant sadist who loves spankings? Don't let a commitment to a label impede your explorations and limit your freedom.

A label or two can be a useful place to start exploration, a conversation, or as a way to be turned on by hearing them from a lover's mouth, but may not be the perfect option for everyone. And if one label doesn't suit you, try, try again! You might be a dominant, end of story. However there are dominant masochists, slave-identified sadists, owners who switch... the permutations are only limited by your personal limits, desires and boundaries. As you grow into your kinky self, you will find some labels stick for the duration, some are fleeting, and still others you'd never considered may well be perfect for you many years down the road. Long-term success in the kink community walks hand-in-hand with authentic

I do love to play dress-up! And I love to be comfortable. I refuse to let my style choices be dictated by the comfort level of someone else. When I first entered the kink scene, I was shy about being naked: I was not fetish-model skinny. Then I saw people of all shapes, sizes and abilities doing all manner of things in all styles of dress and undress and realized that I was always going to be me, in a custom corset, leather skirt and boots, or in a pair of Crocs and a sundress.

expression, and forcing yourself into a given stereotype, box or label may be at odds with the true fullness of who you are.

Own your ethics and don't check them at the door.

When you step onto the path of self-discovery and exploration through kink and all that it includes, you enter as an individual, with your own inner compass, morals, ideals, limits and belief system. There may be pressure to change, or adapt, and there may well be people who strongly believe that the way they've chosen is not only good for them, it is good for you, too. Being buffeted by the opinions of others can seem overwhelming, especially if your ethics are at odds with the flow of the majority of people in the broader community. Taking stock in yourself, trusting that you know you best, and that your beliefs ought not be compromised according to the whims and vagaries of others, can help ground you. Doing what you know is right for you will go a long way towards keeping an even keel when the seas of public opinion get rough.

If you don't like it, don't do it.

This seems obvious, but peer pressure is a bitch. Not everyone is into floggers, pudding wrestling, group sex, or straitjackets. But when you walk into the party, or see miles of discussion on the Internet about how the ultimate high is inverted suspension while being set on fire and eating caviar, suddenly you may find yourself caught up in the passion of public opinion and cast around for someone to hang you up, light you up and feed you sturgeon roe. And if that is truly what you desire, go for it (after proper training of course). However, subjecting yourself to an activity simply because it seems like the cool thing to do can lead to a rather empty feeling.

This goes for all participants in a scene. Dominants and top-identified folks are also pressured to be fluent in all sorts of skill sets because it is often expected of them to do so. Being able to throw a ten-foot bullwhip with stunning accuracy takes a great deal of time, energy and practice. If whips don't particularly turn you on, but you think you have to throw a whip to be cool, then your heart probably isn't in the task. It doesn't matter what the cool kids are doing.

It's fine for you to say "no" to something, even if it is a classic staple of kink. In fact, it is vital that you say "No, thanks!" when you don't want to do something. Permitting others to pressure you, acquiescing to it, then having "buyer's remorse" isn't fair to you and it isn't fair to your friends, lovers and partners.

When in doubt, wait it out. Give yourself time to consider and ponder your desires. Then do what fuels your imagination, your desires, and your passions.

Respect others in the scene.

Interacting with respect makes it more likely that others will respect us in turn. It's also just a nice thing to do. We have explored some ways to treat yourself with respect when entering the scene. Flip these ideas around, apply them to others you may encounter, and you are starting off on a path of positive interaction and respectful communication.

Respect their boundaries.

Just as it is critical for you to have your boundaries respected, it is vital that you honor the boundaries of others. Sometimes, people who have been around in the scene for a while will assume that a boundary or a "limit" is something that should be pushed, or that someone only has a boundary because they are new, or because they just haven't tried it. Pushing someone else's boundaries is not a decision that random folk can make: if someone has said "no" to something, do not pester them on that point. This means listening when folks say "no," and also when they say "yes." A graceful acceptance of a boundary establishes you as someone who treats people well, and helps to create one of the most valuable items of capital in our community: trust.

Full-time? Part-time? Sometimes? Play-time?

There are people in the community who call it home. You will encounter individuals for whom kink is their full-time experience, such as individuals following a path of mastery/slavery, sacred kink, or leather. On the other hand, that kinky stuff may be something in which folks indulge only occasionally, or only as part of their bedroom activities. Respect the degree of involvement of the people with whom you interact; one approach is not "better," more "serious" or more "real" than any other.

Respect voices and opinions.

There will be people who will offer you advice and opinions, and who will freely share their thoughts with you. And this is great! Of course, opinions are like assholes... we all have them. And not all opinions are created equal. It can seem like some people offer their opinions and advice with the weight of authority, and that they need to be taken seriously. Experience, talent and perseverance often are hallmarks of those who have proven themselves knowledgeable and reliable... but sometimes just hanging around long enough gives people gravitas beyond that which they're entitled to.

If someone is offering advice, teaching or sharing information, you can, if nothing else, respect their effort. Be open to listening to what they are sharing before making snap decisions as to whether or not it has value. That sassy young whippersnapper who has only been to one play party, yet spouts off about safety, may be a doctor with real-time knowledge backed by a certain amount of authority. And that twenty-nine year veteran of perversion may well be ignorant of power exchange dynamics. Keep an open mind about the value of the information being shared, see how well it resonates with you, take what you need and leave the rest.

Respect every type of body.

You will encounter folks who are thin and fat, tall and short, ebony-dark and pale-skinned. There are individuals covered in fur and shaved smooth, with implants ranging from breasts to horns and everything in-between. There are male, female, intersexed, transgender, and third-gendered bodies of all sorts. Whether people use wheelchairs or sport high heels (or use wheelchairs while sporting high heels), they each have their own beauty. Mocking or denigrating other people in any way displays a fundamental lack of respect. You may disagree with a choice someone has made in how to modify their body, or you find a particular body type does not spur your libido, and that is your right as a discerning human. However, respectful treatment of others, regardless of your personal opinion, may open you to growth and learning, and can challenge some of your assumptions about yourself and other people. When you treat people of all physical types with respect and dignity, you foster a truly open and accepting community.

Respect people's complexity and humanity.

People are not one-dimensional cardboard cutouts. They did not show up to make all of your hot, sweaty, delicious twisted fantasies come true. We know, we know... total downer. But the fact remains: they had a life before this moment with you, and will exist after you leave. Just as you aren't there to fulfill the fantasies of the person in front of you, they aren't here to fulfill your every fantasy and whim.

Respecting people's humanity first is a great way to get to know folks and create quality interactions. Crawling across the dungeon on your knees and licking the sleek sexy boots of that hot dominant, or grabbing the nearest seemingly compliant submissive by the hair and bending them to your will, may seem hot as hell. But first and foremost, we are humans – with thoughts, feelings, emotions, strong suits, weaknesses, fears and dreams. Treating folks as fully manifested beings rather than instant fantasy objects can help you to get to that hot hair-pulling boot-licking scene later on.

Don't touch other people without explicit permission.

Some people love touch, and some subsections of the community can be very touchy-feely. Others enjoy formality and may only wish to shake hands, while still others eschew physical touch from strangers or find handshakes physically painful. There are those for whom any sort of touch is a profound intimacy, and others who embrace and kiss on first meetings. You will, in all likelihood, feel more comfortable in some situations and less so in others. But there is a great way to minimize awkwardness and boundary overstepping: ask permission.

Sometimes you can take cues from other people around you. Other times, appearances can be deceptive. The fact that someone is being tied up and manhandled by a bunch of people is not an invitation for you to jump in uninvited – ask someone if you can touch the bound person, too, before you do. Hovering in tight proximity can feel very invasive for some folks, too. There are rare parties where a "free-for-all" attitude is encouraged, and others where rigid protocols for addressing dominant and submissive individuals are stipulated. Read the rules and guidelines of these gatherings before you attend.

You lookin' at me?

Most people who are involved in scenes that take place in open play space do so because they enjoy sharing their scenes, their energy, and like to be watched. They might have an exhibitionistic streak, or are pushing their boundaries around playing in public. We encourage you to be a respectful voyeur. The kink community is a great place to people-watch.

However: enjoying the scene or checking out a playstyle you've never witnessed is one thing, staring and gasping in shock, leering at someone manically, or drooling actively is another. Invasive voyeurs do not contribute to the positive atmosphere of a gathering, and being pushy in your voyeurism can quickly get you labeled as "the creepy kinkster." There are some exceptions, of course.

There are sex clubs with a kinky slant where leering anonymous voyeurism and even wanking are encouraged as an addition to the down-n-dirty environment.

If you are at an event or a gathering, and someone is staring at you and you are uncomfortable, say something. Suffering in silence helps no one. That "creepy kinkster" may not even realize what they are doing, and politely but firmly mentioning it might be the catalyst they need to raise their awareness. If you aren't comfortable doing so, mention it to the party hosts, dungeon staff, or event organizers. They want everyone to have an enjoyable time, and usually want to know if there is something troubling one of their guests. That way, everybody plays, and everybody wins.

Hey! That's my stuff!

Never presume to grab hold of people's bags, toys, jewelry, wardrobe, or any other of all those things and accoutrements that people may possess to facilitate their kink. Unless it is freely offered, or a sign indicates that something is for public use, always ask first. Sometimes folks will say yes, but grabbing without asking is rarely viewed as a charming behavior. This is especially true for collars, jewelry, and leather items, which may have profound meaning to the wearer or bearer.

Be aware of your conversational intimacy.

What you perceive as being intimate may not be the same as what others perceive as being intimate. You might consider that conversation about the size and magnificence of your genitals to be totally casual, while others might find it to be too much information. Discussing your bruised ass might be par for your course, but might be wildly inappropriate even for your closest friend. If you aren't sure, ask. Saying "Hey, I had a great scene, may I share it with you?" gives you the opportunity to respect their limits. Likewise, if someone is sharing in a way that is beyond your comfort level, let them know. Respect the time and place. In the elevator at the kink convention while you are crowded in with a family of five is not respectful of their boundaries.

Treat people how they wish to be treated.

The Golden Rule (aka the Ethics of Reciprocity) seems like a no-brainer, a default rule that we are all taught from childhood. "Do unto others as you would have them do unto you." or some variation thereof, is a maxim that crosses cultural, religious and national boundaries. In our communities. this rule can occasionally become a bit muddier. Some people see behaviors like holding open a door or referring to someone as "Sir" or "Ma'am" a basic courtesy, while others may consider such behaviors to be part of a power dynamic. Some people wish to be addressed with fancy formal titles, for others a first name suffices.

If in doubt, start by being civil, pleasant, and nice overall. Holding a door for someone, or saying thank you for someone who held a door for you, is lovely. However, do not automatically take polite behaviors as indications of deeper interests and desires. Respecting that others may not follow your paradigm will ease your process of discovering and growing within the various communities. Respect your own boundaries and values, and those of others, and remember that how we wish to be treated may not mirror the desires of others.

Respecting someone does not mean liking someone.

You can respect an individual's skills, advice, ideas, experience, station (i.e. dungeon monitor), and still personally opine that they are, to put it politely, a flaming douchebag. There will be people with skills and talent you respect, but who do not share your personal, spiritual or ethical beliefs. That does not shove them out of the running for being treated with basic courtesy. Neither should courtesy or respect be mistaken for service or submission. Just because someone is nice to you doesn't mean they want to fuck you. And just because you don't like someone doesn't mean you ought to treat them with disrespect.

In Chapter 7, we will dig a little deeper to explore some terrific and some troubling behaviors that you should be aware of as you venture into the community.

Respecting the space.

Every space you enter is someone's home, or somewhere they have spent many hours (or years) helping create. Their effort should be respected:

- **Read the event waivers and rules.** If you are going into a space, find out what the rules are, and, if asked to sign anything, read it first.

- **Follow the rules.** Rules are there for a reason. If you are uncertain of what a rule means, or why it is there, ask questions outside of the play space/dungeon for clarification. They may be due to regional laws, discomfort around certain types of play, or past incidents.

- **Explore the culture and "unspoken rules."** There may be specific protocols or behaviors expected in a space, and it may not have occurred to hosts to write them down. People may be perceived as rude if they do not know the unspoken rules and culture. If possible, find someone familiar with the environment to help clue you in. Party hosts and event sponsors would be well advised to help folks respect the space by communicating as much as possible as clearly as possible.

- **Clean up.** Clean up after your scenes, after your food, after yourself in general. Strive to leave the space improved over when you first found it. This makes you an awesome guest, and likely to be invited back.

- **"Well, they didn't SAY I couldn't!"** Consider asking if it is OK – asking permission is a better policy than begging for forgiveness. Sure, the hosts might not have listed that activity as a "no-no," but only because it hadn't occurred to them to indicate that unleashing a swarm of bees in a crowded dungeon was not cool.

- **Find out what you can do to help.** It might be nice to bring food to share, to volunteer to help with setup or clean-up (party hosts love this!), and to acknowledge the hard work put into the event by sending a thank-you note afterward.

Beyond the dungeon: Respecting people outside the community.

Respect must extend to people outside of our community with whom we will inevitably intersect. This includes our coworkers, family, friends, hotel staff, government officials, other folks at a restaurant, and even total strangers. As we discover our bliss, it is important to remember, as we are living in the default world, that we respect the choices and lifestyle of non-kinky folks.

- **"Vanilla" bashing.** "Vanilla" is a term used within the kink community to refer to individuals not participating in kink, who do not identify as kinky, or who don't understand or like kink. It has taken on a rather pejorative flavor, and is often used to denigrate people who don't choose, or aren't aware of our communities. If we bash others, we invite reciprocal intolerance. Kinky sex is only better sex if you like kinky sex. Kinky sex is not "better" or "more enlightened" – and anyway, you have no idea what is actually happening in the bedroom of yonder random "vanilla" person.

Bashing anyone is bad because bigotry sucks. So does being condescending or trying to seem superior. Tut-tutting over the "poor vanillas" who are missing out on the awesomeness of kinky sex is like capping on a lesbian because they "just haven't found the right man." Vanilla, as a spice, is expensive, complex and fulfilling, and those who live that life are worthy of respect.

- **Avoid slamming the kinks of others.** Making rude, derogatory or insulting statements about weird leather folks, crazy swingers, messed-up masochists, wacky vampires, polyamorous dorks, M/S freaks, creepy furries, etc., doesn't help anyone. Someone out there probably thinks your kink is pretty weird, wacky or wrong. Try to avoid antagonistic, judgmental and abusive speech.

- **Clean up after yourself.** Hotel staff did not consent to a viewing of all your slippery dildos, and your party hosts aren't going to be thrilled to pick up your body-fluid-soaked paper towels, used condoms and assorted trash. If you are at a convention event at a hotel, put your toys away before the staff come to clean. If you leave a big mess, leave a big tip. If you're at a private party, help out by picking up.

- **Be street-appropriate, not just street-legal.** Many events have guidelines for attendees along the lines of "Please be street-legal in public

Years back, I met and became lovers with a guy who I assumed was "vanilla" and who self-identified that way. He did so defensively, having had several friends who were in the kink community and who teased him for not being as sexually adventurous as they were. He was tired of that air of superiority and stoically maintained that they had no knowledge of or business judging what he did behind closed doors as less "evolved" sex. I found it fascinating that this supposedly "vanilla" guy easily engaged in rough sex, and in role-play fantasies that involved rape and incest, and generally had a very 1950s era household sensibility. When I gently questioned his referring to himself as "vanilla" when he engaged in such kinky activities with so much abandon, he shrugged. "That's just the way I am. Ain't nothing kinky about that," he drawled. And who was I to disagree? We enjoyed several years of "vanilla" perversion, privately, and with lurid abandon.

spaces" on their information sheets. They often mean street-appropriate, especially in hallways, elevators, arriving at the event, etc. Grandpa and the grandkids did not need to see you in a G-string (even if it has a matching bra), or the t-shirt in question-able taste ("A Woman's Place Is On Her Knees"), even if these are, technically, street-legal. Think about what is "street appropriate" in the city you are in; the answer may be different in San Francisco than in San Antonio. You are representing a larger community, and drawing negative attention isn't the best way to ensure that we will be welcomed into these spaces in the future.

- **Keep the answers appropriate to the persons asking the questions.** When interacting with the default world, you will run into people who are genuinely curious about what the hell you're up to in your shiny catsuit carrying five big bags. If the folks in the elevator ask why you are dressed in a gimp suit, consider an answer such as "a private costume party" as compared to "a kinky sex party." Shocking answers do not always make friends, and those people didn't consent to hear your scene report. Some folks really are curious, and some kinksters really do wish to serve as ambassadors. It is helpful to brainstorm a few responses in advance (and see Chapters 4 and 11 for ideas on how to explain this stuff in friendly terminology), and adjust your responses to the receptivity and curiosity of the person asking.

Remember, you are an ambassador for our community. Represent yourself, and our community, with respect for the world around us.

Personal Responsibility

Your experience comes down to you. Yes, you will have loving partners who will journey with you, and yes, you will have friends who will watch your back. But at the end of the day, it is up to you to speak for your needs, wants and desires, as well as to keep an eye out for your best interests.

Sometimes, coming into new communities can feel like a "reset" button has been pushed. Everything's brand new and scary; you're back in junior high on the first day of school. And while it may be new, you are still coming to this experience as an adult, and you can (and should) bring your adult self and experiences along with you on your journey.

If someone oversteps a boundary of yours, express this, advise them, and make sure they're aware of the conflict. If nothing is said, nothing can be addressed. It can be difficult to take responsibility for expressing an issue or conflict, but in the long run no one is served by your unwillingness to speak up. Air your grievances with compassion and respect for yourself, for your boundaries, and for the humanity (and fallibility) of others. This approach can go a long way towards mitigating difficulties and resolving conflict.

Check Your Assumptions

As humans, we make assumptions. Some are helpful: assuming that stepping off a tall building will result in death is an excellent way to avoid deceleration trauma. Some are safe enough: we assume what temperature it is outside based on what it looks like from inside. Some are trickier: we assume someone's taste in music, their economic status, their age or their gender identity, based on the clothes they wear. And some are troubling: we assume the person walking behind us is a threat based on their skin color.

Assumptions get us into trouble, all the time. People, being people, carry this assumptive tendency with them as they become part of our communities. The following are some common assumptions that folks may have when learning about kink, and we'd like to take a look and maybe debunk a few of them along the way.

"Everyone is just like me!"

INDEED, NOT.

There is a vast spectrum of genders, orientations, economic classes, politics, body types, abilities, mental/emotional capacity, religions, beliefs, ages, ethnic backgrounds, relationship structures, behaviors, philosophies, careers, interests, hobbies, erotic desires, internal identities, external identities and levels of experience in the community. You really cannot assume anything about anyone based solely on their physical appearance or presentation.

"Age equals experience."

NOPE.

There are folks who are under twenty who are experts at their craft, and people in their eighties who are just trying out kink for the first time. The number of years that someone has been involved in in the community is also a flawed indicator of experience. Someone who has been in the scene for one year but been going to parties and classes four times a week can possess more cumulative experience than someone who has been in the scene for ten years but who only plays once a year.

"Big toybags and hot outfits equal experience."

NAY, WE SAY.

A toybag (the container full of tools and toys to use in a kink encounter/ scene) has no bearing on experience. That top may have bought those six gorgeous whips and floggers last week. That slave in full Gorean chains and regalia may have just opened a UPS package and declared themselves fully trained. And the low-key player with neither elaborate toys nor extensive fetish wardrobe may be a well-respected pillar of the community. Get to know people, ask around, observe, and keep an open mind.

"If their label complements mine, they will want to play."

SORRY!

There are a few challenges with this assumption. If, for example, you see a dominant as a "doing and controlling" partner and a submissive as a "receiving and controlled" partner, then the first assumption might be that any top would want to play with any bottom. This is nowhere near a safe assumption. That particular dominant might not have a particular chemistry with a particular individual. They may have a partner at home, and are simply looking for friendship, or they simply may not desire to play or "scene" tonight because they had a hard day at work.

The second assumption is that a top would only want to play with a bottom. The thing is, labels can sometimes be flexible. They might also like playing with other tops, with slaves, with a human puppy, or with someone who identifies as "vanilla." Do not rule out a potential play partner just because of the labels they use: all kinds of creative matches exist in the kink community. Attraction, chemistry, curiosity and desire trump a whole lot of labels.

"If I know their kink identity, I know their personality."

NIX THIS ONE.

Some toxic assumptions can impede and damage respect within the community. If you think dominant individuals must be bossy assholes, or that someone who identifies as submissive will be a spineless doormat, you will find – based on our experience – that your assumptions are some serious bullshit.

Many of these types of assumptions are based on fictional literature and media, with fantasy and misinformation, and that they have little to do with reality.

Try to approach each individual, to engage in every encounter, with an open heart and mind. Rather than simply making assumptions about who they are, what their story is, what they are into, or how you would fit in their world, try remaining open, respectful and curious. People can and will surprise you with their many facets, and you will surprise yourself, too.

Language, Names and Social Styles

In the kink community, there are many words, terms, acronyms, abbreviations and jargon that get tossed around, and these are always changing and evolving. Start by examining some examples in Appendix 1: Kinky Lingo. In addition, some people have titles or "scene names" that they use – sometimes to obfuscate their actual identity, and sometimes because they more accurately reflect their deepest selves. One of the first points of confusion that people encounter are honorifics (such as ma'am, sir, master, mistress) and diminutives (such as girl, boy, slave).

Asking someone how they wish to be addressed is a great way to avoid inadvertently stepping on toes. And if you are not comfortable addressing someone in a particular way, you do have the right to declare that boundary. You might also with to ask people if the name by which you hear them addressed is for public consumption: hearing someone referred to as "my pet" or "my liege" may not be an invitation for you to follow suit and address them similarly. It might be a public manifestation of a personal relationship. Again, ask questions first.

Keep in mind that the name or title that you find presumptuous may be of profound importance and significance for the bearer of that moniker. Finding respectful compromises helps us find communication styles that work for all.

Sometimes people will use slang terms. They may seem overly familiar, or exceedingly distant and cold. The person who has manic body language and gets in your face while talking might be an aggressive jerk, or might be a person from New York. The person who avoids eye contact and seems to be evasive in their speech might be a passive-aggressive jellyfish, or they might be painfully shy.

If someone refers to you as "Sir" or "Ma'am," don't assume that they're making assumptions about their dynamic with you; they may just have been raised in the south of the United States, or have spent many years working in customer service. Giving folks the benefit of the doubt and remaining compassionate will help to bridge the sometimes awkward encounters we are all sure to have.

When moving from one-on-one to group conversations, take your cues from those around you. Some talks are boisterous shouting matches; others are measured and thoughtful discussions. Participating is fantastic. So is listening, and paying attention to the people around you sharing their own stories and experiences. Remaining flexible in your approach and patient as you are learning, as well as remembering that you are never too old to learn, will help you become and remain someone with whom people will welcome interaction and discussion.

Some protocols begin even before communication has started. Some people who are involved in TPE (Total Power Exchange) relationships might have protocols that are tough to understand at first glance; a TPE slave might be enjoined from speaking without the owner's permission. And if you encounter someone who plays in animal mode, it might not be appropriate to strike up a conversation about the cheese platter with the snorting, stamping human pony next to you. Take as many cues as you can from other folks; respectful questions can also help clear things up. And if you are one of the people with stringent protocols that might not be self-evident, please treat the curious with compassion rather than defensiveness. Scornful and dismissive responses to someone who is simply curious or unaware of your dynamic only places you in a poor light. Help educate, and look on it as an opportunity to help a fellow traveler on the kinky highway.

There is some crossover between our sex-positive sub-

There are people who are referred to as "master," "mistress" or "slave" so-and-so, and I have friends who will refer to people by whatever title they carry. This is not a protocol that works for me. I will only refer to someone as "master" if I am owned by them, or if I personally have firsthand knowledge of their mastery. I make it clear to them that my choice to call them so does not indicate my slavery to them, but my respect for that title. Same applies to calling all slaves as "slave such-and-such." I don't laugh in the face of someone introduced to me as Sir Lord-N-Grand Master Dragonpoop. I will, however, say "My personal protocol reserves titles for my owner. Is there an alternative way I may address you?" and proceed from there.

cultures, such as between the swinger and BDSM communities, but the difference in cultures can create misunderstandings. Some individuals with a background in the swinger community may have a "Yes until No" culture – that is, people will proceed as the interaction unfolds until someone has reached a boundary, at which point they will so advise their partner (or partners). Others will work within a model that requires a constant stream of consent in all directions, letting you know exactly what they desire in any given moment.

The BDSM communities often use a slightly different approach: generally the involved parties have agreed up front on where they wish to go in an activity and what they'd like to do; that boundary is in place for the duration of the scene – a "No until Yes" culture.

People fall all across the gender spectrum in our community. The binary of "male" and "female" shuts out a wide swath of folks (as explored in Appendix 4F). Consider asking people how they wish to be addressed. Avoiding assumptions will take you further than letting clothes, shoes and external appearance rule the day. Gender pronouns can be tricky in some parts of the kink community. The female-to-male transgendered individual to whom you have spent the past two years addressing as "he" suddenly shows up in a sparkly dress, five-inch heels and a full beard. What do you do? Asking them what pronoun they would prefer tonight gets my vote.

Of course, there is fluidity in these generalizations, and each approach can be successfully utilized depending on the needs of the people involved. This is another case where being mindful of the background of others can be helpful in mitigating miscommunications.

Though we've been encouraging you to ask questions, take care when considering when to ask those questions. If people are huddled and engaged in a private conversation, barging in, or hovering at the edge of the conversation, might be unwelcome. And please, do not ask questions of people when they are in the middle of a scene. Even when you think the scene is over... wait.

Regardless of how careful you are, you will step on toes. A heartfelt apology goes a long way towards avoiding further communication gaps. And this is true regardless of your standing, time within, or role in the community. We are all people first, and need to take responsibility for and own up to our errors.

I've been "coming down" from a very intense scene, in cool-down mode, and had people roll up asking questions about what I'd just done, if I was OK, where I was gonna be speaking next, and why they hadn't heard back from me about that e-mail they'd sent last week. If you aren't invited into the space of a scene before during or immediately after, it is a great plan to keep your distance. Your question can wait.

Rather than a generic "Oh, sorry!' consider using "I apologize for _____" or "I'm sorry for _____," specifically referencing the infraction. We've found that this strategy opens up the possibility for dialogue more than a generic apology.

Maintaining Privacy: Yours and Mine

Many people leading alternative lives under the radar of the mainstream are not "out" about their full journey. This is a perfectly valid choice: they consider their sex lives to be private, and really not to be shared with the general public. Others are involved in professions where the knowledge of their proclivities could endanger their careers, or have family members who would not be supportive if news of their kink side were to be publicized. Members of kink communities have lost custody of children, been dismissed from jobs, been shunned by family and loved ones, and faced violence – criminal, non-consensual violence – at the hands of others because of their orientation. So when we say privacy is a big deal, we really mean it.

The numbers of "out" community members are growing. However, "outness" should be an active choice; each kinkster gets to determine if they will use their full legal name, show their face, and have complete transparency about who they are and what they do.

When you are introduced to someone as "River Peaseblossom," asking their "real name" is presumptuous and rude. Besides, what makes the time they spend as Peaseblossom any less real than the persona they inhabit in their professional world? Or, for that matter, how do you know that their parents weren't hippies who really enjoyed Shakespeare? This is how they wish to be addressed, and so it should be. If, at the office, River goes by the name "Linda Smith, head of marketing for BigInternetCompany.com," that is none of your business.

Should she decide, once she feels comfortable, to share the name by which she is known in the default world, great. But even then, there are pitfalls. If you run into Linda at the mall which she is hanging out with her mom and sister-in-law and you shout "Yo, River Peaseblossom! You looked great in the dungeon last week! See ya at the munch!" you have potentially put her in a tough spot.

Think before you speak. Don't ever "out" people in public spaces. In fact, even in kink-friendly space, yelling someone's personal business is a no-no. Unless you have asked for and been expressly granted permission to share someone's personal data and details, don't do it.

The same applies to gender identity. Some people use the framework of our communities to explore their fluidity around gender. If the lovely, sexy flirty gal you met at the last munch strides past you presenting as male, blurting out "Hey, weren't you a girl last weekend?" is not only inappropriate but disrespectful of their privacy and their journey, and can also compromise their safety. For some, this is the only safe space where they can undertake such journeys, and a thoughtless blunder can put them at very real risk.

Scene names can sometimes have several manifestations. Some people have a name they use in the pagan community, a name they use when they swing, another for BDSM play parties, and their human animal name... not counting the name on the government-issued identification. A friendly "Nice to see you again... um, how shall I address you?" works wonders for helping to manage that awkwardness and avoid potentially problematic faux pas. If you know there is a likelihood you'll run into your kinky friend in public, ask them how they wish to be addressed, if at all, in public. Some people will prefer you pass on by without acknowledgment, some are willing to chat if they are alone but not if they are with a co-worker or family, and some are completely open to being acknowledged. Respecting their wishes will go a long way towards maintaining respect.

No matter how scrupulous you are about maintaining the privacy of your identity, you may run into situations where you have to make decisions about how closely you will hold your personal information. If you decide you wish to attend a local munch or play party, often your legal information needn't be revealed. However, some organizations and events will need to obtain your legal information. If you are attending an adult play party or a kink convention, the hosts have a very real legal obligation to confirm that no minors are involved. You may be required to pay for the event with a credit card. If this is too big a concern or risk for you, don't attend those events. Only you can make that call.

Event hosts are scrupulous about maintaining privacy: their reputations are on the line and producers are invested in maintaining the safety and comfort of their guests. If this still gives you pause, it is likely it will impact the quality of your enjoyment of that particular event.

Sharing stories

So much of what we do can be exciting, scary, thought-provoking, puzzling and enlightening – it feels like we need to tell everybody! With instant access (and we mean instant) to social networks, blogs, email discussion groups and the like, the average pervert has a virtually unlimited virtual audience available to them. Listening to the experiences of others, asking questions, swapping stories around the campfire, or blogging your experiences is a great way to join in the non-stop flow of discussion and dialogue in our community.

However, it is critical to err on the side of caution when discussing intimate details of intimate activities. Not everyone wants the details of their sex lives published on the Internet, or chatted up around the buffet table in the dungeon party.

If you are going to mention that you had an awesome flogging scene last night, rather than gushing, "I was playing with Mistress Madness at the Dark Dungeon X party last night – she is so amazing with a flogger... she has a really beautiful red-and gold handmade cat-o-nine-tails with an inset crystal handle. She is so talented with dirty talk during a scene, especially with that Australian accent of hers, and has the sexiest ass I've ever seen!"

... you might consider saying, "I was playing with a new play partner last night. They were really great with a flogger, had excellent energy, intriguing toys, and I thought they were incredibly sexy, too!"

The former, while wonderfully detailed, gives away the person's identity, details of their property, and is maybe more information that the average person needs to know. Now, if you have asked Mistress Madness if she is happy with your detailed report posting, gush away! However, defaulting to the second option helps protect you and your partners.

This is even more true for posting and linking photos or videos. Many kink events restrict the use of photographic equipment of any kind. However, people often have kinky pictures of themselves and their friends, partners and lovers doing all manner of kinkiness. Even a picture taken at the dinner table at a munch has the potential to out someone if it shows up online. Before you share it on your friendly neighborhood fetish site, ask everyone in the picture if they are OK with being revealed in this manner. Some will say no, some will ask that their face be obscured, some are fine with being shown but not with any name associated, and some will want full photo credit and links to their own website.

When it comes to sharing your own information, we recommend proceeding with caution. Social networking has created circles, chutes, ladders, hidden doorways and amazing information streams that carry data all over the internet. Facial recognition technology makes it possible for a photo that isn't tagged with your name to be linked back to you. Consider what your risks might be if suddenly everyone knew you enjoy consensual BDSM. If you can be out, that is fantastic; you're very fortunate. The more kinksters out there about their kink, the less pathologized it becomes in the eyes of the casual observer. However, if you have any concerns, respect them and consider them before you take the plunge and post photos of the hot temporary piercing scene. In Chapter 5, we will further explore profiles and social media, with some helpful tips and considerations.

So, now that you have an awareness of kink culture and etiquette, the question stands... when do you get to do all this kinky stuff? Where do you meet kinky people? Where do you go? Are we there yet?

We're glad you asked!

Chapter 3

So Many Choices! Events, Groups and Gatherings

Which Event Is Right for You?

IN THE PAST, kink events used to be rare, and gaining access to them was often a lengthy, difficult process. Now they are everywhere, it seems, and of unimaginable variety.

As you read about the various types of events, see what grabs your attention. Not all of them will appeal to you, nor should they. Becoming aware of the different types of events may help you focus on the events that will best fit your needs, wants and desires, and improve the return on your time, money and energy.

Research

As you look into the event you are considering, keep a few questions in mind:

- **What type of event is it?** Is it a munch, a dance club night, or a three-week escape to Jamaica with fetish performers and a full latex dress code? The type of event will determine how much it costs, how much planning is required, what to expect, and what to wear.

- **Who can attend?** Most kink events have age requirements for entry. These commonly start at the age of majority (when you are legally an adult). If this is an event where alcohol is served, the age limits are adjusted accordingly. Some events have further attendance restrictions. They may only allow people of a specific gender (in which case, you'll want to research whether that criterion is based on birth gender, legal gender identification, or internal identity). Or they may be only for people under 35, people over 55, or members of the sponsoring club — to name just a few examples.

- **What "hoops" does it take to attend?** Some events are listed in the local newspaper and anyone can drop in. Others require pre-interviews online, by phone, or in person. Still others require a current member's recommendation and/or sponsorship to obtain access. Some will ask you to RSVP or register and make your payment before being given an address — or the address may not be provided to you until the night before the event. Some events require a legal ID, while other clubs will ask potential members to submit a photograph and formal application in advance.

  Local legalities and culture may affect how "out" a community is, how large gatherings are, and how difficult it may be to get information about the community. A kink club or organization may have been burned by people in the past, have concerns over local laws, or fear becoming targeted victims of prejudice against alternative lifestyle choices. If the requirement does not seem reasonable to you, ask the event organizers why it is there, and then decide for yourself whether you want to jump through that hoop. Just because you have been in the scene for twenty years does not grant you a universal kink pass – if you are new to an area, not known by these specific folks, or local jurisdiction requires it, the hoops still apply. Graciously respecting the protocols set forth by a group with which you hope to interact is a fabulous social lubricant. And we strongly advocate for all manner of lubrication.

- **What are the expectations for behavior?** Though the list of types of events later in this chapter gives a starting point of what to expect, every event is its own unique little snowflake. Regional variations, cultural precedents, and the age and size of the group will all contribute to the flavor of each function. Asking in advance (or reading the event's website and information pages for clues) about expected protocol, behavior, formality, sexual activity and/or social interaction can help you set an appropriate tone. This is totally optional: people often show up and wing it – but sometimes it's nice to have a leg up... as it were.

- **Is this event accessible?** Some events are in in venues only accessible via stairs, and may not have wheelchair ramps. This can present a complication for those with mobility challenges. Other events may be in remote areas, away from public transit, creating problems for those who don't have a car. Sometimes the accessibility concern has to do with finances: for some folks, the fee to enter an event or attend a larger convention is prohibitive. If the event seems not to be accessible to you, write in advance and see if there any creative solutions. There may be service elevators not usually available to the general public, the hosts might know some folks who can give you a lift, or there may be volunteer or scholarship options that reduce fees.

Don't settle

When we first get involved in a new activity, we can't always discern the subtle differences between the energy of various groups and events. If you find out that you enjoy roller-skating, you may not be aware that there are casual roller-skating rinks as well as folks who go out skating in parks on weekends, and that neither of these shares much socially or physically with joining a roller derby team. So it is for kink. So keep a few questions in mind as you do your research, to make sure you are not settling for what seems hip, cool, or simply conveniently located.

- **What kind of person are you?** Do you detest big crowds? Maybe that 1600-person conference is not the best place to make your pervy debut. Have a phobia about bugs? The kinky retreat at a rustic campground in rural woodlands probably is not the best place for you. Does the idea of intermixing alternative spirituality and alternative sexuality leave you cold? Consider not attending the event that focuses on drum-circle fueled hook-pulls, prayer gatherings and rituals.

  While thinking about what does not turn you on, also keep in mind what *does* get your motor running. What appeals to you? Do you enjoy watching big spectacles? Consider going to that fetish ball and seeing all of the over-the-top performances. Do you have an altruistic streak? Try getting involved with events that focus on fundraising for a great cause.

- **What drew you to the kink community?** In Chapter 1, we touched on some reasons people choose to get involved with the kink community. Your answers there can help you decide how best to get involved. For example, if you want to focus on play, look for events that have a play party or available dungeon time. If you are interested in education, look at class lists and descriptions of what is being discussed. Single folks looking to meet new people can look for events with mixers, meet and greets, and speed dating options (though you can meet new people other places as well – check out Chapter 5 for more ideas).

- **With whom are you exploring?** If you are embarking on this journey with spouses, partners, friends, or family of choice, what are the needs of everyone involved? If you are looking for educational opportunities, and your partner is only interested in going places where you can get naked, a hands-on class on about a specific sexual skill may be a better match than a weekend of cerebral conversations. We don't have to get the same things out an event as our partners, but dragging someone along to something they will deeply dislike is not going to encourage your growth or maximize everyone's pleasure.

Different kink events will have different financial requirements The price of admission can vary wildly – from free, to "bring a pot-luck item to share," to $5-$250 for a class, and $30-$4000 (not including your airfare) for a conference, vacation, intensive, cruise or retreat. Much can be ascertained by reading their material in advance. Invest your time/energy/money in what feeds you and works for your needs, wants and desires. The closest option does not necessarily mean the best option for you. It might take you a little longer, and you might have to exert more effort, but in the long run you'll have a better experience if you invest your time wisely.

If travel is not an option

So you live in a rural area, with your nearest munch in the heart of the big city. Or perhaps you have mobility and time constraints that preclude long drives. If you only have one munch to choose from, or one play party you can get to – you can still have a blast! Here are a few ideas on how to make it work for you.

- **Extend your friendship circles.** You don't have to limit your connections to potential play partners. Though you might not be hot for one another, they may have resources for you, or have friends, and friends of friends, who could be right up your alley.

- **Create an "Invasion."** Have you been the only kinky spankophile of color in the dungeon? You can increase your chances of meeting like-minded perverts by networking in advance. Putting out a call for a "Kinky Spankos of Color Invasion!" can increase your critical mass. Whatever your fetish or focus, there are plenty of other folks who share it; you just have to reach out and organize! Ask everyone what dates would work best for them, put the call out... and see who else can be brought out to play by knowing they are not alone.

- **Have folks come to you.** Connect with people online, or network like crazy at the events you *can* attend. Get to know folks, and make it attractive for them to attend events near you. Or see if there may be a niche for a new event. If your locality has another event that may be of interest to the broader community, i.e. a Renaissance Faire or a motorcycle run, planning a concurrent event might lure folks to make a trip of it. If you live somewhere beautiful, encourage the kinky to explore and get their freak on while on vacation: living in Maui is enough of an excuse to throw an event and have people willingly travel to see you.

You can, of course, start your own group, and we think that is fantastic…but we suggest checking out what is already going on locally. Maybe there's a way to make what's there work for you… and if you live in a small town, there may be only so many perverts to go around. In addition, many smaller events are held in someone's home, and it may have taken them many long hours, or even years, of work to make it happen. Just because the current state of affairs isn't satisfying for you is not a reason to trash others. Consider brainstorming with them to see what you can come up with together, rather than telling them that their event sucks and attacking them on a personal level.

Can/Should You Join This Group?

Many different types of groups occupy the world of kink: organizations, leather families, leather clubs, fraternities, sororities, societies, covens, boards, non-profits, social clubs, unions, discussion groups… and that's just for starters. General/open membership groups allow you to pay a fee or fill out a few forms and you become a member. Others require pledging to the group; eventually, through sweat equity, initiation, and other required rites of passage, you may be considered for full membership. Some are open to the public, some are by invitation only, and some require that you be vouched for by current members.

Humans tend to run in packs – different types of packs can fulfill different core needs for different people. What are your core needs? Be honest with yourself: are you looking for companionship, friendship, sex, belonging, support, a way to do community service as a group, validation, a sense of identity, love, spiritual connection, fun times, or something else entirely? Not every group is offering the same things, or will be the right fit for everyone. Every group is inclusive in some ways, and exclusive in others. A particular group may not be the right one for you to join, but you may still want to go to their public functions.

Some clubs also have specific requirements for joining. Do they require that all members attend meetings every single week? Fly to the national gathering every year to renew membership? Give money to charity? Have sex with all the other members? Play at a certain "level"? Own the specific wardrobe required by the group?

Some groups have very formal protocols for joining, for working your way up the ranks, and obtaining full membership. Some groups in particular have rules and protocols around who is permitted to wear club insignia or uniform, and how members earn that right. This is called "earning your colors," and the

> I remember one of the first times I went to a play party in an area with a very small community. I was blown away! Since there was only one play party most folks could get to, the lesbians, gay men, straight couples and fetishists of all stripes were all at one party. They all helped each other out, and the energy was wild. Dykes held the hand of a straight boy getting fucked; a leather-man was teaching a straight couple how to do play piercing... HOT!

process is one that allows everyone who sees those "colors" to know how much work went into the right to wear them. A tool for building camaraderie and a sense of family, part of the richness of such ritual is the challenge it takes to go through. Each group has its own social traditions. In some parts of the leather community, instead of earning colors, you earn leathers: the right to wear specific caps/covers, hankies, collars, or to use specific titles is "earned" and awarded by senior members of the group or club. Through the process of passing down rituals, the new members also learn cultural history and mythology, and become part of the group.

There may be some groups that exhibit traits or characteristics which can seem unhealthy or straight-up dangerous. Encouraging camaraderie is great: forbidding contact with your friends and family, less so. If you are unsure whether the group you are considering joining is healthy for you, please see Appendix 4I.

Finding Events

OK — you want to find an event! Well, if you *promise us* that you will look through the list later in this chapter, detailing what you can expect to find, how to approach it, and what some of the best practices are for attending the different types of events — so that you don't walk into a munch wearing a rubber chicken suit or show up at a community wake expecting to get laid — we'll jump on in and talk about some of the ways to locate kink community events.

Internet search engines

Go on your favorite search system and start plugging in some of the following words that jump out at you: **BDSM, SM, Leather, Gay, Lesbian, Queer, Kinky, Kink, Rubber, Bootblack, Swinger, Fetish, Hedonist, Fetishist, Pervert, Sex...**

Did you get a whole bunch of porn? You will, if you do that. However, if you add some of these words to the search, it gets better: **Event, Social network, Blogs, Conference, Convention, Party, Gathering, Munch...**

Now, add your location: large city, state, region, province, country. It narrows even further! Play around with the language and see what you can come up with. Creative searches are an excellent way to bump into helpful information.

Kink event listing websites

Some websites are specifically built to list events for our communities, and we list some of them in Appendix 4B: listings for swinger events, BDSM events, leather events... there seems to be a list for everything. Some pages charge for listings, and thus may not include smaller events that don't have a big advertising budget. Though not always complete, these list pages are a great place to look around, gain inspiration, and be blown away by the variety out there. Once you get onto the sites for the events themselves, make sure to check out the FAQs (Frequently Asked Questions) to see if the event might be a good fit for you.

Social network sites

Social networking sites may be a great tool for traditional networking, but they're also used by kink populations to network. Please look at Chapters 2, 5 and 7 for some pointers on online etiquette, and don't accidentally "out" yourself on your entire social network by saying you are going to a kink event. However, if you have a kink-specific profile, or are consciously "out," these networking sites can be a great place to find out about upcoming events.

Even better are kink-specific social networking sites. Join up, log in, build yourself a profile, list your city (or a city nearby) on your profile or in the search engine, and *voila!* Most kink-centric networking sites will show you events and gatherings nearest you, and also list the profiles of other site members who will be attending. Many will also have tools for communicating with other attendees beforehand, allowing you to get the skinny on what has happened in years past, and glean tips on making that specific event a success for you.

Reviews and advertisements

Grab a copy of your favorite kinky magazine, and you will find advertisements for some big (or selective) events. There may also be reviews or post-event write-ups on events that have already happened. Read them! What does the author have to say about the event? What is that author's bias? Are they writing to generate good copy, or giving a reasonable assessment of the event, with both pros and cons? Is the review sponsored by the event (or written by the event producer)? Reviews can also be found on a variety of websites, blogs, kink news columns, and more.

Advertisements can also come in the form of flyers in nightclubs, postcards at other events, paid ads in local kink/gay newspapers, and notices at sex shops. Consider where you see the ad appearing. If an ad is plastered on the side of a bus promoting a "fantasy erotic masked ball" complete with scantily clad silicone-enhanced models, the percentage of folks there to ogle the spectacle may be higher than at an event advertised via a postcard handed to you at your local munch.

Word of mouth

At the end of the day, just like in meeting the right partner, finding the right event often occurs via word of mouth or personal introduction. Yes, you can find a lot of great stuff using the above approaches, but once you're traveling within kink circles, it becomes much easier to find other events. The winding maze of discovery by word of mouth may not lead you straight to your goals, but it can be an interesting adventure.

Just like with reviews, word of mouth comes with speaker bias. If someone says they did not have a good time at a given event, ask them why. What about the event didn't work for them? If they say that it was because an ex-girlfriend was there... this is not a reason for you to avoid the event yourself.

As you're looking for that perfect gathering, keep an eye on the types of events that intrigue you. Are they the ones that mention specific words or have philosophies that resonate with you? Is it the advertising imagery that grabs you? There are some people who rule out events just because they do not have glossy photographs as advertisements, or because those images do not feature people that look like them. Ask around for folks who have been to an event before – do the photographs reflect what you will really see there? Will you feel welcomed there, or is it a better event to attend as a bystander, tourist or voyeur: playing dressup, then going home? All of these approaches have their own merit, and may or may not appeal to you, or may appeal at various times in your kink career.

Types of Events

With so many events out there, it can be useful to break them down into categories for ease of examination. In this next section we explore many types of gathering – to give you an idea of what the event is about, suggest how to get involved, and help you gain some understanding of the culture for each type of event.

Remember – every gathering is unique. Even if you went to a party in your hometown nine months ago, it may be different today. There is always turnover in populations, venue changes, and transformations to the vibe. In addition, there are regional variations and exceptions to every rule: at the end of the day, what to wear to go to the Montreal Fetish Ball may be different from what is appropriate to wear on the street on your way to the Flagstaff Fetish Ball. Plus… people are inventing new variations all the time!

Munches, Brunches & Meetups

Concept: People gathering together in a semi-public or public location for food or meeting other kinky people in a safe, usually non-kink environment. Some munches are general (e.g. kink munch), and some are very specific (e.g. the Kensington Diaper Lovers Munch). Munches are also known as coffees, happy hour, meet-ups, round-ups, salons and more. Variation: Sloshes and Liquid Munches, where the munch takes place at a bar venue and drinking is OK.

What You May See: People sitting around a table, eating food, socializing and laughing, and being discreet about explicit, sexual or kink conversations – if any are even taking place.

What to Wear: Jeans and a black t-shirt through business casual. The diner is not the place to wear your fetishwear unless you've been explicitly told otherwise.

Hints, Tips and Tricks:

- **Ask** "Is this the munch?" before launching into your list of questions on fist-fucking… just in case that table is *not* the munch.

- **If you are shy** or anxious about attending, consider going with a friend or "munch buddy."

- **Introduce yourself** to the munch host(s): this is an excellent way for new folks to meet people.

- **Don't understand the slang being used?** Politely ask what a term means, and most folks will help provide definitions.

- **Bring those questions** about the kink community with you – this is a great place to ask quietly and discreetly, or it may start a great conversation if the munch has a private room.

- **Be yourself.** It is just dandy to be shy, giggly or uncertain. In fact, it is often preferred compared to showing up with a fake attitude and pretending to know it all when you don't (or even when you do).

- **Be respectful** to the wait staff and pay your bill. Don't alienate your community by not paying your part of the tab, or by not leaving a tip. Tipping is sexy.

- **Ease off** – just because someone is there does not mean they want a date for that night, or some person clinging to them. This is not a hook-up night, this is a place to talk and connect to people as people. Resist actions that might be seen as creepy, overenthusiastic, or overbearing.

- **Don't** get wasted/drunk, and be "that" person.

- **Please note:** If you're considering creating your own munch, make sure to see if there is already one (or five) in your local area. Is a new one really needed? Are you booking opposite anyone else's events that might cross over? Examine social media sites, especially kink-specific sites, and see whether you can team up, cross-advertise, or build the project together, instead of stepping on each other's toes.

Some munches take years to build popularity, especially in rural areas. Make sure you choose a place you like visiting anyway, just in case you as the munch organizer(s) end up there alone this month. Get word out about your munch (see Finding Events, above, for ideas on how folks look for munches), and don't take it too personally if it takes a while – or if it explodes the first month, as it may if there's a need in your area.

Fetish/Club Nights and Dance Parties

> **But what if I run into my non-kinky friends or coworkers or associates?**
> If you run into a classmate or co-worker or acquaintance, guess what? They are kinky (or at least kink-curious), too! This can be awkward at first, but pull them aside and have a conversation about how to treat each other at the office. Most folks agree to simply not discuss it and pretend it never happened. Others create shared stories on why they now know each other better.
> So, you were spotted at the munch location by your non-kink acquaintances? Consider simply saying you are there to meet up with a group of friends for dinner. It's true and simple.

Concept: Slither into your finest fetish-wear, see and be seen, dance, take in a performance, or party until dawn. This may or may not be with kinky people, as some fetish nights are produced for and by nominally "vanilla" folks having fun playing dress-up.

What You May See: Black shiny clothing or Halloween outfits, fetish finery, folks excited by their one pair of handcuffs, and a lot of people dancing to gothic/industrial music.

What to Wear: Black, with shiny clothing being popular. Other colors may be an "edgy" fashion choice, though blood red and dark purple are popular as well. Events with a raver under-tone may also feature trippy futuristic style. If there is a theme to the night, dress to the theme if possible, or default to black.

Hints, Tips and Tricks:

- **Look at photos** from past events to gauge what to wear and what to expect from your local fetish night.

- **Be prepared:** pack a pair of earplugs (for loud music), your ID (most fetish nights are 21+), a friend to go with you (of course, stepping out solo is great, too!), your wit (especially if you can't dance), and cab fare or a designated driver for the ride home in case you drink adult beverages.

- **If the venue has a play area,** introduce yourself to the person running the space, and ask before you play. A few pieces of gear is plenty – this is not the time to haul out your 60-pound roller bag of expensive whips.

- **Please Note:** This is a dance club, not a BDSM or sex club. Don't get bounced from the club, or, worse yet, busted by the cops for having sex in a public venue, or for doing hardcore kink that may turn off the folks coming out just to dance.

   That hot sexy person with whom you are flirting may be intoxicated. Know your own limits, too. Avoid heavy scenes and toys that can obstruct respiration (like gags or strict bondage) and consider asking "What are you on?" rather than "Are you on anything?" during your negotiation. This helps people to be forthcoming about their own possibly altered state.

Be aware of your personal comfort zones. Practice your "No, thank you," and stick to your boundaries, just in case someone is being overbearing.

Leather Bars and Kink Cafes

Concept: A place where kinky people can come and hang out with other kinky people.

What You May See: Folks in leather vests, sitting on bar stools, some dancing and cruising, making out in dark corners, and the occasional special event night where folks dress to the nines. In the case of cafés, imagine the same folks, only they're sitting at tables drinking a latte and working on their computers between flirting with folks. Or perhaps just kink people who just happen to be in the same space, all working on projects, surrounded by kinky art.

What to Wear: Jeans and black leather vest, or something else "classic" leather/kink. Cafes are more open in wardrobe choices, and casual or business casual is encouraged, with perhaps a kink themed t-shirt.

Hints, Tips and Tricks:

- **Get to know the locals.** Get to know the personalities. Tip your bartenders and baristas, and casually chat with them about what it is that you are looking for. They might know the perfect person for you!

- **Practice "cruising."** At some leather bars, non-verbal communication is normal and encouraged. See someone you like? Look, look again, and if they maintain or intensify their eye contact, move forward, letting them make that last little bit of effort in the approach. Or work up your courage and politely approach them. If you do go cruising, keep a condom, lube, dental dam and/or your preferred method of barrier protection on you... just in case.

- **Kink cafes are often** just that – cafes. People do not cruise as actively there, and you are just as likely to find people discussing philosophy or physics as kink. Get to know people beyond their kinky interests.

- **Patronize the establishment.** These venues can only stay open with our support.

- **Please Note:** If you see someone at the bar or cafe, they may just be there for a drink or some social networking. Don't hound them for information or smother them with attention, unless you're sure your company is welcome.

  If the flirtation becomes more physical, do keep in mind that a kiss or a butt-grab is not a contract for play. It may just be flirting. Don't take it too personally if flirting is all that's on the table.

Fetish Balls and Performance-Based Events

Concept: Dress up and go to a big fetish-themed party with a big fetish-themed show!

What You May See: Costumes, kinky stage shows (such as rope bondage, hook suspension, angle grinders spewing sparks, fashion shows, fire spinning, burlesque, drag king/queens – sometimes amateur locals, and sometimes professionals from around the world), DJs and the occasional live band, people heating up the dance floor, and the occasional vendor.

What to Wear: Dress from simple fetish to downright extreme. If there's a theme (e.g. Apocalypse, Latex, Kink Prom, Victorian, Vampire), get inspired by it! Look at photos from the last incarnation of the event to see the caliber of effort folks put into their wardrobe at your local fetish ball, but if in doubt, wear black that looks good and that helps you feel very sexy.

Hints, Tips and Tricks:

- **Some of these** have very specific fashion requirements for attendees (e.g. Skin Two Rubber Ball) – ask in advance or risk being turned away at the door. The wardrobe requirements help create a fantasy atmosphere, but you don't need to spend hundreds on clothes unless it turns you on – think creatively, and brainstorm in advance.

- **Eat before you go,** and stay hydrated – dehydration in full latex is just asking for a health disaster. Scout for the bathroom when you get in, as the women's restroom facilities often have quite a line due to complex wardrobe choices.

- **Unless you know** there will be a play space, leave your toybag at home. Do keep your ID, some money, and your cell phone on you, hidden in your cleavage, packed in your jock strap, or hidden in a disguised pocket in your outfit.

- **Please Note:** Some fetish events have play areas for everyone, others have areas to play for "known players" whose scenes become background performance art for the "tourists" to enjoy, some have a set show and no play area, and some are dance club nights with no show at all. Ask in advance before getting your hopes up.

  Take care of your feet and body. Those high heels may be less sexy if you have to stand on them, and climb stairs in them, all night long. If you are wearing the extreme tight-lace posture corset and ballet boots, consider packing a backup outfit to change into in case you need it after four hours.

  If walking a long distance to/from your car, bring a jacket to wear over your fabulous outfit, as you may want to keep a lower profile on the streets. Be extra cautious if you are in an unfamiliar or sketchy area. If you are concerned about your safety, ask one of the security folks at the event to help find you an escort to your car, or to call you a cab.

  Gauge your energy in advance. You don't have to stay all night, and it may take you an hour to leave with all the good-byes and crowds.

  Many fetish balls have photographers, and your presence is read as permission to be photographed. If you are not "out" at the office, buy yourself a nice mask for the event.

Private/House Parties

Concept: A gathering of kinky people at a private home to do kinky things together or in each other's presence.

What You May See: People socializing around the snack table in one area of the house while spanking, flogging or sex happens in another area of the house.

What to Wear: Show up covered or in street clothes (this is a residential neighborhood and the hosts really don't need the paparazzi); once you're there, strip down or dress up to whatever makes you feel sexy and ready to get your kink on. Each house party has its own culture, so ask in advance what kind of gathering it is and how much folks dress up.

Hints, Tips and Tricks:

- **Ask in advance** about the concept of the party. How big is it usually? Is this more of a BDSM, swinger, fetish, or some other type of party? How early do folks show up? How early do folks start playing? Is there a specific play area, or is there play in the kitchen too? When does it usually end? Some house parties also have an introductions hour, an opening ritual, or a time that the door locks and no one new can come in. It's much better to find out this stuff in advance.

- **This is someone's home**. Leave it in as good or better condition than you found it, and treat the home and its belongings with respect. Offering to help set up or clean up, bringing something for the snack table, or showing up with a gift for the house is a great way to be an excellent guest.

- **Ask for the tour!** By letting folks know you are new, or new to this party, you will often get shown the house and favorite play areas, be introduced to new people, and get to connect with whoever is helping run the party.

- **Please Note:** Don't spread the word without permission. If you want to bring a guest, ask if you can bring a guest. Your hosts may say yes, or they may inform you of community politics or personality conflicts you were unaware of. This is true as well for asking to come to a party – they may not know you well enough to give you their home address, or they may be looking only to add specific new elements to their party right now. This caution includes not spreading the word about who was there without their permission.

Your behavior at the party reflects on you, and your sponsor if someone vouched for you. If you get banned from a party, your sponsor may be asked not to come back as well.

Keep your conversation volume down around scenes that are happening, or take the conversation to the snack area. In fact, find out how loud noise carries in this neighborhood – screams at 3:00 AM may wake up the neighbors. This is especially true outside, on the sidewalk or in the backyard.

Many folks find out about private parties by getting to know people at munches, or by having had long discussions with folks online. These events are rarely publicly posted, as they take place in private homes. In other cases, they are "after-parties," where folks go after the fetish ball, big hotel event, or other event is over but nobody's ready to break it up and head home. In these cases, they often spread via word of mouth near the end of the main event.

If you are invited to a conference or kink event after-party, and see a well-known presenter, fetish model, or local event producer, remember they're there for pleasure, not business. Don't ask them details from a class or when their next big thing is, unless they bring it up. After-parties are often a chance for folks from the big events to let their hair down and finally decompress and play after a long weekend of work.

In this age of social media, think smart about how you share your experiences. The whole community may not have known about, or been invited to, the party, and hosts may or may not be OK with details being shared. In fact, they may prefer if what happened at the party stay at the party, with no photos allowed and no blogging about the party beyond personal reflections on un-specified events. The flip side of this is that some parties take a lot of photos (or streaming videos) of their kinky antics and will post them all over the Internet. Assume that you yourself should not take pictures or otherwise share information unless you have asked. This includes sharing information before the party... online calendars are often publicly accessible, and posting your hosts' address with a note "kinky sex party" may not be appreciated. This is especially true if they have children, are not "out" to relatives, or live in a state with especially stringent "house of ill repute" laws.

Exploratoriums, Samplers & Tastings

Concept: Explore kink techniques, try out a new toy, or show someone a different type of play.

What You May See: Different areas or theme rooms with people moving from station to station being whipped, pierced, bound, tickled, etc., often for the first time, by volunteers who are experienced with a particular toy, piece of equipment or technique. Some also include five-minute mini-classes for attendees on how to perform the activities with their partners, how to be the receptive partner to the "top," or vendors selling supplies enabling folks to enjoy this play on their own.

What to Wear: Jeans and t-shirts or casual street-wear with a sexy flair. Some folks will dress to the nines, but it tends to be the exception rather than the rule.

Hints, Tips and Tricks:

- **Try something new.** Just because you try it does not mean you will have to do it ever again. In fact, learning what you do not like is just as important as learning what you enjoy... but no one is making you try things that make you uncomfortable. You want to try out an activity as the top/active partner? Ask if there is anyone interested in being your "demo bottom."

- **Ask questions.** This is a great time to pick the brains of folks when they are not in a play-based environment.

- **Speak up.** If you want to experience what that paddle feels like on your thigh rather than your ass, ask! Perhaps you would prefer your partner at your side holding your hand while you get spanked for the first time? Just let the person running the station know.

- **One-time use gear** (e.g. piercing needles, saran wrap) can be expensive when folks are doing them for lots of people. Offering to help pay for those expenses if you want to do a lot of stuff is a great way to show someone you value what they are donating to the community.

- **Please Note:** This is not a play party. Volunteers are offering to do mini-scenes or techniques with you as a form of community service, not to form a relationship with you. Three to ten minutes tends to be average per station. If you are having a great time, you may, politely,

> **Constructive Criticism**
> Didn't have a good time at the party, gathering, or event? It might be very tempting to hop on the Internet and complain about it to the world. However, that neither improves the event nor earns you friends. Consider dropping a note to the event organizers after the event with information about what you enjoyed, what possibly had room for improvement, and how you or others might be able to help make it better. Saying "it sucked" is not nearly as useful as "I wish there had been more areas downstairs to play. I have some extra play equipment; can I donate it for next time?" There may be factors for this specific event of which you might not have been aware. Remember – all events are run by people. People have feelings, and may have put a lot of energy and love into an event, regardless of your opinion of the outcome.

inquire about making a date, but do not take it personally if they decline — it is likely not about you.

Think twice before getting naked. It can be very exciting to try out new stuff and some folks get really excited — but consider where the exploratorium is taking place. If it is happening in a rented hall or at a street fair, ask first if it is acceptable to undress.

Shower in advance. Especially if you are going to be getting into body bags or being restrained with tools to be used by others afterwards, leaving your body odor, makeup, perfume or lotions/oils on equipment is rude.

Every exploratorium will have different stations based on demand and who stepped up to volunteer at the event. If you wish your fetish had been represented, consider volunteering at the next one by dropping a note to the organizers in advance. Some exploratoriums will have 101-level stations, while others will have more advanced techniques and tools available. If you are uncomfortable with what you are witnessing, make sure to take care of yourself by walking away from that station.

Local Classes & Education

Concept: Kinky Sex Ed for adults.

What You May See: People sitting around in a circle talking about their kinks or their relationships, a panel discussion on a kink-related topic, someone demonstrating a type of BDSM play in front of the room while others observe and take notes, or a room full of folks practicing that new bondage technique they just learned.

What to Wear: Jeans and t-shirts or casual street-wear with a sexy flair. It isn't necessary or expected that attendees will dress to the nines, unless the class is about specific clothing fetishes. The exception may be classes held at a local dungeon or sex club, and even there casual (or black) is usually fine.

Hints, Tips and Tricks:

* Come ready to learn! Bring a notebook and pen, a bottle of water, a good attitude, and an open mind to take what you can from the educational opportunity. The chairs may not be comfortable, so bring a pillow if concerned. If it says to bring supplies, bring those supplies

to be able to best follow along and learn — but if you don't own the supplies, email in advance and see if there is extra stuff to borrow.

- **Consider going to classes** that fascinate you, but also classes and topics that baffle you or turn you off. Sometimes learning about a topic can help us dispel myths, grow as individuals, empathize with our partner's journey, or create connections with new people even if we are not into a topic. And if you *are* into a topic? What a great way to flirt with someone who shares your interest!

- **Use the bathroom** and turn off your cell phone or media devices before class starts. It's hard to pay attention when you need to pee, and answering calls or having side conversations in class is bad manners.

- **Ask questions** and dive deeper. If you are intrigued by a topic, do inquire with regard to additional resources on where to go further with the material. The presenter might have a handout or a favorite website, or be able to turn you on to a local connection.

- **Please Note:** Find out who can attend and what it takes to attend. Do you have to be a club member, or is the class open to the public? (If the class is open to the public at a sex club, this is an excellent time to check out the space.) Is the class free, on a sliding scale, are tickets needed in advance, is it pay at the door, or are donations requested? Don't show up at the door and be frustrated when turned away for a sold-out or pre-registration-required class.

If the class listing stipulates "no late entry," they mean it. If you do show up late and are permitted entry, enter quietly, close the door quietly behind you, sit near the back, don't disrupt the class with questions that may have already been answered, and remember you can ask questions after class.

Give credit where credit is due. If you learn a technique from a specific mentor, presenter or friend, give them props for their hard work. Pretending to have invented a technique you did not invent is uncool, and diminishes your credibility.

There are many, many different types of classes out there nowadays! They are held at sex-positive adult-themed shops (many of which offer discounts if you shop that night), dungeons and play spaces, sex clubs, universities and colleges, private homes, back rooms at restaurants, theater spaces, and rented halls. They are organized by local groups and clubs, visiting teachers, community members, or play party hosts as a way to entertain and educate before a party.

Classes vary in length from thirty minutes to four hours or more (see *Intensive Education* below for longer educational formats), and can be lectures, sharing of life stories, conversations, small group discussions, hands-on learning opportunities, moderated panels, PowerPoint presentations, demonstrations of technique, samplings of ideas, improvisational theater, stage shows... you get the idea. Some educators are locals who are stepping up for free to share a few ideas with folks who requested it, whole others are professional educators who present internationally on a variety of topics whose books you can purchase and have signed after class. Even someone teaching their very first class might well have something useful to pass on to you.

Not every class, teacher, or format will appeal to everyone. Try a different style of educational opportunity or instructor if that one didn't work for you... but understand that you simply may not be into every topic. In fact, if you feel the need to leave halfway through the class, take care of yourself... but if it was because you found yourself offended, consider staying to the end, as you might learn important points, or come to understand at least why the participants do what they do.

Public Dungeons, SM Clubs and Play Spaces

Concept: A venue where kinky people can do kinky things with other kinky people, available to anyone who pays to come through the door, or with work required for a basic membership.

What You May See: A variety of BDSM equipment (such as spanking benches, bondage beds and St. Andrews Crosses) in a space often painted black (or the occasional Japanese, medieval or medical theme room), low lighting, and people spanking, flogging or binding their play partners.

What to Wear: Some venues are very casual, with jeans and kink-themed t-shirts considered acceptable, but even in casual spaces tennis shoes or flip-flops are usually frowned upon. Some spaces expect patrons to dress in the highest fetish finery. Most are somewhere in the middle, with a variety of corsets, kilts, latex, business casual, lingerie and leather pants visible. When in doubt, wear black.

Hints, Tips and Tricks:

- **Read** the venue's rules and guidelines in advance. Knowing what the rules are helps keep you from accidentally ruffling feathers. Find out

if they allow sex on premises, whether this is the right place for someone into your specific kinks to feel welcome, and if they have a bag
check where you can leave your toybag when not playing. Most clubs
have a list of Frequently Asked Questions (FAQ) and rules available
on their website or as you enter the club.

- **Check out the orientation night!** Most public play spaces and dungeons have class nights, open houses, and orientation nights where
  you can check out the space, see if they have gear to borrow, hear
  about the rules, get a feel for the culture of the space, have a free tour,
  and then decide if you want to join.

- **Network in advance.** Many clubs have online discussion groups – post
  that you will be visiting and see who else might be going. If you have
  specific interests, consider letting others who share your interests
  know so that you might have an Invasion. Networking in advance also
  helps you learn about theme nights, as often clubs will have specific
  nights for sub-populations or special interests (e.g. gang-bang night,
  latex fetish night, foot worship night).

- **Get to know people.** Make friends in the social area, talk with folks
  about their experience at the club, and consider coming back a
  different night too. Some places may take time to warm up to new
  people, and other times you can talk to locals who might play matchmaker with potential playmates or mentors who share your interests.

- **Please Note:** This is not a brothel or house of professional domination. Offering to pay people to play is often a good way to be banned
  from the club, or to put the space at risk. Paying that entry fee does
  not guarantee that you will find someone to play with or get laid. It
  promises you a place to play, a place to meet folks, maybe some snacks
  and beverages, and little more.

  Read what you are signing before you sign. Most public clubs
  require liability waivers and hold-harmless waivers, and may ask
  you to pay serious fines if you break one of their rules. Don't sign
  anything if you are not comfortable with it, or ask if you can opt
  out of clauses (they may say no, but hey, no harm in asking).

  Don't hog the equipment. If they only have one sling, no matter how much of a fist-pig you are, it is considered bad manners

to take it over for more than an hour, especially if folks are waiting to use it.

Your price for entry may vary. Though some clubs are truly one-price-for-all, many clubs have different rates for people of different genders, singles vs. couples, local celebrities, or people dressing to the nines. If you can't afford the price, ask about volunteering at or for the club in exchange for a volunteer discount.

Private Dungeons, SM Clubs and Play Spaces

Concept: A venue where kinky people can do kinky things with other kinky people, available to those who are in the know, have jumped through multiple hoops, or helped build the space in the first place. Variation: Floor Parties, where folks rent out a floor of a hotel and convert it for one night/weekend into a kinky play area for known players in their area. Another variation is a setup referred to as Shared Spaces, where a group of people, couples or families of choice pitch in to share rent on an apartment or house that they turn into a play space and share access.

What You May See: The same stuff you'll see at public dungeons and play spaces, but with a more select gathering of folks or sometimes more extreme play.

What to Wear: Whatever the rules of the club encourge you to wear. Some clubs are kink casual, others are high formal to help build up the fantasy experience, while a handful have explicit dress code requirements.

Hints, Tips and Tricks:

- **Donate your time and resources** to connect with the group. If you have a piece of equipment to lend, can help with cleaning, or have skills to help drywall a room, your resources can help you make friends and connect with the space.

- **Some kinksters feel** that their private club is the place they feel more at home than at home. Treat the space like someone's home... because it is. Though some private clubs have paid help, this is the exception rather than the rule; usually, everyone is volunteering to help take care of this place they care about, creating a deep sense of intimacy along the way.

- **Please Note:** It may not be fancy. Some dungeons are exclusive for reasons of privacy, not because they are elegant. In fact, it may be two pieces of equipment in a poorly lit basement with Enya on repeat. Ask before you show up in your haute-couture neoprene ballgown.

  You may not be able to join. Some private dungeons are for groups of friends to enjoy each other's company, or for only one specific demographic.

  Cover your kink attire when outside, or change at the venue. Drawing attention to the party negates the purpose of the word "private."

Fetish Nights at Swinger Clubs/Bathhouses

Concept: Sex club special event where they spice it up a bit.

What You May See: People having sexual encounters wearing their hot fantasy PVC and enjoying a pair of fuzzy handcuffs or riding crop.

What to Wear: Dress for basic kink, or two degrees sexier than the venue normally dresses. Thus, in bathhouses where folks are normally nude or wearing just a towel and a smile, a pair of boots and a leather chest harness added to your nude form is a great start, while at a swingers club, sexy lingerie, a collar and some high heels are often in vogue.

Hints, Tips and Tricks:

- **Talk to the venue hosts** when you get there. Some do orientations, but others are happy to answer such questions as "what is the wildest thing you've seen here at this fetish night?" If their answer is mild bondage and a hot flogging, this is probably not the optimal venue for your abduction and gang-rape fantasy.

- **Bring your own supplies.** Though some sex clubs have condoms and lube available for use, gloves, dental dams, and options for folks with latex allergy are rare. Bringing your own safer sex supplies in a small "trick bag" of some sort is a great way to not be caught in a hot moment without the right stuff. This also applies to your kink toys... and you aren't off the hook either, bottoms! Bring your own kit, and perhaps a pair of wrist cuffs, an impact toy or your favorite nipple clamps if you are hoping to play. Not everyone will have toys.

- **You don't have to hook up** if you don't want to. A lot of folks come to such clubs to connect with their partner in a sexy environment, or to ogle the eye candy. In fact, for many kinky people who have been part of the BDSM community for some time, a night like this might be their first foray into public or semi-public sex, so they may choose to attend with folks they know well. Opportunities are often available for anonymous sex hookups too.

- **Please Note:** Many sex play clubs are more attuned to and reliant upon non-verbal communication than SM clubs. For instance, a come-hither glance may be seen as a form of cruising. Thus, someone may touch you or you partner without verbally asking in advance.

Just because that person owns a tool, don't assume they know how to use it. Though this statement is true everywhere, this kind of sexy night can be even more misleading, as many folks are here to spice up their sex life, and may not be part of the kinky sex community or have any kinky skills. A whip dangling from a belt may be a sexy prop rather than a sign of expertise.

On occasion, these venues will rent out their facilities to kink groups, organizations and clubs. In these cases, treat the event as either a public play party or a private play party (with a bit of a sexual edge), depending on whether it is open to the public, or by-invitation-only. Find out whether the regular population of the swingers club and bathhouse will be there, often being "tourists," or if it will only be a sexy venue, with the fetish, BDSM or leather group using it as a rental.

Club Operations, Boards & Meetings

Concept: The behind-the-scenes meetings and gatherings that help all the fun actually take place.

What You May See: People sitting around a table at a restaurant, in someone's house, or holding a formal board meeting – debating the value of venue costs, sharing challenges from recent events, or discussing whether someone should be allowed to join.

What to Wear: Leather clubs may require attendance in full colors/uniform, while most other groups are more casual. Jeans and black t-shirt are an easy default, as is business casual clothing.

Hints, Tips and Tricks:

- **Bring your notebook!** If someone mentions something you want to remember for later, writing it down is often the best system for actually doing so.

- **What do you have to share?** Everyone can help make the kink community a better place. You can give back to your community in a variety of ways, including teaching, leading, holding a board position, volunteerism (in advance or at the party), blogging, writing about upcoming events, event building, helping make equipment, offering quality advice, running registration systems, and more!

- **Please Note:** Don't show up and complain that it was boring. It was an administrative meeting. Yes, some kinky groups mix up their administrative meetings with fun, sexy times... but most are straight-up administrative meetings. That party you want to go to will not magically happen without some serious work behind it.

Watch and listen before investing/taking sides; neutrality may be a more appropriate approach than playing partisan politics. If in doubt, remember to respect all parties involved, even if you don't agree with them.

The Big Hotel Event

Concept: A conference on and about a diverse selection of kink, in a hotel, convention center or other large venue.

What You May See: People attending classes on a variety of topics, shopping in the vending area, exploring desires in the dungeon/play space, listening to keynote speakers, donating at fundraisers, partying at special events, and/or milling about and flirting in social/

One of the cooler side-effects of presenting at so many different conventions is that, over the years, I really have seen how much a kink convention reflects the prevailing attitudes, social ebbs and flows and how well you can build relationships over time and distance. There are some folks I only see at conventions, and I value their friendships for the grounding presence they provide in a whirlwind of activity. It can seem daunting to walk into a big convention, teeming with a thousand people, but knowing that my friends will be there makes it worth the sometimes frenzied pace. Focusing on one-on-one interactions helps me when I am feeling overwhelmed and discombobulated.

networking spaces. Cons come in all shapes and sizes, and size does matter. Below is a rough breakdown of large event types. Local events usually draw heavily from local talent for presenters and attract people within a small geographic radius. Regional events may be sponsored by a larger organization or several groups working together, and attract attendees and presenters from a broader region. National events are usually annual, and can become a destination event for people from all over the country. International events are often pretty sizable, with presenters flying in from all over the world and kinky folks travelling in to meet up and share with people they might not otherwise ever have the chance to meet. Your thirst for knowledge will vary; try to decide what your desires are when selecting a large hotel event. Do you need just a little sip, or are you parched for sensory input?

	Size	Great Thing	Drawback
Tall	50-200	You can meet all the attendees and build a sense of community	Often less variety
Grande	200-600	Sense of shared intimacy retained with much more diversity	Don't get to meet everyone, even if you try
Venti	600-1500	Lots of programming and diverse personalities	Can feel anonymous, and many events this size can seem like clones of each other
Big Gulp	1500-250,000	A mind-blowing array of colors, sights, sounds, and information	Can be overwhelming, and may have drama between communities

Keep in mind that some huge cons are more local events, and some smaller cons will bring in presenters from many different countries: it depends on the ambition, resources and vision of the event producers.

What to Wear: Semi-casual clothes you feel sexy in during the daytime, fetish and sexy finery at night. If the event rules say everyone must be "street legal" – they mean what would be acceptable on the street of that town, not pasties and a jockstrap.

Hints, Tips and Tricks:

- **If the big event** has an orientation session, go to it. It is here that you will learn the local culture and rules, meet other new folks, and get the skinny on how to best operate at this specific hotel event.

- **Study the schedule,** circling the stuff you want to do. If the schedule winds up looking like it has a severe case of ringworm, step back, think about what you *really* want to do, and clarify your priorities. Budget time for conversations after class, the scenes you hope to do (and buffer plenty of extra time between them if you have multiple dates planned), and time to make it to the vendor area. It is really easy to get sucked into wanting to do it *all*, but that's not really possible – pace yourself and leave space for random magic moments to happen. This includes, in some cases, making sure you take meal breaks for yourself in the midst of densely scheduled events.

- **The venue may be sprawling:** consider comfortable shoes.

- **Want an escort** to your hotel room, feeling concerned about something you just saw, or having a health challenge? Event security, medical team, staff, or dungeon monitors may be able to help.

- **Please Note:** Be prepared for strong/explicit language, a sexually charged atmosphere and seeing or hearing about new things – including some extreme types of play, or kinks you might think strange or unusual. The variety of human sexual desire is vast, and for many folks their first big kink con can throw them for a loop. Folks can be equally surprised by the amount of laughter, silliness, joy, friendship and happiness at such events.

  Watch your language, attire and behavior in elevators, restaurants and other shared spaces. Grandma and the grandkids do not need to hear about the anal fist-ing class, and the waiter did not consent to watch-ing you spank your lover. Remember — respect.

Some venues ban the use of phones entirely. Some allow limited usage in specific areas. Take your phone call outside the main programming spaces. Talking on your phone in the venue may not be against the event rules, but it is rude, and may cause people to worry about whether you are taking a picture of them.

Cons make for great eye candy! I love the variety of body shapes and sizes I see at events, and have been wowed at the costumes… and of course the spectacle scenes! Nothing says WTF like walking into a play space where there is a bishop spanking a schoolgirl, seven human dogs wrestling, four women in matching ball gowns having a quiet conversa-tion in a corner, and someone hanging from ropes in midair. All in one space! I feel like there is room for everyone's desires.

If you are concerned about photos, find out what the photo policy is at the event: often, event wristbands are color-coded to indicate whether the wearer is OK with being photographed. Event photog-raphers are very diligent about respecting these bands. Sometimes, there are specific areas where photography is permitted or encour-aged, jump on in or avoid these places as best suits you.

Cons, conferences, gatherings, festivals, and extravaganzas are great places to people watch, feel safety in numbers, connect with new people, and re-connect with friends you might only see once a year at *your* event. For those who build a strong connection to a specific event, the loss of such an event can be traumatic, and changes to the event may be taken personally. Remember that events are run by people, and that the loss of that one presenter who got sick, or the cancellation of that panel discussion which you were so eagerly awaiting, doesn't have to "ruin" your whole time. There are other things to choose from: make the best of this new opportunity to explore.

Remember — you can help make the event even more fabulous than the pre-set programming! For example, if you are a joyous exhibitionist, the con is a great place to show off. Craft your performance-based, high-production or theatrical scenes in advance, and have it become the scene others will enjoy and talk about year after year. Putting on a show can help create a sense of excitement for everyone at the event.

Kinky Camping, Runs and Retreats

Concept: A kink event in the great outdoors. They often have a communal, immersive environment conducive to flying our freak flags and being our kinky selves away from the eyes of the non-kinky world.

What You May See: Tent camping, cabin camping, folks having late-night conversations by the fire, outdoor dungeons, bondage in swimming pools, fucking on the grass, and slings hanging from trees.

What to Wear: Sunblock and bug spray. Beyond that, the culture varies dramatically from leather and Levis camps to nudist to latex lovers' retreats to full Gorean fantasy events...or just folks in shorts and tank tops. You may dress to impress, or you may end up dressing for the humidity.

Hints, Tips and Tricks:

- **Look at the weather report,** but pack for all contingencies. Better to have packed that heavy sweater and rain tarp and not need them, than to be caught in a flood with only two leather jock straps and a collection of dildos.

- **Ask what kind of camping event it is.** Is this solo cabins, tenting, shared cabins? Is it a fifteen-person family-of-choice gathering with light play in someone's large back yard, or a huge affair with indoor theme spaces, programming, and hundreds of acres of land? Asking in advance will help you prep for success and also not be let down by a "rural, rustic and roughing-it" gathering when you were thinking "spa retreat."

- **Theme parties?** Pack that extra toga, animal mascot costume, or dress leathers so that you can play along and make memories with everyone else!

- **Consider making your cabin** feel like your home. A bit of décor can go a long way... but remember that whatever you pack in, you have to pack out. Coffee maker and air mattress – sure. Inflatable hot tub, fold-out dance floor, four sling frames and a complete light kit? Sure... if you are ready to do the work at the end of the week too.

- **Please Note:** Bug spray is helpful in the wilderness. But licking insect-repellent-laced flesh is not a great move. Consider a quick shower before that body worship scene.

Some kinky camping events have programming that may not appeal to everyone, such as kidnappings/abductions, age play scout events, human pony festivities, and more. Study the program in advance, and if there are things you will not enjoy, see if you can be somewhere else when they happen. This may not be possible at all events (e.g. if the entire group does a big main ritual on Saturday night), and thus may help you decide if the event is good for you.

Ask what spaces at the campout have specific rules, such as the dungeons, meal hall, or pool. Sex in the pool may seem sexy, but it is contrary to good pool hygiene in a group environment. And those chemicals can kill your friendly body flora. Consider having sex next to the pool instead!

Shopping and Swap Meets

Concept: Shopping events, spaces or stores for kinky stuff, or with other kinky people.

What You May See: Vendors hawking their wares, while folks representing all levels of alternative lifestyle involvement peruse, try out items (with clothes on), enjoy the eye candy, gather inspiration and shop the day away.

What to Wear: Whatever you normally wear to go shopping! If the shopping space is at a kink conference or a fetish pride event, fetish wear may be encouraged... but otherwise, you are going into a shop, so wear street-appropriate clothing for coming and going from the shop or venue.

Hints, Tips and Tricks:

- **Ask the vendor** how a toy works, or if they have that hot outfit in your size. They are usually happy to help! This is a great way to actually feel how powerful a Sybian machine is, before you spend thousands of dollars on a high-tech industrial-strength vibrator.

- **Get measured in person** for special-order items (like chastity belts and corsets). Even if you can't afford it today, if you know for sure you will be buying it soon, make sure it will be a good fit and work for you.

- **Support** your local and community vendors. Yes, you can buy that book online for fifty cents less, but shopping it "in the family" is a great way to build community.

- **Check out the free table.** Many kink shopping events have give-away areas that may be as simple as a table with condoms and flyers for local events, or far grander affairs.

- **Bring your own shopping bag** or toy case with you. Not all shopping events (especially kink swap meets) have bags to take home your newfound goodies, and you may not want to walk through the street carrying a whip.

- **Please Note:** Budget in advance. It's easy to get carried away and convince yourself that you "really need" that inflatable rubber suit. Perhaps you do. But can you still make this month's rent afterward?

  Check for quality. Is that item hand-crafted by a kinky artisan, acquired by a kink vendor who knows what it is going to be used for, or mass-made overseas with little to no quality control?

Pride Parades and Street Festivals

Concept: Taking to the streets to celebrate pride in sexual identities, and conduct political activism and outreach through public exposure.

What You May See: People on floats, riding motorcycles, or marching down Main Street, spectators cheering along, and often a big gathering with vendors and info booths at the end of the parade route.

What to Wear: Dress to your level of "out." You will see wardrobe varying from drag queens and dominatrices in elaborate regalia to folks wearing pride message shirts – and, of course, spectators in jeans and tank tops.

Hints, Tips and Tricks:

- **Wear sunscreen and drink water!** Pride parades are usually held during the summer, and no one wants a sunburn or dehydration.

- **Marching?** Consider comfortable shoes, or at least a fabulous pair of boots that will enable you to march the entire length of the circuit and still be functional the next day.

- **Spectator?** Some really large pride parades are such productions that sometimes spectators show up the night before to set out lawn chairs, blankets, or arrive early to set up their pop-up tent, camera equipment and snack area. Others are much lower-key, with people making sure to show up early enough to have a good view of the parade and beat the rush.

• **Please Note:** Pictures will be taken... by random spectators and the media alike. If you are uncomfortable having your image out there, consider investing in a nice mask or fun makeup. Or dress casually and, if asked, feel free to underscore that you were there to support friends.

Individuals of all ages may be there. *All* ages, from one month to a hundred years old. For many, this is an outing for both family of choice and family of origin. If you are bringing your child with you to a pride parade or street festival, be prepared to answer questions in their language and to their level of understanding. If you are uncomfortable being your fully authentic sexual self in front of random individuals, this may be a chance for self-reflection concerning public behavior. Opinions abound on this topic, and only you can decide what is best for you and yours.

Party safe. Though many cities are more lenient around public nudity laws during pride parades and street festivals, this is not the case everywhere. Please think twice before engaging in activities that are not normally legal in your jurisdiction... it can be easy to get swept up in the energy of the celebration. This also includes, in areas where prejudice and injustice are part of the cultural environment, to consider attending pride parades as a group — the parade may have been so amazing that we forget not everyone everywhere is as inclusive and welcoming.

Most pride parades are for the LGBT (Lesbian, Gay, Bisexual & Transgender) community, but often have a kink, BDSM, or leather contingent (including heterosexual kinky individuals marching). There are a handful of kink-focused pride events, such as Folsom Street Fair in San Francisco — which in 2010 had over 400,000 individuals through the gates, huge vendor areas, parties in the city during the entire month beforehand, leather pride banners on the street lights of the city for a full mile, and dance parties that lasted late into the night.

Other kinds of street action take place as well. There are street sex-ed clinics, block parties, information booths on kink and alt sex at other types of festivals, and, occasionally, large political activism activities (such as marching

It is very easy, while at a huge event like the Folsom Street Fair, to forget the entire city isn't your pervy playground. SFPD will let a whole lot slide while people are on the fairgrounds. As the fair winds down at the end of the day, it is fascinating to hang out about a block away from the fair's gated exits and watch the police handing out tickets the guy who forgot that a cockring and a pair of engineer's boots just won't cut it for the walk back to the hotel and the gal who just can't understand why her labia piercings need to be covered up. Pace yourself, stay aware, and bring a change of clothes!

on Washington, or protesting at state capitols).

Leather Contests and Title Competitions

Concept: A leather/ kink contest or pageant. They may have a skill-based, political or explicitly sexual focus.

What You May See: People on stage in sexy outfits vying for a title or honors through questions, performances, and speeches, while judges sit to one side judging, and an audience watches and/or cruises each other. If it is a skill-based event, like a bootblacking competition, there will be competitors showing off their skills for attendees. You may also see stage entertainment, demos, an opening act, funny MCs, a serious presentation of the national flag, step-down speeches, and someone getting laid in a dark corner of the bar.

Though some local events are stand-alone competitions, many are "feeders" for larger regional, national or international titles. That means that the winner of the local event will go on to compete at a different event. The international events are often truly international affairs. For example, International Mr. Leather, held annually in Chicago, which features contestants from five countries, hosted more than 15,000 attendees in 2008, and includes a world-class vendor market, parties, special dinners, and more.

What to Wear: Dress to the theme of the competition, or as close as is comfortable. Leather title competition? Wearing leather trousers, vest and boots is a safe choice, but dressing in rubber or a corset and heels would be OK too, as might crisp jeans, boots, and a leather vest. Some events will only allow in those in appropriate theme dress. Former title holders are expected to show up wearing their sashes/vests/medals so that they may represent the history of the event when former titleholders are called to stage.

Hints, Tips and Tricks:

- **See and be seen.** Dressing up, getting inspired, and people-watching are all good fun. You may end up hooking up, but more likely you'll have a chance to socialize, flirt, be inspired to the history of the community, and see people who only come out on occasion.

- **Bring money for the charity fundraiser** (there usually is one), drinks (local titles are often held at bars), to have your boots blacked, and for cab fare home just in case.

- **Find out** what the judging criteria are for the people vying for the title. This might include a "fantasy" (a skit or an act, usually set to music, that demonstrates a particular theme or idea that the competitor finds compelling, or hot as hell, or both), a speech (especially in political titles), pop questions, a specific skillset (such as bootblack or educational titles) and an interview... but many are criteria that audiences can get in on, through cheering or directly supporting their favorite candidate for their sexy look, overall audience interaction, and ability to fundraise.

- **Please Note:** In many communities, contests may start late and go long, so if you're there to support someone, don't make a date for right afterwards.

    Leather press and LGBT media regularly cover title competitions. If you are not OK with having your photo taken, try very hard to stay out of their way. Again, a basic mask can be your friend.

    Many contests are sponsored by bars or alcohol companies. If you have a history with substance abuse, be aware of your capacity to be in the venue to support those running.

Intensive Education

Concept: Kinky learning experiences that allow for immersive education, ranging from six hours to a week-long retreat to a weekend a month for eighteen months.

What You May See: People sitting around in a circle talking about their relationships, a room full of folks practicing how to "throw" a whip, or ten different educators taking turns filling students with amazing ideas.

What to Wear: Ask in advance. Some are casual affairs, while some require all attendees to be in specific wardrobe/uniform or nude.

Hints, Tips and Tricks:

- **Ask what the format will be.** The intensive may be a single educator speaking on only one topic or speaking on many topics. It may be a small number of presenters teaching right after each other, building on what came before (unlike the big hotel event, where education is a "choose your own adventure"). It may be an anarchistic or attendee-driven format, using the "un-conference" model to create exactly what attendees are asking for once they get there.

- **Sign up early.** Most intensive education opportunities have very limited numbers, and tend to sell out in most areas.

- **Clear your other obligations,** if at all possible. Being able to truly "immerse" yourself in the experience is part of the journey, and constant calls from the office or text messages from your cranky cousin can be distracting.

- **Please Note:** Be kind to yourself. Your brain may get full, or you may have breakthroughs and revelations. If you need to go get some water, take a short walk and then come back, most intensives are willing to help make that happen.

Leadership Conferences and Alternative Academia

Concept: Leaders and academics gathering to discuss theories of sexuality, community structure, and other "meta" concepts.

What You May See: Rooms with people all passionately listening to or sharing on topics of sexual health, community building, or discussing the challenges being "out" in their field.

What to Wear: Business casual, business formal, or jeans with leather vest and dark shirt, depending on the specific event. Though showing up in fetish finery to the lecture at Harvard may grab attention, ask yourself if it may pull focus from your message or redirect conversation.

Hints, Tips and Tricks:

- **Bring your notebook,** business cards, resources, and smart phone. This is a chance to network on your own behalf, as well as to connect event attendees with people in other regions doing similar work.

- **Insert some joy into the proceedings.** Make sure to grab lunch with a friend, update your social media network so your "home team" can cheer you on, or do other things to keep yourself (and others) smiling or at least on a good note with one another.

- **Please Note:** This may not be "exciting" if you are not wired for academia, or if stuff like politics and community leadership doesn't get your gonads galloping.

  Your feathers *will* get ruffled. Someone *will* piss you off. And, eventually, you'll be the ruffler or the pisser, so to speak. If you go to enough gatherings of activists, academics or leaders, you will eventually disagree or agree with someone enough to raise your blood pressure. Have a plan in advance as to how to process what comes up for you.

  If representing kink out in the world of academia (such as guest-lecturing at a local college), keep in mind whether you are providing a balanced perspective on this complex community and set of desires, or if you are simply providing shock value or titillation.

When Kink is Just a Slice

Concept: A big event that is not about kink, but that has a kink contingent or nearby party. Some examples include science fiction conventions and Burning Man.

What You May See: Captain Kirk in a slave collar, pirate wenches with whips, and modern primitives on the playa sporting dust-covered leather cuffs.

What to Wear: Whatever the local culture is will determine your wardrobe. Then, add a layer of subtle kink over the top.

Hints, Tips and Tricks:

- **Finding out someone is kinky**, as well as into this thing you are also into (Burning Man, Renaissance, Sci-Fi, Anime, Paganism, Furries, etc.) means you have multiple shared "axes of freakdom." Having mutual interests can be good for making long-term connections.

- **Bring kink resources** for the larger kink community with you. You may meet people who are kinky, but did not know there were such things as munches, kink conferences, etc. You can help educate them if they are interested in learning more (or lend them your copy of this book).

- **Please Note:** Don't make assumptions about just how kinky or not kinky someone is based on their wardrobe or a collar. Especially at science-fiction, anime, and role playing game conventions, kink as fashion statement is quite common.

The private party may *really* be private. They may not want folks knowing about the party, and sharing the location, even with that really hot hottie on whom you are crushing, may get you removed from the invite list.

Many of these events are all-ages gatherings. Be discreet about your kink interests, unless behind closed doors or veiled in a topic appropriate for the venue and population as a whole. And since it is all ages, be aware that that person in the collar or carrying the hand-cuffs might be fourteen years old.

Faith and Spirituality Gatherings

Concept: Kinky people expressing their faith together. Sometimes kink is the manifestation of the faith, sometimes the faith is given a kinky spin, other kinky folks come together to practice their more classical religious or spiritual rites.

What You May See: Hook pulls and flesh suspensions, a leather-friendly Seder, naked drumming around fire pits, or a group of people who happen to be kinksters attending church services.

What to Wear: This will depend entirely on what kind of gathering it is. Some may be "sky clad" (pagan-speak for naked) or in body paint, while others are in dress leathers, street clothes, or perhaps their Sunday best.

Hints, Tips and Tricks:

- **Come with an open mind.** You never know, you might have a good time, whether or not you have a transcendent experience.

- **Find out what kind of gathering it will be.** Will there be fire walking, singing of hymns, hours of silent meditation, speaking in tongues, reading and discussion of doctrinal texts around a living room, sitting in a sweat lodge, cathartic flogging ritual work, a leather tribal revival, building a giant altar together, or something else?

- **Be authentic.** Try not to worry about being too weird, or not weird enough. Just... be.

- **Please Note:** You are not guaranteed a magical experience. Though some of these gatherings may have moments of shared revelation, inspiration, or transcendence, there is also a chance that you may be bored, confused, or offended.

  Don't proselytize. Even if your kink is an integral part of your faith, or your faith is an integral part of your kink, and you have been deeply touched, other people may not "get" it, nor should they have to.

  We all carry preconceived notions of different faiths as a whole, and of which one should or should not be kink- or sex-friendly. Kink faith/spirit events are Pagan, Christian, Jewish, Muslim, Shamanic, Vodou, Tantric, Radical Faerie, New Age, "Non-Secular" and more. You may be comfortable with some of these, but not others.

Virtual Communities and Gatherings

Concept: Kinky people gathering on the Internet to discuss, connect, flirt or play.

What You May See: An online bulletin board, social media system, someone's webcam, or collection of virtual people mingling and playing with one another in a virtual world on your computer screen while you sit at home, or having a LAN party (folks with computers all on the same network or in the same room while on the same online system).

What to Wear: Whatever you are comfortable in. Some people hop online nude, while others are in jeans and t-shirts, or full fetish regalia. Wearing an outfit that turns you on can help connect your virtual community with your phyical experience.

Hints, Tips and Tricks:

- **Make and manage** your online profiles to reflect what you are looking for and how you want to connect with others. See "Managing Your Virtual Self" in Chapter 5.

- **Find online communities** for your specific desires. Even if no one else in your area is into Marshmallow Fire Play, someone else online probably is, and may even have a discussion group for it.

- **Be on time** for your virtual gathering – and make sure that you confirm what time zone the meeting time is set in.

- **Please Note:** Share inspirations, but respect copyrights. Pretending that you wrote something, or took a picture, or are someone you are not is a great way to piss people off.

Be aware of how much time and energy you are spending online. Compare it to how much you get out of the experience. Make sure the ratio of input to output makes sense.

Get involved with conversations after reading what others have said on various topics, listening to the podcast being discussed, or having actually looked into the issue or event in question. Posting new/original material is a great way to connect, but so is giving thoughtful response to the writings and thoughts of others... while talking out of your ass, or trolling, is rarely appreciated.

Other Major Categories of Events

Special Interest Groups (SIG) and subculture gatherings

Special Interest Groups (SIGs) cover a wide variety of topics. They are places for people with a shared fetish or kinky passion (or shared experience of challenges) to connect with one another, rather than trying to find these folks amidst a sea of general kink. SIGs might be classes, munches, conferences, parties, or something else entirely.

We have seen SIGs on such topics as: rope bondage, masters/dominants only, slaves/submissives only, latex fetish, food play, age-based roleplay/littles, spanking, professional sex workers, new people to the scene (aka newbies/novice), flash-mob kink, human animals, anal fisting, mutual masturbation (aka jack and/or jill parties), hypnosis, 18-35 years old (aka The Next Generation, or TNG for short), age 55+, tantra/sacred sex, as well as specific religious affiliations, sexual orientations, gender experiences, and much, much more. In fact, some SIGs are not about a sexual desire, but are instead about social consciousness, such as political activism, people of color, health care reform, or interfacing with law enforcement. If you want a SIG for your special topic, feel free to create one — either as a stand-alone group, or as a sub-group of a larger organization. This is, of course, after you see if one already exists.

Remember, though — just because someone shares your fetish, does not mean they share your politics or are automatically going to be your best friends. In addition, different sub-populations have different cultures. For example, many gay men's furry (animal mascot/costume) spaces are often known for having casual touch between strangers and friends alike (which often applies to a smaller degree in gay men's kink spaces in general), while heterosexual power exchange spaces can be very constrained in levels of protocol and permission needed for touch.

Fetish model, adult film & pro events

These events are a chance to meet your favorite performers and professionals in the sexuality community, learn about new ones, watch them receive awards, network with them and their clients and fans, and, potentially, hire them. You will see professionals in sexy outfits hawking their DVDs, magazines, or sexy selves, while non-professionals ogle them, ask questions, get signatures, shop, or dance and party until dawn.

Some events allow you to book photo/video or domination sessions with the professionals. Pay people for their time, whether financially or in fair trade: this is their profession, and they should be respected for their work. Ask what their rates are. Remember, you're paying not only for your fantasy or the project at hand, but all the gear, prep time, space rentals, their training, and the ability to get what you are looking for. In turn, remember that laws on sex work and professional domination vary from region to region. Every individual has their own boundaries as to what they will and will not offer or do, and whether on the side of the professional or the client, those boundaries *must* be respected. Don't offer to pay extra for unlawful activities during your session... that is *illegal*.

Pampered pleasure

Kink-themed cruises, spas, bed and breakfasts, and all-inclusive vacation opportunities or resorts are a chance to explore our desires while indulging in life lived large. If you can dream it, it might just exist. Human pony farms where you can sleep in a barn, a matriarchy where all men are slaves while on site, spa retreats in Palm Springs for single leather bears into other bears, cruises for swinger couples to party their way across

I went to a kinky B&B in Australia that had a 24/7 on-call slave. I could push a buzzer in my room, and her vibrator would go off, knowing I needed something. My Boy and I of course decided we needed her to bring us water at 3 a.m. after playing until late, because, well, how could we not?

the Caribbean and go deep-sea fishing in full latex ... these are all fantasies that have been made real.

Some are very rustic, some are high luxury. Asking for photographs of the venue in advance, or asking others who have gone before, can help you set your expectation level. In addition, ask if there are extra costs beyond registration. Some of these opportunities are truly all-inclusive, while some may have extra cost for additional opportunities, or may not include travel costs in the price tag.

Charity events and fundraisers

Though many charity events and fundraisers take place at title competitions, hotel conferences, and pride festivals, some stand alone. These include auctions of all kinds (silent auctions, live auctions, online auctions, auctions of scenes with well-known kinky people as well as locals and celebrity perverts), raffles, beer busts, people doing embarrassing/humorous things in exchange for funds raised, selling swag (pins, t-shirts), bootblacking, taking pledges for kinky/fun acts (such as a masturbate-a-thon), classes, dances or play parties with proceeds going to charity. Budget in advance to donate a few dollars beyond the door entry (or a few extra cans of food); you may inspire others to do the same — and it adds up.

Ask for whom, or for what organization the charity monies are being raised. Fundraisers may benefit titleholder travel funds, kink charities, local organizations, food banks, women's shelters, breast or prostate cancer research, HIV hospice, LGBT centers, and many more. However, not all things called fundraisers are actually there to raise money. They may be "awareness raisers" — which are important, but different. If you know what the charity is, you might have creative ideas on how to help — for example, if you don't have money to give, you might have frequent flyer miles to donate to a travel fund, or clothes to the local homeless shelter.

And remember, if the fundraiser is something involving bootblacking... tip your bootblack. The art of leather care takes time and energy to develop as a skill set, and even if the bootblack is donating their time to the cause with funds raised going to the charity, tipping beyond the amount listed will help them pay for the cost of materials used and show them they are appreciated.

All ages / family gatherings

The intricacies of family life within the world of kink have become increasingly complex as our communities age. There are parents, grandparents, and extended families of choice raising biological children — and sometimes these kinky people want to hang out with other kinky people and their kids in an explicitly non-kink environment. This concept was introduced in the polyamory and lesbian communities, but has caught on in various parts of other alternative communities, including the BDSM, leather and kink worlds. These gatherings might include barbecues or ice cream socials with people having non-kink conversations and kids getting to play games with other kids. These can be fantastic ways to get to know people beyond their kinky selves, and create multi-axis friendships.

Keep the conversations kid-friendly, and if in doubt, ask the parents of said child what level of discussion is appropriate. Different people raise their kids with different levels of kink exposure, and though the generalities of the alternative lifestyle might be known to them, it is not appropriate to discuss details or explicit information with children. In addition, think twice about listing these events, as a host, on adult-only websites: a family-style gathering is probably best left off of kink-centric social media.

Relationship commitments and celebrations

From simple ceremonies of one person on their knees quietly receiving a collar while both parties make vows, to huge affairs with rings exchanged in full fetish regalia and an orgy afterwards, or something else entirely off the map — the kink community, like every other community in the world, has moments where individuals, couples or groups make commitments public before family (of birth or choice) and friends. Every relationship has its own style and its own approach to these rituals.

If invited to attend, ask what kind of celebration or ceremony this will be. Is this a wedding, collaring, branding, gifting of leathers, or earning of colors? Will it be solemn or celebratory? Also ask what your role is, if that has not been made clear. Is there an unspoken request to have you bear witness, be in a gang bang, sign legal contracts, be part of a paddling gauntlet, or watch something beautiful/extreme? It is best to confirm rather than assume. In turn, just like any other commitment ceremonies in the default world, do not invite anyone else without asking first. The venue may only have room for forty people, there may be catering issues, or the celebrants may be selective of whose "energy" they want present.

Memorials and honoring our dead

Every tribe mourns those who have passed on. Funerals, celebrations, remembrances, and wakes all take place within the kink community. We shed tears, tell stories, scream our rage, give each other hugs, and occasionally throw parties in our friends' memory.

As part of this process, it is important to remember the notion of respect. Respect the needs of those who have been left behind. Some individuals may be in trauma or suffering deep grief; they may want to hear the funny story about their deceased partner or friend, or may not. Respect the deceased, and who they were. This does not mean putting them up on a pedestal, nor does it mean pointing out at a funeral that they were not who some might be making them out to be. This also means asking who is welcome at these gatherings, and knowing that in some cases these gatherings may be a mix of biological and chosen family, kinky and non-kinky alike.

By remembering the departed, we honor the memory of those who came before, both as good examples and otherwise, and pass on their tales and lessons to the next generation. Bequeathing leathers, toys and objects from those who have gone before fosters a sense of tradition. With more and more multi-generation biological families in the kink community, it will be interesting to see how this tradition, as well as acknowledgement ceremonies for the beginning of life, will shift in the years to come.

...And Even More?

The previous 27 categories of events and their variations are a great start. Now it's your turn. Dream outside the box — look out there, see what you might find! New variations and approaches to alternative lifestyle events are evolving all the time, but the classics are classics for a reason.

Now that you have an idea of what kinds of events might appeal to you... it's time to begin planning for making attending these events a success. Who defines success? You do, of course!

Chapter 4

The Pre-Game Plan: Planning, Budgeting, Packing and Getting There

Planning

"Luck is what happens when preparation meets opportunity"
-Seneca, Roman philosopher, mid-1st century AD

HOPING TO GET LUCKY at kink events? Whether you're looking to score a hot playdate, make new friends, or be at the right place at the right time for that life-changing experience, you can help make luck happen by being prepared. We want to help maximize your potential for awesomeness, and be as successful at events as possible.

Make allies in advance

That's right — allies. Not just playdates, booty-calls, hook-ups and beat-downs. Friendly accomplices can introduce you to people, help you navigate the event, and give you tips on how to make the experience successful for you. Allies can also morph into fantastic friends, collaborators-in-kink, partners in crime, and, yes, maybe hot dates. Of course, if you do want to network in advance for "dance partners," feel free to peek at Chapters 5 and 9.

If you are concerned as you research event types that no one of "your ilk" will be there — there are some things to consider. Ask yourself whether that really matters. Can you have fun if you are the only young person, only queer person, only single person, only person of color? If yes, then don't sweat it. If no — how can you change that? Make it so! Ask if others in

When I first started attending parties in the SF Bay area back in the mid-'90s, I would often be on the young end of the spectrum and frequently the only black person at the class. Most people I ran into were middle-aged, middle-class white people. It was unusual for me to see younger or browner faces. One or two times I'd see another POC (person of color) and sidle up to them, asking why I hadn't seen them around. Frequently I'd get an answer along the lines of "Oh, I came to a few events and didn't see any other POCs, so I figured I wasn't welcome." Meanwhile, the broader BDSM and leather communities were wondering what they could do about the lack of diversity. Even though I was still quite new, I was tapped by a local BDSM educational group to put together a panel discussion on "Issues for People of Color in the BDSM Community," and I scrambled to get representation from non-white kinksters. It was controversial, and something of an unholy mess, but the turnout was shockingly... diverse. People who hadn't been to events in many moons turned out. If you build it, they will come.

your peer group are attending, as they may not have a public profile. Put a call on a SIG discussion list, announcing that you are planning to attend a particular event. See if you can rustle up your own posse! Let others know it would rock to have more human puppies, denim fetishists, kinky knitters... all at this event. They might not have signed up because, you guessed it, they thought they would be the only one of that demographic in attendance. If you act as a beacon, suddenly you have other folks responding, you move toward critical mass, and now you have quite the party!

How much planning should you do?

There are many different approaches to event attendance. Whatever style you choose, we suggest preparing in advance, plus maintaining a degree of malleability and an open mind. If you have spent hours poring over the class schedule and booked yourself for as many sessions as possible, that captivating conversation in the cafeteria may divert you from attending a couple of classes. And that can actually be pretty great. That conversation could change your life, provide you with new ideas, or initiate a friendship.

There are those who love to plan every minute of their pervy day at kink events in advance. They make "dance cards" (a running schedule of planned play-dates and encounters), use calendar applications, and confirm dates weeks or months ahead of time. On the opposite end of the spectrum are those who remember to show up, and consider that pretty darn good.

For those who fetishize advance planning, consider whether you are leaving enough open space for magical moments, scenes that go well and deserve some extra time, and random conversations to happen. For those who barely plan at all, consider whether you or others are aware of your desires, and whether having a degree of infrastructure might be helpful in facilitating the manifestation of your fantasies. There is no "right" answer to any of these, simply questions to ponder as you find your way and strike the balance that best suits you!

Budgeting

Budgeting is not just about money. The art of budgeting also includes time, resources, and energy.

The real cost of events

So, what do you need to consider when considering financial budgeting? We're glad you asked!

- **Registration/entry fees.** Every event has a different ticketing policy. Some will allow ticket purchases at the door, while others require registration paid a month before the event opens, with no exceptions. Most events give discounts for those who register in advance. This saves attendees money and fulfills an important role in event hosting: events will often utilize the funds from early registrants to cover travel expenses for presenters, hotel bookings, and event supplies. In fact, some events may be cancelled if not enough folks have declared interest and commitment by registering early.

  Even for free events, RSVPs give the party or munch hosts the opportunity to know how many people they might expect and how much food/space to reserve. When you register for events, consider researching the cancellation or ticket transfer policy if you think there is a chance you may have to bow out. Some events provide for complete refunds, but a return of a percentage of the ticket price or the potential to transfer your ticket to another attendee are far more common.

- **Time off work.** Many of the larger events run Friday through Sunday, which means taking time off work Friday if you want to catch that 2:00 PM class. If you work weekends, or are attending longer events that require taking multiple days off work, budget for this, too. And that does not include time needed to travel, time to pack your bags (which, if you have nosy kids, parents or roommates at home, can be a scheduling adventure), or recovery if you catch cold or experience "Con Drop" (aka post-event blues, which we discuss in Chapters 10 and 11).

- **Baby/pet sitters.** Have kids or pets at home? Where will they stay when you are away? Will you need to pay for babysitters, budget the time to drop them off with the grandparents, or pay for them to go away to summer camp while you are off on your erotic escapade? Some kinky people create care co-ops, with pets or childcare being rotated between a team of folks: one stays home while the other four go off for adventure, and next time someone else in the co-op stays home. Whatever choice is made, try to normalize the experience for them: the kids don't need the graphic details. It is probably enough for them to know that their parents are going camping with friends, heading to a relationship convention, or having a date weekend. Children usually just want to know that their parents love them, and that they're in a safe and happy home.

- **Flight/travel.** Travel takes money and time. Whether you fly, drive, carpool, take a bus, train, ride a bicycle, rev up your hog or walk, advance planning can smooth the journey. Plan the route in advance, arrange the details, set aside the money, and leave some extra time for safe travel, side excursions, and getting lost. This is especially true when visiting a city that is new to you. Not only will you be unfamiliar with the terrain, but you may want to stop, get touristy and snap some pictures to show the co-workers and family back home.

  And budget all those little incidentals. You know what we're talking about: the baggage fees, your third energy drink, that extra tank of gas. They add up.

- **Where will you stay?** Even if it is a one-night event, you might want a hotel room if you are partying until late or have a long commute. You can save money by crashing with a friend, or a fellow event attendee, but consider if there is a hidden cost — is there an expectation of time spent together, sexual encounters, or having to hear all about their last breakup?

  In the case of hotel rooms, what will it cost? Does that include hotel tax, city tax, and state tax? Is there an event discount you can get by being part of the convention's room block? In the case of big hotel events, registering under the con's block code might help the conference by accurately reflecting the number of attendees present. This is especially important if the hotel contract for the convention requires a "guarantee" — a certain number of room nights sold lest the convention pay a fee.

- **What will you eat?** You need to eat to play. It's just how it works. Not budgeting for food is a recipe for disaster, as it were. Get a minimum of two full meals a day, preferably more. And we don't mean a bag of chips or a candy bar. Real food, with real nutrition, is needed if you want to do any real play or intense thinking.

  Food at hotels can be expensive. If concerned about prices, consider bringing your own food, asking for a refrigerator and microwave for your room, or arranging collaborative meals with other attendees.

Also, consider budgeting for the price of the keynote banquet, or a late-night run for a midnight snack after that really hot scene has your body demanding protein.

- **What will you drink?** For barfly-identified kinksters, the cost of alcoholic beverages adds up. Budget in advance so that you don't end up spending your taxi fare on more drinks and wind up making poor choices on how to get home. Even teetotaling can add up when bars charge four times market value for a soda.

- **What will you buy?** You walk into the vendor area and oh my god there is that amazing thing that you have been looking for ages and you must have it...where's that credit card...?

  Budget in advance for shopping. How much can you spend before it becomes more than a moderate stressor on your financial life and relationships? What system will you have in place to make decisions about purchases and avoid buyer's remorse or overspending? Taking time to consider your shopping plans, and discussing them with friends or with partners in advance, is a useful exercise.

- **What do you need beforehand?** Not only do we buy stuff at events, but we buy stuff in advance. A new roller bag, 600 disposable hypodermic needles, a new pair of boots to wear to the Saturday party, cute underwear... it adds up. That expensive travel kit might seem like a wise investment, but will a handful of plastic baggies do the trick just as well? Keep track of what you have, and think carefully about what you actually need.

- **What are the extras?** Registration may only get you into the door. Sometimes, there are extras — add-ons and special events under the umbrella of that big event. Is there is an extra fee for the meal plan, specific group dinners, performances, supplies for the cane-making class, or for staying extra days? Have you set aside funds for donating to the event charity or bidding on the silent auction?

- **What event souvenirs do you want?** "Swag" is a slang term for a particular event's promotional merchandise. T-shirts, mugs, hankies, water bottles...often they are not included in the price of registration. Swag is a great way to remember the event, tell others that you were there, or create a collection of merchandise commemorating every event you have ever attended. Many leather community members have a large collection of "run-pins": the pins acquired from the events they have attended, as a way of starting conversations and recording cultural history.

- **What are your energy / stress levels?** No matter how much we love events (and, trust us, your two authors love events), they do take energy to attend, and can at times be stressful. In some cases you may actually emerge from your "vacation" more taxed when you dove in, and need time to decompress afterward. Some folks get really amped up in the days, weeks or months leading up to an event. That can be about the emotional pressure they or their partners put on themselves in the planning, or in theorizing what might happen at an event. Remember to chill out, please. Ultimately, this is about you enjoying yourself. If you know going in that you are prone to jitters, make sure you budget for that stress. If you know you always freak out the night before leaving for an event, schedule some chill time in advance. Honor your emotional process and make room for it.

  People may stress over what to tell their co-workers or family, when to schedule daily check-ins with partners or kids back at home, how to manage telecommuting while at the event, what to wear at the dungeon party, and more. Some of these energy expenditures are worthwhile. Other stuff... not so much. Only you can decide.

- **Where are you going?** If you take time off work or need to arrange kid/pet sitting, folks will ask you where you are going. They are probably neither attacking you nor trying to ferret out your "dirty little secrets." Most likely, they're just curious, or making polite small talk. However, for those who are not "out," this conversation can feel nerve-wracking. We recommend consistency of answers and something as true as possible.

  I/we are going to...
  ... a weekend-long date.
  ... a relationship/communication event.
  ... a self-improvement weekend.
  ... a camping trip with friends.
  ... an educational event.

... a costume party.

... a role-playing event (you know, like Dungeons & Dragons).

... a theater event.

... a religious retreat.

... a vacation.

... a Burning Man warmup / cooldown party.

... a visit with family or friends.

... a night out with the girls/guys.

Remember, folks just want to connect with you and be happy for you.

They probably don't want all the lurid details (unless you know they do).

How do you afford it?

So you really want to go to that big event, but you've done the math and it seems really expensive. Remember, though, that you're investing in education, connections with new people, and memories that can last a lifetime. In fact, there are people who come to only one big kink event a year, or even one in a lifetime, and are able to grow an amazing home-based kink life out of such outings. Some folks just want to say that they went that one time.

The big kink event can become your vacation. You can cut costs by buying your ticket right when registration goes live, hunting the Internet for cheaper airfare, and sharing a room with someone you know. Finding events in driving distance can save on airfare, and sharing the drive can reduce gas costs.

People in the kink community have varying levels of disposable income, and some folks reading this will happily drop money on going to a big kink conference every month or two, with shopping, flights, and more. Many of these folks are also the ones who we have seen contribute to charities, support scholarship funds, and donate in other ways to make the event excellent for others. Thank you so much for all of your support of the community. And for those who have more limited financial resources and still make it work, thank you for making the effort and jumping in to make it happen!

What are ALL your resources?

If money is not readily available to you, consider taking a look at all of your available resources. Do you have time, energy, or expertise that an event might be looking for? Perhaps the play party would happily let you in for free if you can help clean the space after the party is finished, or the big hotel event will "comp" you in exchange for managing their online presence if you have those skills and resources. Many events have volunteer opportunities, staff positions, scholarships, at-cost positions, or offer the possibility of working for the event's vendors. Your life skills and professional expertise in the default world make a place for you in the kink community: event planners, accountants, security professionals, nurses, project managers and many more find an eager welcome from folks planning events. If you are a massage therapist and can't afford a weekend pass, maybe you can afford a few hours to give massages to the staff in exchange for your fee.

Packing Your Bags!

So you know where you're going, your tickets are in hand, and it's time to start figuring out what to haul along with you. Let's get packing!

- Does the event have any special events you with to attend? You may need to whip up a toga for that Roman orgy theme party.

- Do any classes you want to attend require bringing specific props? You might need your own yoga mat for the "stretching for sex" class.

- Are you doing anything at the event beyond attending? If you're volunteering, presenting, hosting a theme party, judging a contest, or doing anything else extra, you may have special packing needs.

- Do you have any mobility or accessibility concerns? Bring along extra batteries for hearing aids, and check how best to integrate your service animal into the event.

It can be tempting to bring it all: every wardrobe possibility, every toy you might even consider using. Think twice. Remember, at the end of the weekend you have to re-pack the car, and airline baggage fees add up quickly.

If there is stuff you really want to have with you but you're not sure whether you can bring it on the plane, check the airline's policy carefully. If there is still a question, or you really need that katana sword or collapsible police baton, consider shipping it in advance. Many hotels will allow registered hotel guests to send items in advance, though some may charge a small handling fee. And driving can be an issue as well — laws vary from state to state and country to country about what you may possess and carry. It would be a shame if your "Good Cop / Bad Cop" scene was derailed because you weren't aware that your props were illegal!

I fly a lot. And, once in a while, baggage gets misdirected and your leathers don't land when you do. It is smart to carry on a nice change of clothes, and pack enough for at least one day of survival at an event. That way, if bags do get to you late, you aren't skulking around the dungeon in those comfy frequent-flyer pants, slouchy sweater and shabby sneakers.

Whatever do I wear?

You don't have to have thousands of dollars in outfits and toys; in fact, most folks don't. Don't let the porn fool you. Not everyone has a custom couture latex wardrobe and hundreds of pounds of chains in their luggage.

Clothing for kink events is not about how much you spent — it is about dressing for your own personal, sexual and emotional success. That means asking yourself what you can wear to feel fabulous! Many fetish looks out there do not look good on everyone — what will look best on your body type and with your specific attitude and style?

The variety of wardrobe choices are pretty staggering. Common themes include:

- Corsets, stockings, lingerie and/or heels
- Leather, chaps, motorcycle gear
- Wrestling, football, soccer or sports gear
- Religious or spiritual-themed costumes
- Tuxedos, ball gowns, or other formalwear
- Medieval, Renaissance, Victorian and Edwardian clothing
- Punk, rockabilly and gothic
- Zoot suits and flapper dresses
- Age-play gear (from diplomas to diapers)
- Human-animal based costumes
- Modern primitive, tribal or body paint
- Sexy underwear or jockstraps
- Latex, PVC, and other shiny options

By wearing wardrobe that is chosen to make us feel and look sexy, and getting together with others who have done the same, the space becomes an erotic fantasy feast for the eyes. Everyone can make the effort to dress up to contribute to this collaborative experience.

Consider DIY kink fashion. Thrift shops, garage sales and the fabric shop are rich with possibility. Modify that old Halloween costume, or add a PVC tie to the button-down shirt and trousers you already own. If in doubt, black is a safe default, but try digging through your closet and see what you might already have. Mixing and matching from past outfits can sometimes spark ideas for creative new looks without breaking the bank.

> I have a denim fetish, so a really sexy pair of jeans really works for me most of the time. However, if an event has a fetish theme, I go out of my way to try and dress up. It's not about me – it's about creating a collaborative vision for sexual fantasy. If I rocked up in my flannel print shirt to the Eyes Wide Shut party, or to the super-classy dungeon, it would feel like a glitch in the Matrix for me. SM party in Oregon? Hell yeah I'm wearing my flannel print shirt! Fetish event in Manhattan? Not so much.

Now as for footwear – that is a matter of passionate, heated debate in the kink community. Some would argue that highly polished boots and staggeringly high heels are the only way to go if you are serious about your kink. Others think that as long as they are not stained white tennis shoes or ratty sandals, you're probably okay. And then there are the handful of Keds and Birkenstock fetishists who feel their desires are being derided! Someone into age play may need those high-top sneakers to achieve their desired look, and some leatherfolk would never consider walking into a bar or dungeon without spit-shined ship-shape jump boots. Know that in some places, if you don't have on decent-looking footwear at least, folks may not let you in – and also that if you try to wear 7" stiletto heels all night, your feet may hurt. The authors recommend packing backup footwear.

> **Guys, make an effort.** Don't be that dude – the one that shows up in stained pants and a shoddy shirt when your partner spent two hours getting into their fabulous outfit. At least put on clean jeans, a nice kilt, or that suit lurking in the back of your closet.

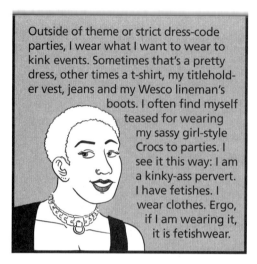

Outside of theme or strict dress-code parties, I wear what I want to wear to kink events. Sometimes that's a pretty dress, other times a t-shirt, my titleholder vest, jeans and my Wesco lineman's boots. I often find myself teased for wearing my sassy girl-style Crocs to parties. I see it this way: I am a kinky-ass pervert. I have fetishes. I wear clothes. Ergo, if I am wearing it, it is fetishwear.

Getting There

Bus, subway, light rail, taxi, train, plane, shuttle, carpool, driving a rental car, driving your own car or motorcycle... there are so many options on how to get there! Be diligent in your research. Yes, there are two airports in Chicago, but one is a free shuttle away from the conference, and the other takes an hour and a half of light rail and fifteen blocks of walking with all your roller bags. And that's assuming you are in a major city like Chicago!

Some venues will not release full hotel information in advance in order to maximize privacy for attendees. Stringent privacy rules might be in place because of past issues. If the local press has in the past released information pertaining to kink event locations and caused a stir, the event hosts are going to do their utmost to protect event attendees from unwanted attention. But they should still be able to give you honest information about whether you can fly in and get a shuttle, if there is public transit available, or whether a car will be needed to get there. Sometimes that event labeled "Dublin, Ireland," is really located forty minutes outside of town in rural County Kildare.

Can I fly with that?

The Transportation Security Administration (TSA) has seen it all. No, really. However, there are many things you cannot carry on flights, such as sharp items, weapons, or bottles of liquid over three ounces. Check a toy in your luggage if it can be mistaken for a weapon, and make sure that the potential weapon in question is legal in your destination. Brass knuckles, weighted leather "sap" gloves, switchblades and butterfly knives, cattle prods, etc., may be legal in your home state, but may provide grounds for arrest once you hit the tarmac at journey's end.

If the inspectors or TSA agent asks you the purpose of a particular item, answer honestly in a way they can understand. If it is an electric butt plug, say it is an electric butt plug, or perhaps a bedroom novelty device. If it is a vibrator, say it is a vibrator, or a personal massage device. Playing coy and coming up with some clever answer can make it seem as though you're something to hide, which isn't a good move. If you are shy about saying "butt plug" or "bedroom novelty device" to a TSA officer, consider not putting it in your carry-on luggage. And don't trip about being proactive – if they ask, tell 'em. If they don't ask, there is no reason to volunteer your personal details.

Some body modifications, collars, and chastity devices are items that will both set off metal detectors and also are not possible to take off. We highly recommend letting the officer know before you get to the scanner that you have jewelry that cannot be removed (they do not need to know that, for example, your owner gave it to you), advising them that you will be setting off the metal detector. They often appreciate the information. The usual procedure is a full-body patdown, being sent through a full-body scanner, or being asked to have a private room screening. Being upfront about your jewelry and mods will minimize fuss in most cases. If you are concerned about it, many chastity devices come with disposable locks that can be snipped off in an emergency. For those who wear collars, consider asking the keyholder for an emergency travel key, just in case.

I carry a personal collar with me. It is a very thick, jointed chrome piece, which resembles an oversized heavy watchband, weighs in at sixteen ounces, and is a rather intimidating piece of steel. It caught the eye of a baggage screener, who called over another TSA agent... who then called over their supervisor. I thought about piping up but I figured I'd wait and see what happened. They pulled my bag from the belt and asked me if they could go through it, to which of course I replied yes. Out came my Wahl vibrator, my rubber horse hooves, some snacks, my headphones, a bunch of random crap, and then the item in question. The agent pulled out this pound of wicked-looking steel links. I smiled, he looked at me, and back down at the collar... for a long, long time. He then wrapped it back up, put it back in my bag, along with the random crap and the vibrator, and sent me on my merry way.

Travel made easier, fun and sexy

Why not make the travel part of the event? As kinksters who travel a lot, here are some ideas we can offer for making it fun or sexy:

- **Rideshare** with other perverts. If you're looking at more than an hour of travel time, consider meeting potential carpool buddies in advance. Fewer sucky moments suck worse than being trapped in a vehicle with someone who grates on your nerves for six hours, then knowing you have to do it again after the event. But if it's a good fit? It's an amazing chance to have great conversations!

- **Play sexy car games.** All the classic car games can be perverted. "Punch Bug" takes on a whole new level when switches and brats play, and word association games with sexual themes can reveal a lot about a lover or friend. We also love the "Anal Game": the model names of cars you pass on the road, e.g. The Ford Explorer, The Dodge Ram, and the Isuzu Trooper become hilarious when you add "anal" in there.

- **Pack a kinky book.** Reading something that has a titillating edge while in transit can help you start getting in the mood.

- **Consider** making your trip about more than just the kink event. Get "off campus" for an afternoon to hit local sights, take pictures, or head out one night to check out a local leather bar or find the local sex shops. Into age-based role playing? Come in a day early and go to the zoo with "Daddy"!

- **Minimize** fretting by making the travel easier for yourself. Print out the directions, check them on multiple systems of navigation, and don't just rely on your GPS. We have seen many adventures go wrong by someone ending up on a road that "does not exist." Better yet, find out if there are driving directions recommended by the venue or event. And while you're at it, make sure to bring along snacks for the car, plenty of water to drink, and plan for regular bathroom breaks.

Sometimes, though, shit happens. Even if the airlines lost your bag, the kid next to you on the flight was ornery, you had to wait an hour for the hotel shuttle... whatever — find the time to shake it off, take a deep breath, and show up with an attitude that will not carry you into a funk throughout the whole convention. You deserve to make the event you are going to walk into be as wonderful and exciting as possible, without letting that cloud linger all weekend long. That fog can get in the way of helping you make new friends or connecting with folks you already know.

Chapter 5

Make New Friends (and Keep the Old): Keeping It Hot without Burning Bridges

A VITAL ASPECT OF JOINING the kink community is to meet other kinky people – people who will become our guides, mentors, friends, lovers, play partners, sounding boards, and more. People we know are journeying through kink as well may have insights for us, or become friends to last a lifetime.

It is important to meet people in your community. Yup, *your* community. You get to make it yours by becoming a part of it – at your own pace, and in your own style.

Countless works have been dedicated to the art of social interaction. There are many different approaches to meeting other people. The following chapter presents a series of tips, tricks, and tools for connecting as authentic human beings within a sexualized and kinky context.

So buckle up, pull out your calling cards, plug in your computer, and get ready to meet your community!

Preparing For Successful Networking

There are so many amazing, open-minded, smart, sexy, geeky, friendly, hot, fascinating, fun, and fantastic humans out there... where do we start? Oh yeah – here. That person holding this book is a pretty unique and amazing person.

The first step in preparing to meet other people is to meet yourself. Sit with yourself for a while. Who is this person, and what are they looking for? Are they anchored in a sense of self-worth, and feel worthy of deserving respect? If not, consider working on that, as low self-value (or exaggeratedly high self-value) can dramatically affect whether you can have healthy interactions with others.

Once you have come to a place of comfort with yourself, it's time to ask yourself a few questions. The first is why you want to meet people in the scene. There are so many reasons! Some include:

- **To make friends** who will be ears to bend, shoulders to cry on, a partner-in-crime, or someone who will be your new kink-friendly best buddy.

- **To have mentors,** guides, gurus and teachers to show you how to do all that kinky stuff.

- **To have lovers,** play partners, hook-ups, or a fun bit of action.

- **To have allies** or friends apart from your partner to avoid being seen only as "so-and-so's husband/wife."

The Mentor/ Protector Thing

Mentors (a person who will guide/teach you, originally used to pass on knowledge through a lineage) and protectors (someone who will watch out for you, originally used to show formal association with a group/house) are lovely ideas. If you are being "protected" by someone, consider if/what you are actually being protected from (is there a real concern, or is this a chance for someone to keep you close?) In turn, if you are being mentored, consider whether they are helping you become your greatest possible self, or turning you into a clone of their bad habits.

- **To network** with folks who run events and parties, and get in on the action.

- **To find** your kinky Ms. or Mr. Right.

- **To connect** with peer mentors on parallel journeys, who you can turn to in times of uncertainty or when you need identity reinforcement.

Some folks don't actually want to meet people. They want to show up and be a tourist — watch people but not really interact with them on any deeper level. That's cool, so long as you own that fact. If you are only here to get titillated and then go home, it is better to know that in advance. Being aware of why you want to meet people will help you be aware of your expectations. If you are looking for a lover, you may project your expectations on what a lover should look like and act like onto the people you meet — before you even know their names. Not everyone you meet will fit into the molds of what you are looking for... or they might surprise you by being exactly what you really need in your life right now, even if they weren't what you thought you were looking for.

Next — do you have a thick hide? We hate to say it, but as we mentioned in the introduction, the kink community is a microcosm, not a utopia. It is full of people. You will meet people who will rub you wrong, whom you will not like, and who will not have read this book. You will find unicorns and trolls alike (see Chapter 7), and they may not always handle you with kid gloves.

This is not to say people will necessarily be intentionally unpleasant. However, our sex life is often something that we as individuals take very personally, and just like religion and politics, other people expressing their personal opinions can feel like a personal attack. As you are entering into the realm of kinky people, know that not every interaction will be perfect. Try to avoid taking people's personalities personally.

In-Person Connections

"What, you mean I have to meet people, like, in person?" Yup.

Meet them where they are

There are lots of places to meet new people, or connect with folks we may have met in passing but do not know very well yet. True, you can meet people at any event, but there are some places that are easier than others, and are in fact built for that very purpose.

The first is munches. These social gatherings are built around the notion of being social. Come up to the table, and say "Hello." Of course, "Hi!" "Heya," and "Um, I'm new, is this the munch?" are totally viable too. Letting folks know you are new to kink, new to the area, or new to this munch is a great way to subtly say that you want to know more people. You can also choose the less subtle route and say that you are excited to be at the munch because you were hoping to connect with new folks, make new friends, and who knows, meet people, maybe for other stuff too. Going straight in and saying that you are at the munch looking to get laid is, however, often frowned upon.

If you have been attending the munch for a while, the arrival of new people is a great chance to expand your acquaintanceship. Ask them what name they go by, and if they would like to tell you a little bit about themselves. Get to know them as people and why they are there before asking them questions about their orientation, identity and personal details of their sexual and kinky proclivities. This will allow them to adjust to the experience gradually, instead of having to defend or debate what they're into before they have even gone to their first play party.

Once you have been at the munch, ask people to introduce you to folks with whom you share kink or other interests, who they think you should know, or with whom they believe you might be a good fit. The more folks get to know you, the better these introductions will be, because the folks doing the introductions will have a clearer idea of who you are, what kinks you have, and what relationship configurations interest you. If you meet someone who you think would be a great fit for someone else you know, playing social matchmaker is a great way to pay it forward.

You can also meet people at mixers, special interest gatherings and speed dating experiences at bigger events. These opportunities are specifically set up with ice breakers, party games, name tags, and other tools for meeting new people. Outside of big events, you'll also encounter the occasional singles mixer and speed dating night. In some areas there are also pre-planned group outings to non-kink venues, where kinky people will announce that they are all going hiking, to a movie, or to play board games together one night, and that other folks can join them.

Available or single?

Compared to the default world, a higher percentage of individuals in the kink community are in open or polyamorous relationships. Thus, if an event is a singles mixer, find out if it is for single people (unpartnered) or for available individuals (could be partnered or unpartnered). If you are partnered and available, make sure to let others know, as folks may believe that partnered people are unavailable, or available people are unpartnered.

Another great place to meet people is at classes. Not only are you there to learn, but you'll be there with other people who are into or curious about the same topic you are! Listen to what people share in the class, and after class introduce yourself and mention what you thought was interesting about what they said. Sometimes, after classes, the conversation will continue at a different venue — ask if you may join in the conversation. They may say that it is just for a small group of friends, but they may just have space for one or two more folks at the table, and you all have the class in common to get the conversation started.

And then of course is the chance to meet people...everywhere. At a big event you can carry a watch, lend your schedule out, let someone borrow your pen, offer directions, grab someone a glass of water, be a demo partner for someone, offer to help clean up around the food area, and more. Not only is this a great way to be a nice human in general, but people notice objects in motion. The person you just helped might start up a conversation with you, but even more likely is that folks will notice you being around in general, creating a positive impact.

Let's get talking

There are lots of ways to get the conversation started. Going up to individuals or circles of folks who are not in the midst of a scene, aftercare, or intense conversation of their own, and saying hello, is one option. So is catching someone's eye and smiling.

Authentic compliments are a great starting place for some folks. Make sure before you offer a compliment that it is actually a compliment. One of the miscues we see time and time again is someone saying "Um, nice shoes," only to have the recipient ask, "What do you like about them?" Blank stares show the compliment was not authentic. Consider giving sincere compliments on a scene of theirs that caught your eye, a fantastic point they made in a class, the photos on their profile, the funny comment they made, how helpful they have been at the event, how much you love their smile/eyes/corset/boots... and the list goes on.

At more formal events, or in some segments of the master/slave, leather, or sex magic communities, it may be more comfortable or appropriate to be introduced by someone else instead of starting a conversation directly with someone new. However, even in such spaces, approaching with a sense of civility and politeness will go a long way. Yes, some specific sub-sects of those sub-communities have very formal structures for introductions (e.g. masters may not speak to slaves who are in locked collars without speaking to their owner first) – but even in such spaces, most folks will react positively if we are polite and friendly.

No matter what route we take to say hello and introduce ourselves, we now get to actually talk. The following are some conversation starters to consider if you are at a loss at events:

"Is this your first time here?"

"What brought you to the event?"

"Have you seen any good classes? What was your favorite part?"

"What sessions are you looking forward to?"

"Did you find anything fun in the vendor area?"

"Can you recommend anywhere good for dinner?"

"Have you been in the scene for a while?"

"What kind of play do you enjoy?"

"Where did you get that outfit/toy/pair of shoes?"

It is less optimal to open conversations with questions about the personal lives of others. Because "outing" can be detrimental, remember to avoid specific questions about people's workplace, last name, and contact information, unless they offer such information first. Avoid pressing for information if any train of conversation seems unwelcome or uncomfortable. In fact, keeping the conversation local and present is a great starting option in many cases, because both of you are here now.

Another conversational route that can be helpful for some folks is to ask people about themselves and their relationships. If following this route, ask yourself in advance whether you are asking to learn about them, or because you are interested in a deeper relationship. This can be tricky territory in some cases though, because "Are you seeing anyone?" can be read as "Are you single and interested in playing/going on a date with me?"

When folks do provide information on their relationships, you may then be exposed to a wider range of relationship structures than in the default world. People may use such words as slave, sir, family member, boyfriend, kitten, daddy, wife, mother, and so much more. It is easy to assume we know what they mean by those words, but they may in fact mean something very different than our initial assumptions. Questions like "What does that relationship look like for you?" can help you learn more about them. And, possibly, about yourself.

As you are exploring being social in kink spaces, consider having someone whose opinion you trust to give you feedback on your behavior without raising your own defensiveness around what they have to say. Sometimes a friend's opinion can help give you good feedback on how you are moving through the world. The feedback of a friend who can lovingly point out that someone was giving signals of being uncomfortable, or let you know that someone was flirting with you, can be invaluable.

Beyond words

Our words are not the only things that convey our message. Our bodies, behaviors and visual cues say a lot about us as well, and affect how we are received by others. Thus, the following ideas are just that — ideas. Consider them, weigh out if they will work for you, and consider your social trajectory accordingly.

- **Bathe.** If you are going to meet other people, be hygienic. That does not mean that you should slather on perfume, cologne or other body products. There are lots of people who are allergic to that stuff. You may really be digging your own scent; we get it, but please, just bathe.

- **Be aware of space.** Different people have different space preferences. Some have a big bubble around them, while others seem to have little sense of personal space at all. Some of this difference may be based on their culture of origin. Watch the reactions of people based on your proximity, and consider whether you might get more traction by taking a step back or forward.

- **Touching... or not.** Some parts of the kink community are very hippie-granola and love to hug and casually touch everyone. Other parts are very hands-off-don't-you-dare-touch-me-or-my-property-without-a-signed-contract-in-advance. Most places and people are somewhere in the middle. Look around, see what the social behavior is in the rest of the space, and then ask someone whether this is more of a hug or handshake group.

- **If you can't ask,** consider going 80% of the way to touching, and let them come the last 20%. Or offer the hug but don't be offended if they say no — it's probably not about you. If your boundaries are different than what seems to be the local cultural norm, understand that that norm is not there just to offend you. Inform the folks in that space of your preference, and when asked if you want a hug, accept it happily or say no, thank you.

- **Consider the wardrobe.** Feeling shy? Consider wearing something fabulous, something you feel sexy in, or a funny t-shirt. Your clothing can help bring the conversation to you.

  Also consider what your wardrobe is saying for you. Is your buttoned-down outfit saying "hyper-conservative formality" when you really crave the attention of people admiring your sexy body? Being involved in the alternative communities gives us the freedom to express ourselves, our sexuality, and our desires in ways that might not fly in the default world.

  There are many ways to indicate your orientation and desires: symbols like collars, hankies/bandanas, silk clothing, chastity devices, specific hats or jewelry and more can have a great deal of visual meaning to some people. Your locked collar might indicate to some your unavailability. Your yellow handkerchief might be there to be used to wipe your brow, but someone else might think it means you are into piss play. Really. If you are unfamiliar with community flags and symbols, consider flipping through Appendix 2.

- **Body Language.** Are your arms crossed over your chest and head down, inferring that you are blocked off and unavailable? Do you keep staring at people and having them mistake it for you cruising them? There are a number of good non-kink body language books on the market, and they are a place to start. If being a wallflower is not working for you, consider standing up, moving around, putting your shoulders back, relaxing your facial expression into a slight smile, and seeing what happens.

Calling cards

A classic idea from the 1800s has found its home firmly in the kink community. Known by many names, this business-style card usually has only your most basic information and scene name on it, though some get more intricate with a sexy picture of themselves, a fun piece of art, or a quote they enjoy. Many folks leave the back blank so that either the person whose card it is, or the person who received it, can write a note to remind them who gave them the card.

When connecting and wishing to keep in contact with someone, consider giving them your calling card directly, or by having a friend pass it on, or dropping it and running – though the first is of course tends to be more successful! If you don't want to give someone your home information or phone number, don't include it on your card. There are programs available online for call forwarding and alternative email addresses that forward along, reducing such concerns somewhat.

I call these Slut Cards! Mine has my name, Google phone number, email address, social media info, and uses the free clip art from the business card site.

I have two versions – one for teaching, which has my name, website, email, phone number and a picture I shot; and my trick cards for my hookups, which have my nickname, social media handle, and a different email address.

The flip side of this is that if you receive a calling card, and you want to stay in touch, you actually have to write them afterward. If you do not, three years will pass and you'll have a shoebox full of these cards and no actual connections to speak of. In fact, if you meet someone in person, keeping the conversation going online or through other streams of communication is important to build lasting connections.

Shy freaks

It is easy to assume that those who identify as kinky are uninhibited exhibitionists who run around all day in ecstasies of guilt-free sexual bliss. And sure, there are folks like that. There are also people who are painfully shy and terribly awkward, who have to muster up all of their nerve just to put up a kinky profile. And wherever you are between those extremes, there is room for you.

The trick is to proceed at your own pace. Most people feel awkward at some point in their lives. You aren't alone in feeling like the lone geek. It is important to respect your shyness, and to treat the awkward parts of your personality with compassion. Comparing yourself with other people isn't going to bring you any peace, because that social butterfly or party animal might be sweating it out on the inside, just like you!

Compassion for your shyness means understanding why you have those feelings. Have you always been shy? Was there a pivotal event or time in your life that drove you to be especially hesitant around other people? Is it new people, places and things that prove difficult? Or are you really conscious of your personal boundaries, and your shyness is a protective mechanism? Knowing the root of your shyness can help you to overcome it enough to get you where you want to be. You may have very real reasons for your hesitations, and if pushing past it causes undue hurt or damage, or you are living with a type of severe social anxiety, consider working with professionals to address these concerns.

For those who have always been shy, collaborating with other shy folk is an excellent way to have an empathetic buddy. Don't be shy about your shyness! Kinky folks tend to want to help out, and if, for example, you are having a hard time working up the nerve to go to your local munch, letting the person running it know this can help them help you feel more comfortable. Shyness cuts across all facets of our communities. Dominant people can be shy, too. Don't let your identity in the community push you to act a certain way.

Aside from yourself, the only person who is going to know you identify as shy is... you. This is one of those places where a "Fake it until you make it!" strategy can work.

Give yourself credit if you step outside your comfort zone, even for the "small" stuff. Sending out that friend request to someone on a social media site is a brave thing to do! Pat yourself on the back, and acknowledge your bravery. The more positive reinforcement you provide for yourself, the more you'll feel comfortable stretching your own boundaries into new and exciting adventures.

You can also take steps to work around shyness in proactive ways! Some of these tactics might include:

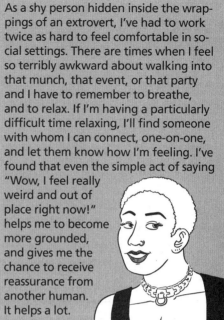

As a shy person hidden inside the wrappings of an extrovert, I've had to work twice as hard to feel comfortable in social settings. There are times when I feel so terribly awkward about walking into that munch, that event, or that party and I have to remember to breathe, and to relax. If I'm having a particularly difficult time relaxing, I'll find someone with whom I can connect, one-on-one, and let them know how I'm feeling. I've found that even the simple act of saying "Wow, I feel really weird and out of place right now!" helps me to become more grounded, and gives me the chance to receive reassurance from another human. It helps a lot.

- Wearing a funny or clever t-shirt as an icebreaker.

- Printing up a business card that says "Hi! I'm shy but I think you're cool! Here's how to contact me!"

- Teaming up with a friend who is less shy than you and having them help you network.

- Volunteering for positions at events where you are compelled to talk to people (like registration at a convention, or the front desk at a party.)

- Treating that difficult moment like your own "scene." Dare yourself to speak to three new people at that party.

- Checking in and debriefing yourself after each event, giving yourself credit for even the smallest victories!

All we kinksters have been awkward outsiders at some point – some parts of each of us don't necessarily fit in the default world, so we seek out like-minded folks with whom we can connect. This knowledge can help you open up to others: we are all bonded by "otherness" of some sort.

A lot of what people fear about connecting with people is rejection. It is a scary thing, we agree. However — rejection is not always a bad thing. In fact, it can really be helpful in building your self-esteem. That new person in whom you are interested who shuts you down has given you a gift. By letting you know immediately the connection isn't mutual, you can let go and move on to more productive interactions. Though it seems counter-intuitive, surviving a "No" strengthens you. It gives you the power to move on and remember that there are many more people with whom you can successfully connect. It may be tempting to mope and feel sad, and wonder "Why don't they like me?" but the fact is, they don't know you. They have their own story about who you are, what they want, and where they are in their lives. It is important not to put too much importance on any single interaction. Put yourself out there, keep a positive attitude, and you can and will connect.

Once you've practiced making those initial connections, you'll have a whole new world opening up to you! Coming up in Chapter 9, we have some great ideas on asking to play, hooking up, and then figuring out what to do once that conversation gets rolling.

Volunteering and stepping up

Another fun way to get to know folks is becoming a volunteer. By stepping up and helping out, you not only meet people, you up your personal investment in the community. Many events and organizations within the kink communities tend to be volunteer run as a labor of love.

A few examples of volunteer opportunities include:

- **Dungeon monitor** (someone who oversees play areas, may require training)

- **Medical staff** (for those with medical backgrounds)

- **Event registration** (helping people sign up for the event, check in, and get information as they come through the door)

- **Equipment setup/teardown** (investing "sweat equity")

- **Hospitality** (keeping everyone fed and hydrated)

- **Decoration and room setup** (making the space pretty and usable for its function)

Volunteeraholic?
Some individuals love volunteering, do it from an open heart, and may do it a lot, but they get a lot out of it emotionally or energetically. Others, however, compulsively volunteer even though they are frustrated, over-taxed and feel drained by the process. Be aware of which you are, and weigh whether you are helping from a place of charity, are being fairly compensated (such as with entry to an event), or if you are doing it because you are trying to fill an emotional void.

• **Demo bottom/top** (assisting presenter in demonstrating a scene or technique)

• **Classroom assistant** (introducing the presenter and/or serving as a liaison between the presenter and event)

By volunteering, you also can forge con-nections with the people who are organizing and running events. If there are no official volunteer positions at a particular event, just offer to help if you can: it means a lot to event organizers and they tend to remember it later... and event organizers know a lot of people. Even an hour of helping out can really make a difference.

Some events require work shifts from every attendee – make sure to choose tasks that suit your personality. By building the event together, you help invest in its greatness. This may seem frustrating if you paid to get in. If you really don't want to volunteer, ask if there is a "vacation / resort" option to get you off the hook.

Managing Your Virtual Self

Not only do we meet people in person, but we also do a lot of our kink con-necting online. Amidst all the porn and pretty pictures are real people mak-ing real connections around their real desires. But how do we meet people between the pixels, and make those real connections, rather than just ending up in a sea of spam and frustration?

What will serve your desires?

The first question to ask, as we did with in-person interactions, is: what do you want and desire? Do you want to get laid, build a relationship, or have a community to reach out to feel a part of? Are you hoping for a one-night stand, or friendships to last a lifetime? This answer will determine where you build your online profiles, as well as what those profiles will include.

That's not to say you can't find one-night play partners on community sites. A lot of people do. It's just a matter of considering what the primary focus of a site is, and maximizing your energy based on your desires. Trying to find a life-mate on Craigslist Casual Encounters may not be the best choice.

There are lots of different kinds of websites. Cruising sites, hookup sites, social networking sites, shared interest sites, event sites, discussion and chat sites, dating sites, blogs/online journals, informational sites, porn sites, personal websites... and more! Some sites are for kinky people only, while others are broader interest but have a few kinky people on there doing their thing in the background. See Appendix 4B for some places to set up profiles and start connecting with others.

Now that you know why you are hopping online and know where to put your profile, you get to write it. This does not mean you copy it from someone else's profile and change your name. Inspiration is fantastic, but plagiarism is not.

I worked for the company that owned ALT.com and Bondage.com – and let me say, I saw more profiles than anyone ever should. Occasionally, I'd take a phone call if a customer had a serious issue. One day, a woman was transferred to my desk, and I needed her handle in order to log into her account and try to resolve her issue. "Can't you look it up by my e-mail address?" she asked, her voice strained. "Sorry, ma'am, not in this system." She sighed and mumbled something. "Could you repeat that, please?" I asked, as I was unable to understand her hoarse whisper. She cleared her throat "Daddymumbl-emumblemumble..." My turn to sigh "Look, just spell it out for me, OK." "Fine, its D-A-D-D-Y-S-L-I-T-T-L-E-C-U-M-W-H-O-R- E." "OK! Got it, thanks." I wondered if she introduced herself as such as, say, her local munch. There's absolutely nothing wrong with having an explicit or saucy moniker... so long as you're fully comfortable with it, and prepared to step into the persona you've created.

You can be as succinct or as verbose as you like, but know that very few people read past the first paragraph when doing their initial scan. If you want to be perceived as a three-dimensional being, consider mentioning more about yourself than a vivid description of your genitals and your favorite three fetishes. Consider as well what details you are choosing to share, as in some parts of the community sharing every single one of your fetishes or interests can leave people overwhelmed or confused about you focus. Some opt for minimalism, while others choose to list everything so that the reader gets the full picture. You can't control how other people will see you, but you can decide to be as honest as is feasible. Keep it straightforward and real, and remain true to yourself.

Check your spelling and your grammar. Read your draft aloud to yourself Have a friend read it over, or at least read it yourself a second time, before posting at 4:00AM. It doesn't have to be flawless, but it needs to be coherent. And remember, you can always change or update it. In fact, your profile is a living document. Updating your profile to reflect your current reality shows that you are engaging the media in question on a regular basis, and not just putting up a place-holder.

Beyond your profile description, your profile name or "handle" will also say a lot about you. For some people, their handle is a simple translation of their scene name. For others, it is a statement of desire, identity, humor, or philosophical beliefs. Others choose to use their legal names. Sometimes, your handle ends up accidentally becoming your scene name whether you intended it to or not, because people will see the handle over and over again, and come to associate that handle with your images, words, thoughts and desires. Thus, think carefully about your handles, just as you will want to think carefully about your scene name.

If you are a dominant, and that's your only identification, great. Or maybe you're a bottom and have no desire to play on the other side of the whip. Some folks are switches, and will have profiles that express this. And there are other people who will create multiple profiles depending on what sort of partner they seek. It's all OK. You might have a profile that puts your top side forward, and another that is more reflective of your desires to bottom. If you are bisexual, pansexual or queer, having multiple profiles that appeal to different people on the gender spectrum may well increase your chances for making a successful match.

Profile pictures

Many people are intensely visually focused, so having an image on your profile is an excellent way to catch the attention of those who will be checking you out. Providing a good photo will increase views to your profile, especially on dating sites, where people will often filter out those without pictures.

The photo does not have to be of your face, though many people have tasteful headshots as their profile picture. There are also those who never put their face on their kink profiles for reasons of personal security or concerns about outing, or simply because they just don't want to. The image might be a hand holding a whip, a collared neck, a spicy photo of your favorite pair of boots, pictures of your favorite toys, a piece of inspiring artwork, or a humorous image that grabs people's attention. Some individuals post images of their genitals as their primary profile picture – something that really appeals to one part of the population but is a huge turnoff for other parts of it. Be aware of who you wish to attract, and post accordingly.

Beyond your primary profile image, most folks also post additional photos to their profile. No matter how many pictures you post, make sure that you are not misrepresenting yourself by saying that the picture you took off the internet is in fact a picture of you, or your artistic work. Credit needs to be given where credit is due, listing the name of the artist, model, or image source if it is not your intellectual property. If you do not know who took it or is in it, say something like "I found this sexy image online" in the description, rather than saying "this is my slave girl" if in fact you've never met the young lady.

Many social media sites enable you to add "friends." Some folks are gleeful collectors, while others only add people they know in real time. It is a courteous gesture to drop a note to someone you'd like to add as a friend, say hi, and ask to connect online. And if, for some reason, they decline, just move on. Everyone has the right to choose how they move through the online universe. And you have the same responsibility to yourself! Make sure you know who you will and will not add as "friends," and you'll optimize your experience.

Social media awareness

Be aware of the fact that the footprints you leave on the Internet are there to stay. Despite security and disclaimers and the best intentions of the vast majority of people online, there is always a risk that your images and words will wind up outside your intended location. And once your kinky genie is out of the bottle, there's no turning back. Search engines have long and detailed memory, and photographic recognition software can perform amazing feats of detection.

In addition to the kinky folks with whom you share a common interest, there may be others lurking about – those who are simply curious, people doing research on alternative sexuality, or people with malicious intent.

What if, for example, you post about the hot scene you had last weekend on your micro-blogging site, which cross-posts to your favorite non-kink social networking site, and your boss spots it? You might hit on some unexpected consequences. Networking with other kinky folks could compromise your privacy as well, even if you aren't the one posting photos of a gorgeous singletail whip.

This isn't to say you should freak out. This is to say that you should take your time, and think carefully. You can always share more, once you are comfortable and know what you are doing. But an impetuous rush to share isn't something you can undo.

A more discreet, separate profile, not affiliated with or linked to your main online presence, can be a great way to start learning what level of disclosure is right for you.

Communication styles

Subcultures usually come with their own protocols for communicating, and the kink communities are chock-full of specialized language and methods for signaling your chosen role. These tags, handles, and non-standard approaches to language can seem confusing. Some folks treat these as inviolate rules, while others seem them as silly online posturing. There will be those who want to type all in lower case letters ("my name is bob"), type all in upper case letters ("MY NAME IS BOB"), refer to themselves in the third person ("this slave is unworthy to be called bob"), or will want to address honorifics and diminutives simultaneously ("G/greetings to Y/you from slave bob")... the variety of approaches is astounding. One thing is for sure: when uncertain, respectful communication using standard, default grammatical guidelines is always a good fallback.

Lasting Connections

When you plunge headlong into this new world, it can be easy to feel as though you have to start all over again, building friendships and relationships, finding new ways of interconnecting. But a great deal of what works well in the default world works well the kink communities. It can be tempting to meet new kinky friends and want to plunge headlong into discussions about kink, to exchange stories, to see if they might be able to fulfill that hot fantasy you've kept hidden away for all those long years. And this is an understandable impulse, but it's a good idea to remember that you are still dealing with people, and people are more than a catalog of fetishes.

Getting to know folks in the kink community is a process — trust needs to be built. Compatibility must be determined. Common interests must be established. And limiting yourself, your discussion and your interactions to what you can get out of the person with whom you are dealing will cut you off from some potentially deep and wonderful interactions.

When we're asked, "How do I get to know more kinksters?" we encourage people to think about successful relationships they'd built prior to exploring kink. When you met someone you found interesting, you conversed, exchanged ideas, spent time together, and got to know them. And this is an excellent strategy for building a solid network of pervy friends as well.

It is tempting and seductive to hook up with people because you have a common kink. And this may be terrific while you are engaging in that kink. But if you desire an ongoing relationship, seeking out shared interests and commonalities will help to build long-lived relationships.

As you get to know people, be aware that not everyone will be your best friend. In much the same way as we have varying levels of social interaction within our lives outside of kink, we will find that different people meet different needs in different areas of our lives in kink. You might have someone you connect with monthly at a munch, or acquaintances you see once a year at a big national conference. You may have emotionally intimate connections online: people with whom you exchange endless rounds of emails and spend countless hours chatting together, but may never meet in person. Or you may make a lifelong connection of the heart and soul in one night. All of these interactions are valuable, and each has its place. Respecting the role each of these plays in your life is the foundation of your interpersonal network, and keeping it strong will give you good grounding going forward.

Shit happens, deal with it gracefully

Of course, not everything is going to be hunky dory. As in any social milieu, there will be stress, drama, bullshit, gossip, infighting, backstabbing and difficulty. Microcosm, not utopia, remember? We aren't here to sell you on a bill of goods that everyone gathers around the spanking bench at the end of the party and soulfully sings a few rounds of "Kumbaya." Having reasonable expectations is one of the keys to successfully navigating these waters. In Chapter 7 we will be exploring the variety of emotional traps, physical pitfalls, and social snares that you are likely to encounter.

Practicing open, honest and straightforward communication is good business for everyone. This does not mean doing everything in your power to avoid conflict, but building well-rounded communication in all directions without building resentment. Working with grace in your casual interactions and friendships means you are constantly working on the muscles that will help you be a clear, open and honest communicator in your more intimate relationships. "Conflict is opportunity" is a motto both authors work from: an opportunity to grow, to gain knowledge, wisdom and experience, and to bolster our ability to be well-balanced perverts.

Chapter 6

But It Followed Me Home!: Pre-Event Negotiation And Planning

WE'VE HEARD IT time and time again... sometimes from our own lips. How could that have happened, that thing, that experience that we didn't want? Often, it's pretty simple. We didn't set systems in advance or stick to them.

This concept applies broadly. Whether we are talking about coming home with an unplanned purchase, a new partner (when we were trying to be monogamous), or a sexually transmitted disease... it can follow us home if we don't do any pre-event negotiation or planning. Or, of course, if we set those limits and don't listen to our own stated intentions, desires, and needs – what was the point?

Setting Frameworks Before You Go

The first part of this process begins by setting frameworks before we go to the event. This means sitting down and thinking about the potential concerns and joys alike, in advance. By running ourselves through what could come down the pipeline, we can begin brainstorming our reactions, our desires, our motives, and how to have our greatest possible success.

Negotiation and authenticity

In the kink community, you will hear the word "negotiation" batted around a lot. Negotiate before you play, negotiate for your desires, negotiate the structure of your relationship. It has been said that this is what makes kink relationships and sex different from those in the default world – that instead of assuming we know how to pleasure our partners, we have discussions to find out what our partners actually desire.

There are many different approaches to negotiation (explored in further depth in Chapter 9). What often gets left out of the repeated mantra of "negotiate, negotiate, negotiate," is that negotiation starts internally: you talk to yourself first. Many different tools are available: you could journal, read books, take notes, work with a therapist, have a long talk with a best friend or an anonymous human on the Internet.

Here are some of the things you might wish to negotiate with yourself:

• Why do you want to go to this event?

• Who are you hoping to interact with?

• What do you hope to get out of the encounter?

• Are there specific types of individuals or activities you are drawn to? Not drawn to?

Consider looking at Appendix 3 (especially the Long Kink Questionnaire) as a place to start brainstorming your turn-ons and your turn-offs. Consider what genders of individuals you want to play with, what styles of relationships resonate for you, and what your body calls for.

Whatever tool you use for examining your desires, take a long hard look at your motives... and we don't mean what you "should" be motivated by or drawn to. Cut the bullshit and really look at what you are going after. It's a bad idea to tell your friend you're looking for a one-night stand when underneath you are called to a lifetime love affair. Are you really longing to be in an open relationship, or are you doing it to placate your partner? Is this 24/7 slavery thing calling to you, or would you be better served with a once-in-a-while play date?

And you know what? You can change your mind. The decisions you made for yourself four years ago were made by the person you were four years ago. Consider re-negotiating with yourself every once in a while, taking a long hard look at the new truths buried beneath the "should" comments you've been telling yourself. Before we can ever hope to have a healthier and more meaningful sexual existence with others, before we can deepen our romantic or relationship connections by being real and vulnerable with them, we have to learn how to do these things with ourselves!

Every person in a relationship will share this information differently. Some will sit down with a workbook and pore through all their desires in a marathon session. Others will plant one seed, step back, and see what grows from it. Some people sit down over a nice meal, others figure it out as they go, and the occasional one chooses to follow a "don't ask don't tell" policy when it comes to kink (something that has its own concerns attached).

Be honest about what will work in your relationship... not just what you think will be most comfortable in the short term, or easier in the long term. And when we say relationships, we don't just mean the people you are dating. Who do you feel you need to negotiate this event or kink community encounter with? Your answer list may be short, or very lengthy, depending on the networks you are already part of.

If someone asks to negotiate with you, remember to actually listen to what they are saying — not what you want them to be saying, or what your inner demons are twisting their words into saying. Consider using a tool like repeating concepts back in your own words to make sure you understand what they are sharing. If moments of judgment arise internally, what is bringing them up?

Are you finding a "button" of yours that they have hit? Perhaps they are saying they want to spank you... and your subconscious mind says that "good men don't hit women." Instead of saying "You're sick," consider words like "I feel uncomfortable being spanked because I was told that men should never hit women." "You" statements can alienate, while "I" statements are your own truth, not projections, and can thus help folks listen to each other with more ease.

Budgets

The next framework that needs to be set in advance is your budget. How much money can you spend while at the event? Many folks figure out that they can afford entry to the event. But once they've made that commitment, suddenly need that one new toy, that one new outfit for the Saturday party, and heck, let's go to the nicest restaurant around too and get the bottle of wine and... and suddenly they've spent three times more than they said they would.

If the big weekend event will be a splurge, set that framework in advance. If you have to be aware of the budget, be honest with yourself up front. This includes setting up your shopping budget in advance – because, let's be honest, you'll probably want to get something while you're there. Events let us support our own vendors, plus you get to try everything on before buying it, and you can order custom items.

We have seen individuals who wander the vendor area first and then debate what to buy. Others leave their wallets in their rooms except for $40. Some listen to their gut reaction and do extravagant shopping, and have included that joyful experience into their pre-event planning. Others plan a set amount that they can enjoy going crazy with, and enjoy getting creative with what they can afford.

Physical limits, needs, wants and desires

Before we can go to an event, we also need to set for ourselves the frameworks of our physical limits, needs, wants and desires. This will include issues like the amount of sleep we need to be functional, the kind of marks we can come home with, or our desire to have a group of folks hold us down and kiss us.

Listen to your body's wisdom; it is aware of what it needs, wants and desires. However, our conscious mind is needed as well, for building healthy limits in advance. Remember, just because your body might enjoy something in the moment does not mean it is a good idea. Consider who else will be affected by your choices. Will those marks affect your work in the default world, or that night of hot nookie send you home to your spouse with an STI? Will that weekend of crazy interactions have you coming home exhausted and unable to work on Monday?

Thinking about these issues in advance will help plant the seed for living responsibly when the kink event comes around. In the case of STDs/STIs, this includes reading the STI Awareness section of Appendix 4E, and becoming aware of your own pre-existing health concerns. And remember, different bodies have different realities: for example, different skin types mark differently; "cell popping" is not always in fact "temporary branding"… but is in fact straight-up branding if you keloid (quite likely if, for example, you are of African descent).

Emotional limits, needs, wants and desires

In addition to the considerations to meet your physical needs, it's important to plan for your emotional needs as well. How much attention from your lover do you think you'll need to feel connected? How much time will you need alone? Are there specific people who you know will be a drain on your energy? Do you really want to challenge yourself to flirt with someone new? Brainstorm these things in advance!

Time

The day only has 24 hours, and there's so much to do! Consider ahead of time how much sleep you will need, the time it will take to eat, shower, and get dressed, and, of course, the time needed for that impromptu conversation that may change your life. There will be other events, you don't need to do it all at once. Consider whether your top priority should be quantity or quality.

Energetic capacity

We each have an internal battery. Some things fuel us, and some things drain us. Sometimes, the drain is worth it, and sometimes the fuel comes with strings

I veer between wanting hours of connection, lots of interaction, and loads of play – to wanting to hole up in my room and watch Discovery Channel. (If it's "Shark Week," you won't see me all night.) I learned that going with the flow is the best way to get my emotional needs met. It is just as OK to relax in a hot bath at the end of a busy day as it is to shut the dungeon down in the wee hours of the morning. Only you can decide what you need!

I love sexy flirtation at 2AM – in fact, it will "fuel" me more than that extra hour of sleep. Knowing that about myself means that I can make judgment calls that will have me feeling happy the next day.

attached. Becoming aware of our own energetic capacity, and what fuels and drains us, can help us budget our energy at kink events.

Your energetic capacity will also help you figure out how much to do in one weekend. Some folks will want to jump in and try new, exciting play. When people try out a new kink activity, it is referred to as "popping a cherry." Some people have the energetic capacity for a single round of cherry-popping, wanting the time to process it afterwards, while other folks are fans of trying thirty new things in a veritable "cherries jubilee." Knowing yourself can help you decide what amount of experimentation, if any, will bring you joy.

Pre-Event Preparation

Okay, so you've set your frameworks, you have a handle on your wants and needs, and you've selected the event you want to attend. You figured out your travel plans, you have tickets in hand (or have checked and verified that you can get the tickets at the door), and you are packed. No? Well, go back and look at Chapter 4 again and figure out your budget, your plans for getting there, and what you're packing. Once you know those, you can then begin the preparation for the actual event.

Styles of event attendance

You can choose from many ways to attend the event. That process begins when you buy your tickets. Do you like to purchase them months in advance, and pride yourself on being registrant 13? Do you prefer to grab your tickets at the door, and don't like to go to events that require pre-reg? Then comes the packing issue – do you start packing weeks in advance, making packing lists, or are you more likely to throw together a bag fifteen minutes before leaving? Listen to your body as you read these options – which ones make you feel uncomfortable? If your body says it's a bad idea, consider listening to that wisdom. Maybe you will be more relaxed if you can pack a few days in advance, or have a checklist – even if your partner is a spur-of-the-moment person.

A prediction: you will forget something. Make a list, check it twice, but be kind to yourself when you realize you left your favorite set of footwear at home.

Consider as well your travel plans – do you buy airfare far in advance and have three different printouts in two locations on how you will get there, or do you like to hop in the car and take your chances on getting lost in traffic? There's no one right way, but there is very likely a right way for you.

Once you are at the event itself, what style of attendee are you? Do you want to...

- Book in all the play that can fit in one event.

- Get lots of sleep each night, with everything else coming second.

- Attend every class possible.

- Sample a few classes by different teachers.

- Try classes on a variety of topics.

- See what "feels right" in the spur of the moment.

- Follow a track of programming, perhaps going to every bondage class and watching every bondage scene in the dungeon.

- Hang out with your partner; everything else is bonus.

- Be a wallflower and watch from the sidelines.

- Converse with friends, happily skipping classes or play time.

- Relax by the pool in fetishwear.

- No sleep 'till Brooklyn!

If you know you're going to chill and relax, you may want to pack an extra book and flip-flops. Meanwhile, if you know you are going to attend every class possible, you can look at the program in advance, print it out, highlight the classes and events you are going to attend, and bring the gear needed. If you're there mostly for the play, you may want to fill your dance card in advance and show up with a trunk full of toys.

Even if you think you know what style of attendee you are, we recommend being open to unexpected developments. You might plan to attend twelve classes in one weekend, only to have your body inform you it needs sleep. Perhaps those play dates will fall through and you'll find unexpected joy watching someone else's hot scene. Being fluid with expectations enables you to have fun even when things don't go as planned.

Setting intentions

Why are you going to this thing again? Go back to Chapters 1 and 3 and re-examine the question. If you're here to make long-lasting friendships in the kink community, why are you worrying about making it to every single class slot?

Does your intention match the event, or are you going to an all-ages event looking to get anally fisted? And if the event doesn't match your goals, and you are going anyway, can you adjust your intentions and goals? Perhaps you can find some different joy or learning from this experience.

Consider, as well, any conflicts in your expectations. Perhaps you told your partner that your goal is to play with them, while telling your best friend that you would take a class and bring them back notes. If the class and the play date are at the same time, you have a challenge.

All the physical stuff

Pre-event prep also includes preparing your body. If you know you'll be doing heavy scenes, consider stretching and working out in advance to build up your body's capacity. Check in with your doctor in advance: how is your heart doing? What is your overall fitness and health, and are you ready to play at the level you desire?

Preparing your body also includes being aware of pre-existing illnesses. Don't bring the "con crud" (the cold or flu that passes like wildfire around a place where people are laughing, hugging, kissing and breathing heavily) with you to the event. Check out Chapter 10 for tips on how to avoid catching it yourself.

Prep For Relationships

Hi there, single person, person not in relationship, non-dating or not-engaging-in-kink-with-your-partner person! We know this section says "Prep For Relationships"… but that also includes your relationship with yourself. So we encourage you to give it a glance, at least... many of the ideas apply to your relationship with yourself.

We hear it time and time again: Person One decides to go to the kink event with their partner, Person Two. Person Two gets bored/gets turned off/ has a bad time, and blames Person One for taking them along. Or Person One goes off to have fun and Person Two is left feeling abandoned. The variations go on and on.

Exploring kink with a partner is a slightly different adventure than exploring kink alone, as is exploring it by yourself with a partner who is cheering you on while staying home. Let's talk about the prep we can do within our relationships, and within ourselves, to have our wants, needs and desires met.

Shapes of relationships

Compared to the world at large, where asking if someone is married or not is assumed to be plenty of information about that person's relationships, the kink community is overflowing with a zillion different relationship styles. There is no requirement that you change your pre-existing relationship structure to match any of these shapes, no matter what High Lord Domly Dom at Dark Dungeon X might say. However, it is useful to be aware of some of the relationship shapes that are out there, as you will encounter them in your wanderings.

Awareness of some of the relationship configurations out there may also help you define your own unique relationship. Are you a monogamous couple that wants to swing together, but only at sex clubs? Fantastic! Perhaps you are a polyamorous triad who is okay with power exchange and service outside the relationship, but all sexual and physical kink play takes place within your closed system? Huzzah! No relationship dynamic will work for everyone, and no two relationships are identical.

- **Monogamy.** Monogamy is generally defined as one person being involved with, or open to being involved with, one other person only. However, beyond that, it's hard to get consensus as to what individuals define as monogamous behavior. People may be sexually or erotically monogamous (sexually or erotically involved with one person), emotionally or romantically monogamous (emotionally or romantically involved with one person), socially monogamous (the world at large knows them as being with their one partner), or have an identity as monogamous.

I started referring to myself as "mono-amorous" because I was dissatisfied with "monogamous" to describe my MO. "Monogamy" refers to a one-on-one marriage, and doesn't parallel polyamory, which means "many loves." While I have dear friends with whom I play, while I might occasionally enjoy an NSA fling, my heart and soul and mind function optimally when I am connected in a one-on-one, emotionally intimate, committed loving relationship. Question labels until you find the ones that work best for who you are today!

If you identify as monogamous, or use the word "monogamy" to explain your dynamic — what does that mean to you? What do the behaviors you expect look like? Does your monogamy have non-sexual exceptions, such as you are okay with your partner being spanked by someone else? Special circumstances, like it's okay only if you're there, it has been pre-approved, or if you don't have to hear about it? What do you define as sexual? Would bondage cross your sexual line, or is it not "sex" in your mind unless both parties had orgasms? How would you feel if your partner had an orgasm while being flogged, but there was no genital touch?

Some monogamous couples are fine with outside sexual play, but not with outside romantic engagements; these folks will have to define what they mean by "romantic engagements." There are those who are fine with outside romance, but not okay with outside play. Perhaps you are okay with your spouse being part of a same-gender gang bang, but not okay with them flirting one on one with anyone of a different gender — or the reverse. Many of these lines are based on how people define intimate behaviors (see later in this chapter), or on what things they feel might threaten the relationship.

- **Polyamory (aka poly).** Polyamory generally means a person being involved with, or open to being involved with, more than one other person. Beyond that, though, it's as tough to define as monogamy. All the variations we discussed under "monogamy" apply equally to poly.

  If you identify as polyamorous, or use the word polyamory to explain your dynamic, what does that mean to you? Are you in a hierarchical polyamorous dynamic with a primary partner, secondary partner, and tertiary partner, and, if so, what time/resource, emotional and sexual expectations might each of those partners have? Do you engage in egalitarian polyamory, where all partners are on equal footing? Are you in a dedicated or poly-fidelitous triad, quad or family? Perhaps you are polyandrous (many husbands) or polygamous (many wives)?

I have always been wired polyamorous, and have been in open or multi-part-nered relationships since I was a teen. However, for a while my partner and I were not seeing or playing with any-one else. We had to talk about that, and make sure that we were okay that our identity was poly, but our behaviors were mono at that time.

More relationships can often equal more bureaucracy, as participants must consider expenditure of all resources, including time, energy, money, space, and emotions. Shared online calendar systems can go from being nice to being vital. However, in these complex days, even monogamous folks have so many relationships—career, children, friendships, volunteer work, hobbies, etc. — that poly-style planning and sharing skills can be important.

- **Consensual non-monogamy.** Consensual non-monogamy (sometimes called "expanded monogamy") is typically one person being involved with, or open to being involved with, more than one other person, in a specific construct that has been agreed upon by all parties in advance. However, beyond that, it's as tough to define as the other relation-ship styles we've discussed. People may have pre-approved event trysts (playing sexually or doing BDSM with a pre-approved outside person at events only), carte-blanche event trysts (playing sexually or doing BDSM with any outside person at events only), swinging (see below), have open marriages (a monogamous marriage as the primary/base relationship with outside encounters or dynamics), identify as "ethi-cal sluts," or build other systems that work for them.

If you identify as non-monogamous, or use the word non-monogamy to explain your dynamic, what does that mean to you? Does "swinging" in your world mean swinging with only one other person who has been pre-vetted, swinging as a couple with another couple (aka "swapping" or "wife swapping"), swinging only if your partner gets to watch/interact, group swinging and orgies, swinging

Isn't It Cheating?
For some people, infidelity (emotional, physical, or otherwise), consensually arranged or not, is something they cannot tolerate. It is by their definition "cheating." For others, it's only cheating when the tryst or outside relationship has not been pre-arranged, while others still only consider it cheating if someone outright lied during or after the encounter. What do you consider cheating to look like? Are you okay playing with someone who already has a partner? Will you feel better, or worse, talking with that partner? Be aware of your own internal compass. There are no "shoulds" here, only what works for you and your partner(s). An open relationship may or may not equal a promiscuous relationship. There are some non-monogamous individuals who will have sex with anything that moves, and others who have zero interest playing with anyone beside their three partners. The same applies with monogamous individuals – some save their sexual energy for their singular life partner, while others sow their wild oats until they settle down with the one right person.

at clubs or specific venues, swinging with anonymous hookups, swinging within ongoing relationships, swinging without sexual intercourse involved, or something else entirely? These same options exist outside of swinging, in kink play too!

• **Professional relationships.** Whether structured through financial interactions or a vocation of the heart (or both), some relationships within the communities are based on a professional dynamic: hired teachers, gurus, tantrikas, sexual surrogates, erotic life coaches, sex workers, dominatrices, professional submissives and more. Attending a party with the dominatrix you have hired requires both internal and external negotiation, and should be given as much consideration as other relationship structures. It is against the rules of some events to pay for play, so check the rules ahead of time.

• **Fluid.** Some relationship structures are based on the fact that they have little to no formal framework; their shape is flexible or fluid. Examples include friends with benefits and friends who indulge us in our desires. However, there are many monogamous, polyamorous, consensually non-monogamous and professional relationships that are open to being flexible and fluid, evolving as the journey unfolds. Relationships are rarely fixed for their entire lifetime.

Consider what shape your relationship takes. Is it one of the above, or something else entirely? Does your partner see it in similar light, or is it like the story of the six blind men describing the elephant – one felt a tree trunk, one a wall, one a piece of rope and so on? Your partner may describe your relationship differently than you — be open to hearing what is behind their words.

Keep in mind, too, that you'll probably find yourself experiencing some flux within your idea of what a satisfactory relationship looks like to you.

As you discover the communities, and yourself, you'll find yourself shifting and changing. Some of this change will come with growing pains, and some of it will surprise you with its gear shifts. Go with it! Part of the wonder of kink is being able to experiment: try on what fits, put down what doesn't and go with what does, knowing that the only limit is your imagination and your willingness to take risks.

> When I was new, I was certain what relationship structure I wanted. Color me shocked that I can now say I've had wonderful relationships with people who weren't my "ideal." From non-kink-identified people who aren't involved in the community at all, to relationships with people who are poly while I am mono. Regardless of how you identify, it is possible to have successful relationships with people outside your "primary identity."

Styles of Partnered Attendance

Once you know the shape of your relationship, you can consider your style of partnered attendance. Just as there are many different approaches as to how one person can attend an event, the functions become exponential as we factor more and more people into the equation. Will you do everything together at the event? Will you arrive as a couple and leave as a couple, but not see each other in between at all? Perhaps you may commit to sleep in the same bed each night, but have separate adventures... or agree to play together, but attend different classes.

Discuss in advance your expectations and intentions for the event. See what will be a good fit to explore together, and what will make more sense to do separately. Plan into the system what you will do to touch base with each other, how often you will check in, and what each of you can do if things are not going as hoped.

If one partner is attending the event while another stays home, discuss in advance how much information the home partner will want afterwards. Will this be a blow-by-blow download session of what you did when apart? Or do they prefer minimal information? Some may be happy to hear the good stuff, but are unprepared to be a shoulder to cry on: it can be challenging for some folks to empathize about your difficult scene when they never even got to go and play. Others are happy to relax at home, awaiting tales of your conquests.

Setting up these systems in advance can be very helpful in making sure that the emotional, physical and energetic needs of the person who did not attend the event are being met as well. It's important that everyone be up-front about their needs: sucking it up and "tolerating" your partner's fun while you mope at home can lead to resentment. It can also be emotionally risky to push yourself to engage with other people solely to keep your partner happy. Getting your needs met hopefully also includes creating a safe environment for safe communication for all.

Consent

When we explore kink and kink communities, the issue of consent is at the forefront. As you explore kink culture, you will hear this word batted around a lot, but sometimes the issue is more complex that it looks.

Consent means permitting or approving someone to engage in specific behavior. Some people believe that silence is consent, but your authors believe that idea to be dangerous; we believe very much in active, conscious consent for all involved partners, and ongoing assent throughout the context of their interactions.

Try to avoid making assumptions. When we make assumptions about other people's limits, wants, needs and desires, we cheat ourselves out of getting to know the full truth of the person before us. Even if you have been in a relationship with someone for a long time, don't assume you know what they will be into, or what they would be unwilling to consider.

What does your partner want to get up to at the event? What in the program called to them? Consider having each of you print out the program and highlight what interests you, and then sitting down for a conversation. If your partner highlighted something that does not appeal to you, consider asking open questions such as "What about that appeals to you?" rather than judgmental ones like "Huh, really? That's weird."

When partners propose ideas to you of what they would like to do, listen to your heart and see if it consents to the experience. It's easy for many people to work from assumptions like "if I say no, they won't like me." or "if I were a better partner, I'd do that with/for them." Those assumptions get in the way of wholehearted consent.

These considerations of consent also apply when you're playing separately from your partner(s). Did they agree to what you're up to (as it applies to your specific relationship), or are you doing what you think maybe kinda might be okay if no one looks at it too closely? In other words, did they say yes, or did they not say no?

Consider as well that different terms mean different things to different individuals. Love and sex go hand in hand for some, while for others they are completely different points of negotiation. Be sure to clarify your agreements. If you said "No sex," where would they put oral sex, for example, or making out with clothes on, in relationship to that boundary? Becoming aware of your own comfort zone, as well as the reasons why those comfort zones are there, can help you better navigate your relationships and kink community alike.

Communication Systems

Every partnership has a different flow of communication. Some rarely talk, but spend a lot of quality body time with one another. Others process the meaning and intention of their relationship on a weekly basis. The variations are endless.

Thus, it's important to clarify first how you and your partner(s) best communicate within the relationship in general. How will this style of communication work into an event like a weekend kink conference? If you are used to getting half an hour of debrief time with your partner after coming home from work every day, and there is no debrief time worked into the weekend, you may unintentionally be setting yourself up for communication challenges.

Consider your communication systems for the following points:

* How will you share your desires and intentions in advance?

* How do you convey your limits, boundaries and concerns in advance?

* What system will you use to plan your activities in advance?

* How often and how deeply will you connect at the event?

* Will you want to set up processing time at or after the event?

* What will you do if you need processing time at or after the event and it hasn't been planned?

It is so refreshing when my partner tells me about their concerns about an upcoming event. Will they get enough of my time, will we have fun, will we get enough time with friends? When they tell me their concerns, I feel safe to share mine as well, from a place of love and respect.

• What system do you have in place if challenges and hiccups arise at the event?

• How will you connect as a relationship post-event?

Chapter 9 addresses ways to share your desires and negotiate to play. However, there is more to share than how you want to play.

If you are going stag or leaving your partner at home, pre-negotiate your communication systems with the partner(s) who is not attending. Will you check in every day? Send a text message before you go to bed each night? Have a single debrief at the end of the event? Give each partner space to do their thing while apart? This applies for people who attend events together as well — if you've been doing stuff apart all day, or going to play with other people, what system will you use to re-connect to each other or share information?

One of the big bonuses to sussing out in advance how you communicate best in your relationship is that sometimes we run into challenges at events. Perhaps you thought that it would be okay having your lover play with someone else, or that it would be fun to spend the weekend alone... and then a moment of envy arises. This isn't a "bad" thing — it's important to be aware of your emotions and what triggers them. But what will you do with that emotion? Do you want a shoulder to cry on, or do you want a solution to the issue then and there? Is this a "drop everything and reconnect" situation, or is it a "check in and let's talk about this in detail after this event is done" scenario? Being clear on such issues can help ease you past the rough patches with minimal emotional jostling.

This situation can be especially challenging when a partner has a change of heart. It can be tempting to say, for example, "But you said it would be okay for us to play with other people," but that doesn't help. Your partner is having an emotional response, and hearing what's going on with them is more important than proving who is right or wrong. If your partner is having a challenging moment, it is likely that they need your support. They may have consented to something in advance, but the theory of a thing and the practice of doing a thing can be very different.

Communication tools to trouble-shoot hiccups include:

- Establishing protocols for communicating difficult issues.

- Listening without defensiveness.

- Using "I" statements. ("When I couldn't find you, I felt abandoned" versus "you abandoned me.")

- Sharing difficulties and, whenever possible, providing solutions and suggestions for avoiding repeats.

- Staying in the present: it's not necessary to dredge up old wounds when there are issues at present to handle.

- Remembering that our partner cares about us, and staying in a loving, compassionate mindset.

- Maintaining awareness that this situation may be entirely outside of your control, and that simply listening may be the best solution.

- Being aware that this is not a blame game, but an opportunity to communicate and re-establish trust.

- Honoring each other's needs, boundaries and well-being.

- Reminding yourself that if someone is feeling hurt, it does not necessarily mean that you hurt them.

Being open to hearing what our partners are feeling is vital. However, if there is an overwhelming tendency in your relationship for one partner to veto another's choices, if the majority of interactions end in conflict, or if there's often an overwhelming amount of processing around these issues, consider whether one partner has issues, fears or concerns that they have not yet voiced, or perhaps even fully realized. Again, compassionate communication is key.

As you do all this – breathe. Listen actively, don't just wait to speak your turn. Remember, our partners are multi-faceted, complex beings. Without requesting and accepting their truth, you have no way to know what is in their heart and mind. Holding a compassionate and loving space for them to share their experience can go far in deepening trust.

After the event, how much information will you or your partner want to hear about what the other got up to? The answers may change based on the context, but there are a few conversational methods that may aid in more fluid discussion:

- "I learned a new trick, can we try it at home?" When you have a fun new experience, it might be tempting to say "They did this better than you, do it this way." This does not help encourage and foster love and support in relationships. Present your positive experience as a positive for everyone!

- "You seem to really like that. What about it appeals to you?" If we don't understand why a partner likes an activity/concept/person, it can be easy to say "why in the world would you like that?" This can feel like judgment. Channeling your desire to understand through open, leading questions and curiosity can help relieve shyness or reluctance about sharing something new, challenging or just really kinky.

- "I had a really fun time, what would you like to know about it?" When you have a great experience, it can be tempting to share everything. Not everyone wants every detail, and they may just want to know if you are happy, or perhaps want more information in this specific context. Let them set their own comfort level.

- "I'm feeling some difficult stuff, emotionally. Can we talk about it?" It sometimes is tough to avoid saying things like "How could you do that? You hurt my feelings!" These accusatory statements can put people on the defensive. Taking personal responsibility for your feelings, and looking for positive outcomes, can help you to find mutually beneficial ways to communicate from a place of caring.

Take an objective look at the information you would like to share, and consider your method of delivery. Think about the following criteria, as suggested by 20th-century guru Sai Baba:

- **Is it true?**

- **Is it necessary?**

- **Is it kind?**

If you're not hitting two of the three, you may wish to reconsider your approach.

Post-event communication is not limited to sharing stories and processing lessons learned. Creating and using connection rituals can help strengthen bonds. This might include spending quality time together soon after the event, sharing stories with one another, or helping one another undress from your kink wardrobe. Whatever rite you choose, it can help re-focus and ground you back into your default world.

Involving Other People

Before attending events, consider whether you are comfortable with involving others. For some people, doing any sort of sexual or kink play in public is uncomfortable because people outside of the relationship will be watching. That's just fine – not everyone is an exhibitionist. Others might love having outsiders watch, interact, or even become a part of their play. Doing so may feel exciting, or offer a chance to connect with our partners in a new way.

If you are someone who finds the idea of playing with or around others titillating, consider your motives. Opening up a relationship won't "fix" it. Though it may rev up your sex life in some circumstances, trying to use swinging, group kink play or partner switching to repair a relationship in turmoil rarely succeeds in the long term. Remember, the outsiders are people, too; they come with their own thoughts, feelings, emotions and boundaries. Crystal-clear motives and healthy boundaries up front can help avoid unpleasantries in the aftermath.

If you do decide to discuss in advance playing with folks outside your relationship, consider your "target audience." Are you comfortable with your partner(s) playing with:

- Other couples/persons with primary relationships?

- People who have been fully cleared by everyone in advance?

- Folks of the same gender?

- Folks of a different gender?

- Individuals you never have to see again?

- People with whom you share intimate friendships?

- Known players in the community?

- Anonymous encounters?

- Sex workers?

Ask yourself these questions first, then discuss your feelings with your partner. Try to stay aware of why you answer a certain way. Saying "You can't play with other men" can be open to misinterpretation. Saying "I don't like the idea of you playing with other men because the type of sex we have is very personal to me, and feels like 'our special thing'" is specific and clear.

Consider as well what both you and your partner consider to be intimate: kissing, cuddling, sex, fucking, dirty talking, spanking, power exchange, body fluid exchange…. For some folks, "a fuck is just a fuck," while for others, sexual intercourse is a sign of love and interconnection. Perhaps your partner considers caning to be a type of play that is intimate, and might feel emotionally hurt to see you being caned by another person.

We don't always know in advance what will set off our feelings that the intimacy of our relationship has been violated: some folks call these discoveries "landmines." Some of these concerns may be related to boundaries ("I don't like it when you use my special toy on someone else") or they could be specific physical issues (being concerned that your partner is using an intimate toy on some else's intimate parts, creating an STD risk due to cross-contamination). If you do know your "special things" in advance, voice them and share your feelings around them. If your partner is aware how special and intimate a specific outfit, toy, venue or type of play is to you, they are more able to take those feelings into consideration when debating playing with others.

By articulating levels of intimacy, sometimes we are able to stumble upon new possibilities. If your partner considers mouth-to-mouth kissing to be an intimacy particular to your relationship, perhaps you will develop a new pleasure in kissing other parts of a new lover's body. Instead

For some people, if their partner has an online-only kinky lover it's not a big deal: it's all on the Internet, so it's not "real." For others, knowing that their partner has an online lover can be heartbreaking, because that person online gets quality time and a glimpse into their partner's heart. Each evaluation is unique, and you have to decide what is "real" for you.

of dismissing something that upsets our partner as "not that big a deal," we can listen to what their fears, wants, needs and desires are underneath, building a stronger connection with them. What may not seem like "a big deal "to us may have strong roots in our partners, and vice versa.

I was at a cuddle party at a mixed kink event, when a leatherman walked in. He looked around, wide-eyed, and when asked to cuddle, said "no way." Even though he was comfortable hitting people with whips, or doing anal fisting with folks he barely knew, cuddling with a stranger was far too intimate for him.

Find Your Systems and Stick By Them

The next step is adhering to the agreements that you have each made. "But they followed me home!" is not a good excuse for turning your monogamous relationship into a polyamorous one, or for an unexpected $700 purchase when your relationship is on a tight budget, or for bringing home an STD because you failed to follow safer-sex procedures. If you aren't sure whether something is appropriate, consider whether you are following the letter of the limit or its spirit. Are you trying to fool yourself into feeling something is okay when you know it's not?

If you're unsure — ask! Use kind and loving language, rather than sounding harsh or accusatory, to help keep communication fluid. Fluidity gives us the vital capacity to be aware when our systems need to change. We may find that what we said and thought would work in theory may not be okay in practice, or new ideas may come to mind the more we explore. Be open to the possibilities!

Planning for jealousy, envy and other emotions

Though we will go more into emotional experiences in Chapter 10, it's worthwhile to look at them briefly here. Why? Because if we plan for what we will do when emotional challenges arise, we can often bounce back or process through them with greater ease.

Note that we said "when" you encounter them... not "if."

When we are in situations where our emotions can be heightened, some of them will be more difficult to handle. Jealousy, envy, fear... these are not necessarily "bad" emotions that must be suppressed for fear of leading you to The Dark Side. They may well be giving us vital information about our feelings and state of mind. Being able to break down the feelings into more articulated concerns, and having awareness of what to do to help address the issues underneath, can be very helpful.

- **Envy.** When we wish we were doing something, and someone is getting to do that thing instead of us, a feeling of envy can arise. Even when we are excited that a partner is getting to explore their sexuality and identity, if we feel left out we can become covetous or discontented towards the joyful experiences of others. It can foster a feeling of ill-will and resentment, when in our hearts we want to be happy for the person. Expressing that we wish we were doing that thing they are doing, and booking a time to have joyful experiences of our own, can help mitigate envy.

- **Jealousy.** When we are resentful of the time, energy or connection that someone else is experiencing, jealousy can arise. This is also the case if we feel others are undeserving of a happiness we perceive as lacking in our own lives. Being honest with ourselves about what we wish we had can help us challenge feelings of jealousy. We become more able to articulate what is driving the jealousy by sitting with the emotion for a while and observing what precipitated the jealous feelings. Letting your partner or partners know you're experiencing these feelings is healthy. Unleashing anger or passive-aggressive reactions without letting them in on what's going on for you is not.

- **Competition.** Feelings of competition arise when we actively or passively compare ourselves to others. Fights over "which lover got more time/energy/focus/orgasms" start building resentment. Fears around being inadequate bubble up. Remembering that each journey is unique, and expressing the things we love in our interactions, can help deflate competitive feelings by reminding us that our connections are one of a kind and can stand on their own rather than in comparison to the experiences of others.

- **Possessiveness.** When we feel that our partners are objects that we possess, and we desire to have exclusive interaction with those belongings, possessiveness arises. This desire to have no one else touch what is "ours" can make alternative relationship structures challenging, unless we can voice what specific things we want to be "ours." Voicing our desires to be loved, feel special, and feel desired, along with expressing how to help all partners feel unique and irreplaceable, can help work through debilitating possessiveness.

- **Exclusion.** The fear of being left out, deprived of time, or excluded from affection can generate feelings of exclusion-based jealousy. We may worry that if the new play partner is getting hot play time with our lover, that our lover will not have time left for us to play as well. If general exclusion is a concern, consider booking "date nights" to reconnect with a partner and reinforce that you and they are still desirable. If specific exclusion is a worry, consider finding ways for all parties to participate together, such as co-topping, group dinners, or letting someone sit in during play.

- **Fear.** Many forms of jealousy are based in fear. That does not make them bad, nor does it make it the "fault" of the person experiencing the fear. Sometimes the fear is rational, often it isn't. Fears range from worrying a partner will leave if someone "better" shows up, that having sex with someone else will make them fall in love with that person, or, as sexuality educator Aiden Fyre says, "that falling in love with a new person will mean falling out of love with an existing partner." You may fear being humiliated by your partner, or losing them. There can be fears about what others outside a relationship will think. Try talking about what actions preceded the fear response, what the fear is all about, and what actions you or a partner might take to help lower

> **Compersion/Frubble**
> In the polyamory community, there is a term called "compersion"; it means feeling empathic happiness or joy when our current or former partner experiences joy through an outside source. In short, when our partner (or ex) is being made happy by someone else, we are happy for them. This emotion can be romantic, erotic or emotional in nature, and varies from person to person. Not everyone feels compersion (or "frubble" in the United Kingdom) the same way, and being compersive or frubbly is not necessarily a sign of a more evolved individual. In some parts of the queer and lesbian community, "stone" individuals (those who prefer giving their partners sexual pleasure to receiving it themselves) are thought to be people who feel compersion above or to the exclusion of their direct/personal sexual and emotional experience.

the fear response. Consider also whether there is a truth behind the fear that should be addressed, or if a story or projection is taking place that has little to do with the reality of what's happening. Just because our partner wants to be spanked by someone else does not mean they are unhappy with their relationship with us, just as complimenting someone else does not mean that they're putting you down.

Other challenging emotions can arise: anger, hopelessness, frustration, anxiety and more. Becoming aware of emotions is the first step towards addressing them, and knowing in advance that they may arise will help you plan for them. If you know you are prone to depression, make sure you bring along fun distractions that will help you work around those self-defeating thoughts. There is nothing wrong with packing a fun book in your carry-on bag, playing some upbeat music in your room, or booking a soothing massage in the hotel spa (budget permitting).

Feeling your feelings is important. If we stop feeling our sorrows, we've probably stopped feeling our joys as well. Kink events can bring up feelings of joy, elation, delight, sexiness, adventure, growth, empowerment, connection and passion. If you have turned off your emotional body by constantly saying you are okay when you aren't, you may be blocking these emotions as well. Plan in advance for how to process your emotions, positive or challenging, and practice feeling these emotions in advance.

Kink does not create enlightened relationships by default. However, because so much of kink culture revolves around the notion of consent, more people within the kink communities have practiced verbalizing their desires as well as their fears. In turn, when we have had to question our sexual and emotional desires for much of our life, the likelihood of kinksters exploring other parts of their inner psychological workings are higher as well.

Chapter 7

Unicorns, Trolls and Other Creatures: Behavior Awareness in Kink Communities

Mythical Creatures Are Mythical

"OH, THEY'RE JUST being a troll." "We're looking for that perfect unicorn!"

Some terms get thrown around a lot in various parts of the kink community, and they can make it seem like a mythical forest! Two common examples are "unicorns" and "trolls."

Unicorn, as seen in the kink and alterative sexuality populations, refers to a type of individual currently seen as rare and highly sexually desirable: promiscuous bisexual female submissives, straight intelligent polyamorous men who want to co-parent, or hot young gay leather-protocol enthusiasts are, for various people, the precious elusive "Holy Grail" of sex.

Trolls, on the other hand, aren't really sought after by anyone. A troll is an individual who posts deliberately provocative content online, or who comes into groups with the specific intention of causing maximum disruption or getting maximum attention. In some gay male communities, "troll" may also be a disparaging term for an older man who does not fall within a narrow vision of desirability.

Unicorns and trolls are mythical creatures. Categorizing people like this does not allow us to treat people as people; it hinders us from learning who these people are beyond a few simple labels. There is almost always more to people than labels can encompass.

In this chapter, instead of slapping on labels, we will look at conduct that occurs across many communities and group populations – behaviors that all of us have perpetrated at some point. These are not necessarily kink-community-specific actions, and these missteps do not make us inherently bad people – they make us people who have engaged in less-than-perfect behaviors. By heightening our awareness, we can lower the likelihood of falling into these traps, pitfalls and snares.

Try to have compassion for those who have fallen into these behaviors. They have probably hurt themselves or others by conducting themselves in this manner, and that compassion is needed – especially if you were the one who got hurt. This is not permission to check our brains at the door, nor does it forgive the actions, but having compassion for all involved makes change more palatable. Together, we can help strengthen our community for everyone – whether you're living in it or just visiting for the weekend.

Emotional Traps

Frenzy

Frenzy, in a kink context, is a behavior pattern where someone becomes so intensely interested in experiencing everything that they possibly can as soon as they possibly can, that they override common sense or do more than is safe for themselves or their partners. Someone in the midst of "sub frenzy" may, for example, get obsessed about trying new things, coercing or pushing partners or potential partners into "cherry popping." A top or dominant in that frenzy state may be quite certain that everyone is secretly craving the kiss of their whip, and their charm and swagger is all that's needed to push past the defenses of wayward submissives and bottoms.

Frenzy behaviors can include:

* Inappropriate sharing. Perpetually talking about their kink with friends, family, co-workers, the teller at the bank...

* Engaging in BDSM and kink to the detriment of the rest of one's social life. Being kinky doesn't mean you drop all of your non-kink connections.

* Not seeing the difference between a "want" and a "need." You don't necessarily need to play every night and attend every munch/party/workshop.

Enthusiasm is one of the beautiful fuels that feed the fire of sexual exploration. However, just because other people like bondage does not mean that they want to talk about it 24 hours a day, seven days a week. Frenzy and obsessive behaviors can be potentially destructive, and are a way to burn bridges – including the one you are standing on at this moment. It can be physically or psychologically harmful to you and your partner, leading to pressure, coercion or pushing the edges of consent in both directions to get perceived needs met. It can also be dangerous to your career, social life and family connections.

Bottom's/Top's Disease

While frenzy consumes the active and conscious mind, the behavior pattern known as bottom's or top's disease is usually unconscious and insidious. Top's disease is the internal, perhaps unconscious belief that if you are a top/dominant, you must thus treat everyone around you as if they were your bottom/submissive – not just your partner(s), but your co-workers, the random stranger at the grocery store, and every submissive pervert you meet. Bottom's disease, the flip side, is the belief that becasue you are submissive, everyone must be dominant over you, including your non-kinky spouse, the folks at your congregation, your employees, and everyone in the scene.

Forcing others into a role that they have not negotiated is not consensual. And just because someone identifies as a master, mistress or slave does not mean they are *your* master, mistress or slave. Being submissive should not mean being a doormat to everyone in creation, and being dominant should not mean being a domineering ass to the world at large. In fact, many in the kink community consider it a personal violation for people with whom they do not have negotiated relationships to assume a dominant or submissive stance.

White knight

"That poor girl, she needs saving." "That sweet man over there who seems to be lost, let me be the one who guides him to truth." While it's true that being of assistance to others in the scene can be a good and worthwhile thing, individuals who are compulsively moved to act as white knights or protectors may project onto others that they need to be "saved," when they may just need a bit of assistance... or may not want any help at all.

Emotional vomiting

Emotional vomiting is the behavior of grossly over-sharing information at inappropriate times, or in ways that do not help any parties involved. Sharing our stories, asking for help and working through challenges is a natural part of growing and finding our way. As human beings, we improve by processing experiences, and that often includes venting to a friend or even an empathetic stranger. However, there are times and places where this is inappropriate and perhaps even risky – does your mother-in-law really need to know about the turbulence of your D/S relationship with your spouse?

Emotional vomiting can also take place when we reply to people online or in person. They may be sharing their story for their own reason, not as an excuse to have you hijack their narrative. If you see someone post about their challenges, consider offering a shoulder to cry on, an ear to listen, or a few points of advice, rather than using it as an opportunity to vent your own spleen or sob-story. Being a good listener is a practice we can all strive to embrace.

Feeding helplessness

People's power over you is limited to the power you give them. Individuals who hand their authority over to person after person, compulsively or out of a feeling of desperation, may set themselves up to be hurt. Common themes we have seen include slaves who "need saving" from an unknown force, submissives who "need protection" from dangerous individuals, and new people that are "innocent and need guidance."

If you are one of these individuals, you may wish to reflect on the following questions:

- Are you working from a place of fear?

- Do you feel you need protecting simply to keep your special place as someone who is unable to manage themselves?

- What do you get out of being helpless?

- Is an outside source projecting this image on you, are you projecting it on yourself, or is there a real need?

If you are the protector, you may want to consider if you are projecting this status onto someone, thus enabling them to abdicate responsibility for their own choices and actions.

Remember, there's a vast difference between protecting someone and teaching them to protect themselves. All of the survival skills you used in your life before you came into your kink identity must be brought to bear here. Helplessness can feel sexy within a negotiated scene or relationship, but can create problems if you take it out into your community.

Boundary Compromise and Breaking Limits

Compromise is a good thing, right? It allows us to gain something we would not have had if we had been inflexible. Well, this is not the case if you are compromising around limits and boundaries.

Sitting down with yourself before you play with anyone is an

In the midst of a scene, I had a play partner of mine ask to suck my cock. We were both already really turned on, but had not negotiated for that. Instead of having him give me a blowjob and compromise our negotiation, he watched as I masturbated in front of him while he begged.

important part of the negotiation process. But if, in the heat of an intense scene, you discard all the limits you have established for your protection, what was the point of the exercise? If we don't respect our own boundaries, how can we expect anyone else to?

Altered states of consciousness can affect our ability to hold to our own limits. Whether we are inebriated on chemical substances or in the midst of a really hot scene, our will can sometimes become malleable. This is why many schools of thought on kink teach that after a scene starts, re-negotiation should only take place once all parties are "sober" again.

Part of taking responsibility for your safety is making certain that you are capable of giving consent and active assent. You have a duty to yourself and your partners to protect yourself and your limits at all times.

Attention-seeking behaviors

Seeking love and attention is worthy and appropriate. Creating drama for the conscious or unconscious purpose of garnering attention is not. This applies whether that drama pertains to yourself, your relationship, between groups, or other people's business.

Conflict-crafting, rumor-mongering and serial victimization are all examples of attention-seeking behaviors with little positive outcome. Sometimes our unconscious desire for attention, love and affection can be warped into these behaviors, casting us into the role of "drama llamas," which is a tough persona to shake. Whatever the source of the drama, consider whether your "weighing in" is about generating the best outcome for all parties involved, or is about using it as a platform to place yourself in the spotlight.

I'm personally aware of what judgmental behaviors can do to those within the kink community. Because of some of the scenes I have pursued that involve controversial topics and behaviors, I have been ostracized, threatened with violence, called names, lost friends and been told I was mentally ill. Keep in mind, these were all other self-identified kinksters, leatherfolk and fetishists. It took years of personal work to get myself past the impact of those judgments.

Judgmental behavior

Belittling, berating or bashing others for their choices, judging scenes we don't personally enjoy or agree with, being "snarky" about a book or event, behaving rudely to someone based on how they dress, saying that someone is not a "real slave/master/whatever"... the kink community has a surprising amount of judgment for a group of individuals acting on desires that have been judged by the world at large.

One common form of judgment is based on how "real" we think a person is in their kink journey. Do they use their legal name, does their profile have a face shot, do they play in public? When requesting detailed information about someone, consider your approach. "You have no picture up on your profile, prove to me you are not a liar/evil person/predator" is less likely to yield a positive outcome than "Hi, I noticed you had no image up on your profile, and I prefer to make sure that I engage with individuals who are known in the community. Do you have any references?"

Another pervasive form of often unnoticed judgmental behavior you may discover in the kink community is self-judgment. When we worry that we made bad choices in the past, or constantly put down our current desires and interests, we sow the seeds for us putting down others as well. Self-judgment can make it very easy for us to project our own perceived issues onto others. Focusing on our experiences, both wonderful and challenging, should be part of our journey; it will help alleviate the impulse to judge ourselves and, in turn, others.

New Relationship Energy (NRE)

A phrase popularized within the polyamory community, "new relationship energy" (NRE) is the rush of "falling" for someone, when we are first enjoying someone's presence, connection, and newness. Some see it as loving how we look in our new lover's eyes, while others see it as a "high" that can leave our thinking hazy from the rush of emotions. This is often considered the reason so many people get "stupid in love." NRE does not apply solely to romantic or sexual relationships; new relationship energy can also apply to group memberships, teacher/student dynamics, and more.

NRE becomes a challenge when the new rush becomes an addiction. The new partner becomes the one that gets all the "good stuff," while the partner already in place gets to deal with nothing but the bills and your sore back. Or the new relationship becomes a focus of obsession, displacing not only the original relationship(s) but other pre-established commitments and obligations. New emotions and experiences can be mistaken for deep intimacy and profound connection, or can feel like a path that must be explored at all costs.

Of course, there are also times when NRE may in fact be indicative of having fallen in love, newfound intimacy, or a new and wonderful path. You may be challenged by encountering these emotions when you were "just" looking for someone to play with. This can be especially true if the feelings are not mutual. Other involved parties may be concerned about how fast the NRE has appeared, fearing that you may be making irrational decisions. If you're experiencing NRE, this might be a good time to have a sounding board – someone you trust who might be able to give a more objective view on the blissful glow you're feeling.

Physical Pitfalls

Pushing our bodies

For many, kink is a chance to fully inhabit our bodies and push them to the max. Extreme clothing, intense physical activities and edgy sexual energy can lead to startling heights of ecstasy... and injuries. Torn rotator cuffs, sprained ankles, dislocated wrists and nerve damage are just the tip of the iceberg when we push our bodies too far. Top, bottom or switch, no one is immune. And, in the rare worst case scenario, poor judgment around what a body can take, technical errors, or poor decision-making occasionally lead to kinky sex becoming a deadly affair.

Few of us are at our optimum fitness level. For those who work day jobs at computers, live with complex medical realities, or who just don't get as much exercise as often as we'd like, the impact on our bodies can be severe. Any workout without a warm-up increases the potential for injury. We should approach BDSM as a full-contact sport; respect your body by staying healthy, stretching in advance, eating well, staying hydrated, and making sure to cool down afterward.

Our bodies aren't the only problem when hardcore exertion goes too far. The mind can only absorb so much sensory input. Frayed nerves, anxiety around being "the bad guy" in a heavy scene, or post-scene emotional meltdowns can be consequences of playing with such highly charged energies. During play in public kink spaces, people's egos may be on the line; they may feel the need to prove to themselves or to onlookers that they can do more, take more, and be more hardcore – physically, mentally, or emotionally.

Consciously pushing ourselves may be a positive goal, but accidental harm is not. Neither is maintaining expectations that are beyond your capacities. Sometimes the hardest thing to do is to stop a scene when we feel we've had enough. It often seems like people believe they must take all that they possibly can, and then just a little more. Live within your boundaries, and act in your own best interests: self-care is critical.

Lack of spatial awareness

In Chapter 8 we will be discussing play spaces, dungeons and other erotic arenas. One of the physical challenges that can come up in those venues is a lack of awareness of the environment. People may use play equipment as a staging area, individuals may walk though scene spaces and into the "back-swing" of a whip, curious onlookers may ask questions of players in the middle of scenes, and more.

Public kink venues are radical arenas where individuals can come together to create space where fantasy can become reality. At some kink events, several hundred people may be playing in the same dungeon. This close proximity requires that everyone remain aware of their environment, lest they become intrusive or disruptive. Things like excessively loud scenes that distract other players, conversations about non-kink topics near folks in scene, or DMs curtly asking a couple in the midst of aftercare if a space is available can be very jarring.

If you are on the receiving end of disruptive or invasive behaviors, try to give people the benefit of the doubt while informing them that you do need space, less noise, or whatnot — and coming to a mutual agreement between all parties so that all can play well together.

Voyeurs without borders

Watching others engaging in hot scenes is a reason many people go to public play spaces. For those who enjoy public play, it can be invigorating to feel the energy surging through the assembled onlookers. Enjoying freely given energy is one thing; leering, egging folks on, shouting "encouragement," getting too close physically, or trying to become a part of other people's scenes without consent is another, and is not appropriate.

Even if you're only part of the kink community for a single weekend, it's important to keep your voyeurism respectful. Look around the venue to see how much space folks give to the people actively scening — are they sitting in a social area, standing ten feet from a scene, or are they up close but not touching? How quiet are voyeurs in this venue? Take the cues from those around you, or if in doubt, ask someone who is not in a scene or doing aftercare.

Exhibitionists

The flip side of the coin to voyeurism is exhibitionism – showing off, strutting your stuff, and being seen and appreciated. There can be a delicious rush to having many eyes on you, knowing that they are relishing your scene – exhibitionism is one of many reasons people choose to do kink in public. However, forcing others into a scene with you to feed your exhibitionism is not consensual. Check your intentions and behavior.

Not everyone who plays in public is an exhibitionist. Some may be there to use the equipment, for reasons of personal security (perhaps they are playing with someone new and want the safety net of event space and DMs), or because the walls at home are thin. Assuming that everyone is an exhibitionist, or voyeur, is a form of projection.

Social Snares

Acting self-important

When we are navigating a world of sexual fantasy and power exchange dynamics, inflated egos may arise. Healthy self-esteem is vital, but behaviors that include denigrating or belittling others, over-inflating our accomplishments, elitism, and excessive snobbery in order to feel powerful are not healthy ways to bolster self-esteem.

Self-importance can also be seen in high-profile community members, people who have been around for a while and claim seniority and who demand special treatment, and among individuals and leather families who claim areas of clubs as "theirs" (unless, of course, they own the club).

Self-deprecation

When we operate from a place of low self-esteem, or are projecting ourselves into the world from a place of

Power exchange relationships are called that for a reason. You must own your own personal power, and have pride in it, before you start messing around with the give-and-take of power and sexual energy.

worthlessness, exploring kinky community and events can be dangerous. Not only are individuals coming from a place of self-deprecation more likely to make poor choices, they often do not respect their own limits, boundaries and desires.

Fantasy or Fact?
You may hear fantastic or outrageous stories of people's lives and journeys in the kink community. Some of them may be true, some may contain truths, and some of them may not be true at all. Ask yourself, "How does this impact me? Is their story causing harm?" If their journey does not resonate with you, feel free to disengage, or engage at the level to which you feel most comfortable. Whether or not they are in fact the sixth reincarnation of the Bodhisattva of sexual enlightenment may not have anything to do with whether you can learn good breathing and pain processing techniques from them.

Being shy is fine and dandy. Self-deprecation and self-hatred are not. If your pattern is to constantly put yourself down, consider taking a step back and assessing how ready you are to engage in this lifestyle. Being unable to speak up for your own concerns is a real issue when engaging in BDSM: all partners need to be able to express their physical and mental state at any given moment.

Exaggerating knowledge/history

When we pretend to know what we do not, we put people at real risk. If we say our bodies can take two hours of punching when we have never before received a body blow, we are setting ourselves up for potential harm. If we say that we know how to safely do a complex piercing scene, and we do not know how to insert needles safely, we not only risk our partner's health but our own (contamination is a risk for bottoms and tops alike). Broken bones, nerve damage, psychological trauma and more are real concerns in some forms of play, and lying about our capacity has real consequences.

Some individuals say they have done things, been places, or had experiences within kink community and culture that they have not. Sometimes these start out as little white lies to hedge against seeming "too green," but the white lies can get out control. By "donning borrowed leathers," they set themselves up as an authority or elder, when they in fact have far less lifestyle experience than they claim.

For this reason, asking for references is part of some kink cultures. Asking about a potential playmate's previous partners, talking with their friends, watching them play, and simply taking the time to get to know someone are great ways to protect yourself. Not everyone who talks the talk can walk the walk, and just because someone owns a toy does not mean that they know how to use it.

Drama around relationships

Every community is made up of relationships. Friendships, mentorships, and partnerships can all help create a stronger community, or, if they end badly, can lead to drama or fractured trust. Just because a relationship ends does not mean that the feelings around the relationship vanish overnight. Our exes and former best friends are probably going to stay in the same community – which means we must practice how to manage interacting gracefully with former partners. Sometimes the drama around break-ups does not come from the people involved, but other community individuals who feel it is their business "to be helpful."

For those who are event hosts, producers and community leaders, there is a difference between "drama" and real-life conflict. If confronted with a genuine and valid concern that you feel is beyond your comfort level, someone trained in conflict resolution may be able to facilitate a positive outcome. If that still does not work, or if a mutually beneficial result cannot be reached, use your best judgment and be decisive; this can set an example of integrity and boundaries for our community.

It also sometimes happens that the relationships which generate drama are not former relationships, but current ones. There are those people who thrive on being the center of attention, or are energized by being in dramatic situations, and may enjoy dragging others into their vortex.

Biological relationships

As the kink community grows and ages, there are more and more multi-generational kinksters. Sometimes being someone's "brother" is slang for a close friendship, but nowadays it may also mean "born of the same birth parents." Some parent-child pairs set up rules around who will attend various events or parties, some are happy to know Dad is happy but never want details, some are pleased to support those in their family by helping them find resources, and some are comfortable playing at opposite ends of the same dungeon. More than one parent has come out into the scene after their kids came out. Each relationship is unique, and will find its own way to navigate the potential challenges that may arise for themselves or those around them.

Coercion

Being seduced into things in which we have already expressed an interest can be sexy. Being guilted, shamed, terrified or blackmailed into doing things is not. The more obvious forms are easy to avoid (both as recipients and givers), but the more subtle forms of psychological manipulation can be trickier. Some coercive language might sound like this:

- "Is that all you've got?"

- "If you were a real top/bottom/master/slave/player, you would..."

- "If you trusted me, you'd let me..."

- "But you should want to..."

- "I know you're not that experienced, but..."

- "I know you better than you do."

- "Trust me, I've been doing this for a lot longer than you."

- "I thought you were tougher/better/stronger/more experienced/edgier than this."

- "Safewords and limits are for newbies."

Coercion is not limited to sexual or kink play situations. It comes up in our community in cases of building relationships, as well as in places of leadership. Guilting people into "giving back to their community" can generate resentment, and, in the case of people who are already at capacity, can burn out the precious resource of willing volunteers.

Swarming

Swarming is the tendency to mob a new face at a gathering. Someone who is "fresh meat" at the event or party becomes surrounded by people, either all at once or in an overwhelming chain of constant attention. Swarming treats people as commodities rather than as people, and can overwhelm, alienate and chase away the individuals in question. If word gets out that people are being mobbed at events, new folks may well be put off by the thought of attending, and regulars may well feel invisible and unwelcome.

Language challenges

Many people within the kink communities use a variety of pronouns (he, she, they, ze, or only being referred to by their first name), honorifics (mistress, master, sir, m'lady, lord, goddess), diminutives (slave, slut, "it," puppy) and special nicknames. These are all personal preferences, but someone who attaches a strong identity to how they are perceived or addressed in the world may feel offended, hurt, or not seen for their true selves. When possible, ask questions. "What name do you go by?" "How may I address you?"

If someone calls you by the incorrect name, pronoun, or title, take a moment before assuming that they're a thoughtless jerk. Remember that their error is likely not about you, and you may need to help others learn your preferences. They may not have enough information, may be new to a specific segment of the community, or may not have encountered this gender/identity before. Give them the benefit of the doubt, or enlist the assistance of your allies to politely redirect them on their approach to language.

Communication between groups

Incivility, relationship drama, coercion... they all happen at an organizational level as well as a personal level, and are to be avoided. Cliques, bickering and gossip do not serve our community as a whole; if you hear gossip about a group, consider getting multiple opinions.

Consider identifying what your group is into or stands for, rather than what it is not into or does not stand for. Saying a group is "for individuals into exploring fetishes and alternative relationship structures" is clearer than saying "we are not a swinger or a hookup group."

Sometimes the inter-group issues we encounter are based on a lack of inter-group planning. In some cities, you may see no events at all for a month or two, and then suddenly see that there are three parties in one night. Sure, the issue might be specific issues of rivalry, or it may just be a lack of planning and poor communication between groups. Whichever it is, creating additional drama by amplifying the issues is rarely helpful. If you find yourself being drawn into "political" entanglements, consider gracefully disentangling yourself. You do yourself and the community at large a favor by not fanning the fire.

Secrecy

Whisperings of a guru who can teach you the secrets of the Old Ways of Leather, or rumors that membership in a particular group will equip you with deep, dark esoteric secrets – the allure can be real. For some parts of the kink community, secrecy and screening processes can be absolutely necessary, due to outing concerns or fears of social injustice. Some parties, for example, keep the location secret until a guest or attendee has registered and agreed to follow the rules of conduct. However, it's one thing to be asked to give your name and attend a few munches before going to a party, and another thing altogether to be required to divulge detailed personal information to someone with whom you've only communicated online, or to pay exorbitant fees to be accepted into a group.

Choosing to learn or study from others who have "come before" can be a tradition within the leather and rope communities. Having someone conceal vital information until you are "deemed worthy," or being asked to move cross country to live with your a secret mentor, is another matter. If you can't "ascend" or "gain true mastery" without spending large sums, sleeping with the central leadership of a group, or "enduring severe indoctrination"... consider whether a group might be a cult. Appendix 4I includes the "Cult Detection Evaluation Frame."

There is an appeal to secrecy. Back rooms that open up to hidden passageways, earning the right to attend selective events – they can be sexy. Hard-won knowledge has added value. Be honest with yourself: if you're seeking out a secretive or elite group because you enjoy the challenge and the mystery, that's okay. Just be aware of where your limits are, use common sense, keep your wits about you, and make sure that this is a good choice for you.

Liars, unethical individuals and predators

Just like any other population, the kink community has the occasional "bad egg." Liars, unethical individuals, thieves, criminals, unstable personalities, bigots, predators, rapists and abusers are part of every population group on the planet. We dream of a day when this is not the case, but for now, it behooves you to be careful.

Having been sexually assaulted during a scene, I know how difficult it can be to recover from such an experience. The person to whom I was bottoming pushed past a line I'd firmly set, and violated my safer sex boundaries. I blamed myself for not fighting him off. I was sure that I had brought it on myself by making a bad choice. I feared that my mental state, altered as it was from hours of play, was too compromised for me to be a responsible bottom. And this was scary: after all, I "should know better!" I'd been involved in the scene for over fifteen years! I finally realized that I had crossed paths with an unethical person, and that I was not to blame for my own coercion and assault.

Keep aware, and keep alert! Don't leave toy bags full of expensive toys out at events. Get to know people before sharing too much personal information. Trust your instincts. And if you have had something truly awful happen, don't let anyone use easy labels to bury your truth: lies like "real slaves can't be raped," "a top can't be abused," "you asked for it by wearing that outfit," and "no smart person would be taken advantage of like that" help no one, and harm many. Being in a power exchange dynamic is no excuse for abusive behaviors either (see Appendix 4H, "SM vs. Abuse"). Some actively deal with perpetrators by reporting them to the police, others expect their community to help police their own, and some, troublingly, do not take action. Make an informed decision from a place of power, talk to a trusted friend and make the best decision for you.

In the future we will live in a world, and a kink community, where everyone will be honest, open-minded, loving individuals. Until then, take care of you and those you care about.

> **If you are the victim of a crime, or some offence has been perpetrated against you, such as fraud, theft, abuse, rape, and other non-consensual behaviors, it is your right to seek help. If you are faced with these issues, make sure to empower yourself and avail yourself of all avenues of reparation. It is beyond the scope of this book to address every possible contingency or to provide legal advice. To help determine if an encounter was abuse or BDSM, please see Appendix 4H.**

People Are People, Everywhere

Moving towards that future world starts with you. Building trust, responsibility and friendships from a place of consent is a profound act, and ensuring that consent permeates all of our relationships is part of what makes the kink community radical. Instead of making assumptions about desires or interests, we endeavor to consciously explore them, and help others explore as well.

All groups of humans have their issues, failings and foibles. But becoming aware of problematic behaviors can help strengthen our community through awareness. And from this awareness we can build true informed consent in all directions, so that all we kinky creatures can explore our unlimited potential.

Chapter 8

Oh the Places You'll Go!
Dungeons, Play Spaces and Erotic Arenas

KINKSTERS' SHARED SPACES come in a variety of flavors: sensual boudoirs, gleaming metal edifices, cozy pads, raw warehouse spaces, and many more. Everyone who decides to create an environment for exploring their sexuality draws upon their own dreams, desires, and experiences to determine what these spaces will look like.

Some commonalities repeatedly appear, such as equipment and supplies. Some basic ground rules are often in place; some etiquette overlaps between spaces.

In this chapter, we'll explore what you might see when you go to a dungeon, club or play space, and some of the basic rules and guidelines you'll encounter. We'll put you on your way to begin navigating like a pro.

Understanding the Space

Not all kink spaces are the same, in terms of intended purpose or specific rules. We'll cover some of the more common venues you may visit, and give you an idea of what you might encounter there. Keep in mind that every gathering has its own personality, and the scene is constantly evolving: your friendlly neighborhood dungeon may include a hot tub area; a local backroom play space might not have a sling but might have a dedicated aftercare corner.

If you have mobility challenges or service animals, be sure to contact the event organizers or venue manager in advance about accessibility. Some of these spaces may not be not fully navigable, though the number of accessible spaces is growing all the time, and creativity abounds in our community.

Dungeons

Dungeons are traditionally BDSM-focused play spaces. Some are expansive, with multiple floors and theme rooms, while others are single-room spaces in a basement or attic. The venue may require a high-fetish dress code, or may encourage attendees to show up in "street legal" clothing so that the neighbors' interest isn't piqued by a sudden parade of fetish wear on their block. If the dungeon is a converted hotel space (during a kink conference, for example), it may consist of a ballroom containing eight pieces of equipment, with a no-frills feeling – or a team of perverted decorators may have spent long hours transforming the space into an erotic wonderland.

A professional dungeon, often known as a house of domination, may be available for either sessions with erotic professionals (though be aware, most BDSM professionals do not provide genital sex) or for rental by enthusiastic amateurs. Why rent a space? Because many of us have thin walls at home, or partners who do not want to participate. Many professional dungeons also have a collection of toys and equipment that are available to use. If you do not know how to use a tool, talking with the person who is renting the space might be a great way to pick up information one-on-one, though there is sometimes an additional fee if it turns into a full-blown class.

Places and props you might see at a dungeon:

- **Greeter table/social area.** Very few people want to overhear chatting about taxes while they are trying to play, and new people need a place to ask questions. For many dungeons, these issues have been addressed by creating a social area, or setting up a greeter table. Socialization is therefore limited to the social area, and new people who have questions may either find a Dungeon Monitor (aka DM, see p. 175) or go to the greeter table to ask questions. The table is usually staffed by a friendly volunteer who is happy to act as an ambassador to the new folks, and who can also monitor noise levels if the social area is adjacent to play-space. The social area may be combined with a food and beverage area, if one is offered at the party. These may offer anything from red licorice and cola to a full buffet spread.

- **Saint Andrew's Cross.** This "X"-shaped piece of furniture is a classic in the world of BDSM. It usually has attachment points at the extremities to facilitate bondage. St. Andrew's Crosses are commonly used for secur-ing people for flogging, whipping, or receiving other styles of sensation play. Whipping posts, pillories, chain spider webs, Catherine Wheels and flogging frames are other items of dungeon furniture designed to secure fortunate human targets. Some dungeons will place these pieces of furniture in a roped-off area for whip enthusiasts, providing safe space so that passers-by aren't struck by the backswing of a whip.

- **Spanking bench.** This is a four-legged frame where the body is com-fortably supported. It may be structured to support the bottom com-pletely, or be of a more simple construction so that the bottom can bend over and brace themselves. Its design allows increased access to vital and delightful regions of the body, and increases the comfort and endurance of the person receiving the sensations. Many other styles of furniture assist in comfortable support, including bondage beds, massage tables and bondage chairs.

- **Cage.** Cages come in many shapes and styles, from dog cages to standing cages and prison cells. Some have holes in them large enough to access the person inside, while others are solid-walled containment units used for isolation.

- **Medical area.** When temporary (aka play) piercing or cutting is permitted at a dungeon, a specific area is often designated to increase safety. "Mood lighting" may be sacrificed to provide increased visibility. It may be set up like a doctor's office, or have equipment, furniture and flooring that can be easily disinfected. It may feature a gynecological table, dental chair or surgical-level lighting. Most dungeons that permit temporary piercing or cuttings will provide a sharps container for safe disposal of biohazards. If you're planning this type of scene, verify beforehand that the dungeon provides such a container, and carry a portable sharps disposal unit (available at most drugstores) with you, just in case.

- **Suspension frame/hard points.** A suspension frame is a metal or wooden structure that has been specifically designed to safely hold the weight of a mid-air, moving human body. Some venues have "load rated" hard points in the ceiling, with heavy bolts running through support beams, secured on the opposite side. Winches may also be attached. Be diligent in conducting your safety checks before dangling people from a structure or object: some flogging frames are mistaken for suspension frames, and some venues put small rings in the ceiling for decoration only. Check with party hosts and venue managers, and confirm for yourself if a frame or overhead point is actually built for your intended play before risking your partner's health. And hey, bottoms? It's your ass on the line. It's never a bad idea for you to conduct a safety check, too.

- **First aid station.** This is what it sounds like: a place where basic medical supplies are kept. If you need a Band-Aid because a whip drew blood, or water for someone who is dehydrated, this is your go-to zone. Larger dungeons and events often have a nurse, EMT or other medical professional on call during parties, in case of a serious injury or other health concern. In other cases, some events request that a DM or host be the contact point for a 911 call. Again, it's a great idea to check beforehand so that your contingency plan is in place.

What is a DM?

Dungeon Monitors/Managers (aka DMs, sometimes called Play Monitors, Venue Facilitators, Event Assistants and more) are individuals who help a party run smoothly. Depending on the region or venue, they might be there to help attendees find play or aftercare spaces, assist in networking, bring food and water, or have information about the party and the scene in general. They are neither babysitters nor employees, and are not there to clean up after you. At many parties, DMs are there to help enforce party rules, maintain the safety of the party as a whole, or distribute safer sex and cleaning supplies.

Not all parties have Dungeon Monitors; sometimes the hosts choose to have attendees police themselves as responsible adults, or keep an eye out for one another's safety in a communal manner.

At some parties, DMs are empowered to stop or modify scenes. If your scene is interrupted by a DM in this instance, immediately halt the activity in question. Wind down as quickly and gracefully as possible, doing your best to minimize an abrupt come-down. Even if you are in the throes of a very hot scene, and disagree with the DM, comply first and ask your questions later. Perhaps your screams are bringing the unwanted attention of neighbors, or the kids who live at this house got home early. They are empowered to protect the integrity of the space and enforce the rules by which you agreed to abide.

Feel free to ask DMs later, outside the play space, what happened or why your scene was stopped. Polite compliance and respectful dialogue is the best way to maintain safe space. At the end of the day, Dungeon Monitors are individuals who care, and who volunteer their time to help insure things go smoothly. They are, however, still human.

If a DM at an event does have any degree of control over the action in the dungeon, they should be appropriately trained in the rules of the space and the desired atmosphere of the gathering. Also helpful is an awareness of basic first aid, and savvy social interaction skills. A talented DM knows, for example, how to help a top end a scene well rather than abruptly derailing the energy. Being aware and familiar with the safety measures required to minimize risk across many styles of play is a vital DM skill. Individuals who are emotionally attached to control, are easily shaken up, or are severely confrontation-averse do not necessarily make good DMs. Dungeon Monitors in turn should be aware of what their actual capacities are at the event and venue.

- **Cleaning/disinfecting supplies.** With so many people using the same equipment, it is important to make sure body fluids are not left behind after your scene. (This is also critical in helping reduce the possibility of viral or bacterial cross-communication.) Thus, dungeons have supplies such as absorption pads (aka "chux") for protecting equipment and floors, antibacterial wipes for cleaning sweat from equipment, and heavier-duty disinfectant sprays and wipes for cleaning up after ejaculate and other body fluids. Take the time to read the instructions! Many of these sprays need to remain on the surface of the equipment for a few minutes to be effective. Others should be sprayed onto a wipe and then used, rather than applied directly onto a piece of equipment. If a dungeon does not provide effective cleaning supplies, decide for yourself whether you feel safe putting your naked body on their gear.

- **Aftercare room/area.** After kink encounters or BDSM scenes, some folks need time to decompress. This might mean curling up in a warm blanket, coming down from the experience through quiet conversation or cuddling. Others need personal space and/or alone time post-scene. An aftercare area generally provides a "soft" space for doing just that — comfortable couches, cozy bed areas, mattresses on the floor and other padded surfaces, combined with easy access to water and calm music, or quiet.

On-premises sex clubs

In the swinger community, there are both "on-premises" and "off-premises" gatherings. On-premise clubs allow and are set up for sexual encounters to happen on-site. Off-premise gatherings are opportunities for swingers to gather in public or semi-public spaces, and then take the play back to their homes or hotel rooms. In the swinger community, play is usually more likely to mean sex, while in the BDSM community play is referring to scene interactions. The kink and leather communities have their own variation of off-premise spaces, such as at the local leather bar — a space where leather folk will actively cruise, but usually go off-site to play.

Sex clubs provide space for all manner of erotic encunters! These include:

- **Swinging.** People playing with a variety of other people, or their partner, in an open space.

- **Partner-swapping.** Pairs trading partners with one another.

- **Gang-bang nights.** A few central people, with a much larger number of people sexually interacting with those central people.

- **Jack & Jill parties.** Masturbation/mutual masturbation only.

- **Orgies.** Consensual group sex interactions.

- **Cuckold parties.** A wife having sex with other men while the husband watches but does not interact with her or anyone else.

- **Sex worker nights.** In jurisdictions where sex work is legal, the club may have parties focused on sex workers plying their trade.

- **...or other special events!**

Though some rough sex may be welcome, it is good etiquette at sex clubs to ask the hosts what degree of BDSM/kinky play is suitable for the environment they wish to create. Many sex clubs are not enthusiastic about extreme kink in their spaces (as discussed in Chapter 3), but some kink groups want to play in sex clubs. The answer? Private rentals! Sex clubs and bathhouses will sometimes rent out their venue for a night for BDSM groups to come in, set up dungeon equipment in their space, and tear down the dungeon at the end of the night. These spaces become a fusion of energies; other fusions can be created as well. Temporary swinger spaces set up in mansions, back room spaces created at kinky cafes... wherever your fantasy will take you.

Places and props you might see at an on-premises sex club include:

- **Orgy bed.** Orgy beds are furniture created to facilitate... wait for it... orgies. Sometimes they're just a bunch of queen- or king-sized beds pushed together, and other times they're specially commissioned beds that are round or very large. Sometimes these props show up at cuddle parties, where participants are engaged in consensual non-sexual touch.

- **Sex shapes.** Sex wedges, swings, body pillows, supporting frames and other props are sometimes used at swinger and kink clubs to help make your sexy time more comfortable, or more exciting. Achieving and maintaining those extreme poses for double and triple penetration often require assistance. Or perhaps you just need a fun way to be comfortable for longer while receiving oral.

Whatever the purpose, there is a broad range of shapes available to get you where you need to be.

- **Hot tub.** Many swinger spaces have hot tubs; they encourage everyone to get naked, relax, and get cozy. Some clubs permit the hot tub to double as play space, while limiting sexual contact to "above the water-line only." If individuals do not shower before entering, are having sex in the pool (thus exposing other bathers to their bodily fluids), or the tub gets cleaned very rarely – consider for yourself whether the hot tub is a good space for you.

- **Dance floor.** Whether you are called to the two-step, tango, booty drops or disco – the dance floor is a great way to meet new people and get your body moving.

- **No-voyeur area.** Though voyeurs can be fun in swinger clubs, there are some players who want a space away from prying eyes. The area may be for couples (or triads) only, or for "invited voyeurs" only (individuals invited by the above couples). There are also "women controlled" spaces, where women (often a minority in heterosexual swinger spaces) can invite specific people to join them, but single (or groups of) men are not allowed in on their own.

- **Safer sex station.** If we are getting our freak on, it's important to have access to safer sex supplies. Precautions to minimize risk of exposure to STDs/STIs can be found in Appendix 4E. Many swingers' clubs provide condoms and lube, and some are beginning to carry latex or nitrile gloves, dental dams, and other safer sex supplies. If you have latex allergies, or prefer a specific shape, size or texture of condom (there are so many shapes and sizes out there!), bring your own supplies and find a way to carry them around with you.

The back room

Though they are rarer than they used to be, the back rooms at leather bars traditionally were a place where sexual encounters could happen away from prying eyes. The back room play space is actively advertised in some clubs, while in other bars it is a whispered affair only for the regulars. Some clubs allow anyone to play in the select area, while others are available only for known entities.

Places and props you might see in a back room include:

- **Sling.** Though any equipment listed in dungeons may be featured in a back room, the sling has a vibrant history and tradition in back rooms. A sling is usually made of leather or heavy canvas, suspended from four chains hanging from the ceiling or a metal frame. Containers of lube and condoms are often nearby. As slings are made of porous material, and are therefore difficult to disinfect, you may consider bringing your own gloves and chux (absorbent pads) or a towel to cover the sling.

- **Glory hole.** Some back room spaces facilitate or encourage anonymous cruising or sexual play. A glory hole can facilitate this type of encounter. One person waits on one side of a barrier (usually a wall or a door) to offer a "hole," while someone on the other side presents their cock. The excitement, and challenge, with this connection is that you do not know what you will encounter on the other side of a hole — a mouth? An ass? A cunt? A hand ready to give a hand job? Some consideration is useful before sticking your cock through the aperture and deciding whether or not to take on all comers. Be aware that some people will present a cock with a condom in place, others will not engage in safer-sex practices. Consider carefully what degree of safety is within your comfort zone.

Bathhouse

In the generic sense of the word, a bathhouse is a public place for bathing: depending on the region, they will often include a steam room or sauna. In the gay men's community, and occasionally in the women's community, a traditional bathhouse may have been converted to, or double as, an on-premise sex club. Please note: not all bathhouses are slang for sex on premises friendly spaces, and soliciting the nice lady working at the Korean-style women's bathhouse for a happy ending is in very poor taste. Once you've confirmed that the bathhouse you're checking out is a sex-friendly venue, you'll discover that there are often a variety of areas to explore.

Places and props you might see at a bathhouse include:

- **Lockers.** So that you don't have to schlep your stuff, bathhouses offer lockers for your valuables and clothes. They'll also provide towels, sometimes for a fee. Check out the policy before you go. Once there, you can strip down, wear your towel and key, and head off into the space to explore the delights to be experienced.

- **Sauna/steam room.** No matter whether the sauna is a "dry" or "wet" sauna (aka "steam room"), it's a good idea to bring in a towel for your butt — it's hygienic, and besides, that bench gets pretty damn hot. Keep in mind, not everyone in the space is looking to get laid. Play may range from "sweet and mild" to "crazy pornographic" in the level of touch, intimate contact, and sex.

- **Social area.** Social areas at bathhouses are not just for talking and greeting, but may provide magazines with sexual and non-sexual content, beverages, social activities (like card games), or erotic art galleries, to encourage conversation and social interaction.

- **Massage room.** Nope, it's not slang for an erotic massage. Many bathhouses have licensed massage therapists on hand who offer their paid services for clients. Why combine sexual spaces and masseurs? Because it is much easier to feel sexy if you are relaxed!

Sacred sex temple

Those whose kink is part of their faith, or whose spirituality includes some form of kink, may choose to build a sacred sex temple as a space to practice their erotic explorations. This is also the case for those whose bondage crosses over with their tantra, or whose sex magic happens to feature dominance and submission. Temples may feature large mirrors, live music/drumming, and other tools to set the mood and facilitate transcendent experiences. If the space includes massage tables, make sure to check the weight capacity before multiple people climb on top — they are usually built for one fairly static body rather than multiple highly active individuals.

Places and props you might see at a sacred sex temple include:

- **Altar.** This large table or area is a place to acknowledge the energy of a space or leave your own sacred objects to be "charged" with the energy of the ritual you are participating in. It is often themed to reflect the type of kink ritual or work being done that day.

- **Yoga mats and cushions.** Many sacred sex spaces will have these tools available so folks can sprawl comfortably on the floor.

- **Dance area.** Some sacred sex rituals start with, or include, some form of dance, such as bellydancing or ecstatic trance dancing. Another type of expression is a "ball dance" where participants wear balls, lemons or bells attached through temporary piercings in their skin. The dancing here is not formalized dancing with steps; each dancer chooses the movements that help bring them into an ecstatic state, often leaping, whirling and other wild movement. Often, there are drummers or other musicians off to one side providing loud rhythmic music.

Educational spaces

Whether they are called dojos, libraries, clubhouses, social centers, or something else entirely, these spaces are often set as spaces for attending classes and educational intensives, watching live poetry and performance nights, or exploring extensive sexuality libraries. There are folks new to exploring kink who have come to these spaces and been disappointed when no kinky or sexual play broke out on a specific night. Might erotic spectacles happen? Perhaps, depending on the gathering – but it is far from guaranteed.

Places and props you might see at an educational space include:

- **Classrooms.** Specifically set up to facilitate discussions or presentations and classes, these areas will probably look pretty much like any other classroom... until you see the suspension frame set up in the front. The setting is often flexible in order to accommodate different teaching modalities such as lecture, discussion or hands-on participation.

- **Reference libraries / museums.** As people strive to collect and protect the histories of alternative lifestyles, some people have taken on the responsibility of preserving the history of the kink, leather and BDSM communities. From a box of books in a local clubhouse, to elaborate travelling libraries of smut, these historians and librarians have taken on the task of seeking out, gathering, storing and making available to the general public as much information as they can about our kink culture. Appendix 4B has some information on a few of the resources available to you.

Special interest specific venues

Special interest groups often create spaces that cater to their interest's specific needs. Since so many venues are built to cater to the common denominator, people with very specific desires or who want a more finely-tuned focus will often create space just for them. While a spanking fetishist may find plenty of room in a kink event to get their spanko needs met, they might not wish the distraction of a boisterous take-down scene at the next station over. SIG space allows people with aligned fetishes to do their thing in a more homogenous space suitably centering on their kink.

Places and props you might find as a special interest specific venue include:

- **Rope dojos.** Asian aesthetic rope bondage (aka *shibari* or *kinbaku*) enthusiasts have been known to create a rope "dojo," where their art form can be taught on tatami mats, with shoji screens and kimono decorating the space. Suspension frames and/or hard points facilitate suspension bondage.

- **Stables.** For those into "pony play" (human-animal role-playing), a "stable" may be as simple as a corner designated as such, with a blanket and a bowl of water, or as elaborate as a full-scale replica of the accommodations of a biological horse. Some hardcore aficionados will host parties on their own farm, while other will travel to visit such an authentic environment to facilitate their human equine fantasies.

- **Nurseries.** Those into "age play" or AB (adult baby) play will sometimes create "playrooms" or "nurseries" with adult-scaled toys and baby furniture. Everything from a slide to a changing table may be created in outsized proportions, to give the feel of being a baby or kid in an adult-sized world.

- **Messy Play Areas.** Tarps and plastic sheeting are often the order of the day for those who love to engage in messy food play, also known as "sploshing." Parties may be conducted in places easily hosed down (a bare warehouse space may be the perfect locale for that pie fight), or in a carefully covered and draped environment, where the floor, ceiling and walls have been secured and protected.

Note the vibe

Every event has its own "vibe" or "energy." These terms generally refer to the feelings elicited in our minds and bodies as a result of spending time at that event, the spin that the people hosting the party hope to put on the flow of the gathering, and the way the specific event operates. No two parties are identical, even at the same venue on a different night. Each might have different music, decorations, themes, protocols, levels of noise, levels of silliness or solemnity, and, of course, attendees. If you love Gothic-industrial music spun with a live DJ, the play party with canned disco on the dance floor might not be to your taste.

Kink events are social events, and, just like any other social event, some of them simply may not capture your interest. That is sometimes difficult for those new to kink and BDSM to hear — especially those who expect exciting, mind-blowing depravity at every turn. You may hit on a slow night at the local dungeon where no one is playing, or conversely everyone may be playing at the same time, making it too chaotic for you to engage emotionally. Some parties might feel awkward, some music may be annoying, and the energy at some parties may set your teeth on edge.

But fear not: knowing in advance that these possibilities exist can help you to be prepared for this eventuality. Remembering that it is OK to walk away will alleviate the sensation of feeling trapped or pressured to stay.

Sometimes you can bring your own fun or elevate the mood. Slow night? Maybe it's on you to be the first scene in the dungeon. Not digging the music? Politely ask the DJ or party host if there are other options available.

Not every party you attend will have a human chandelier and *Eyes Wide Shut* masks at every turn — but perhaps you can make one of those happen down the road. So much about kink is what you make of it: the energy and the attitude that you bring to the

For the first year I attended public play parties, I was largely uninspired by the music played in the dungeon. When my dominant took over running a series of parties, I made up a CD and asked if it would be OK to play it at the next event. No one ever expected to hear James Brown, Tricky, Prince, Earth, Wind & Fire or George Clinton in the dungeon! But people commented on the new sounds, and other local party hosts soon caught on that a broader spectrum of music elicited a broader spectrum of energies.

Squicks

A squick is something that repulses or upsets an individual. We personally know individuals who are squicked by blood, anything that looks like domestic abuse (e.g. a man punching a woman, even consensually), resistance/struggling, weapons, screaming, emotional coercion, inflatable items, humiliation, belts as a punishment tool, sticky substances/food, religious-themed scenes, and more. Some of these are related to past traumas, while others are culturally ingrained. However, squicks are not always rational. If you get squicked at an event, walk away from the encounter. Our buttons have little to do with other people's motivation or experiences. It is unlikely that the folks playing came to the dungeon specifically to offend or upset you. Talk to a host/ Dungeon Monitor (DM). Decompress elsewhere. Process later what about it squicked you, and know that though some may work through their squicks, others will be squicked by that thing for life. Some of us may even develop a new squick over time in the kink community. We all have buttons, and that is OK.

event have a great deal to do with how much you enjoy yourself. And in the instance where it just doesn't click? It's still a learning experience, and you have better knowledge of what does or does not work for you going forward.

Their kink may not be your kink

There is a mantra in the kink community — "Your kink is not my kink, but your kink is okay." This is an important ideal, because the kink communities are built on the notion of radical inclusivity — that a wide variety of humans with a wide variety of desires can all work together to create safe space for everyone. When we make space for the desires of others, they in turn will make space for ours.

However, if you know your type of play is likely to disturb or "squick" others (see sidebar), be respectful by considering whether it is appropriate for the venue in question. If you're unsure, ask a host. Some venues have warning signs alerting attendees about potentially unsettling scenes that will happen in certain rooms, or at certain times, in order to allow attendees to opt out, while others may keep a play space open late just for those into your fetish.

If you do not understand or are upset by what you are seeing, talk with a DM or host. Otherwise, wait until after the scene is done (including aftercare, in any form), and ask the players themselves. This might be online with a respectful email, or later that night around the snack table. Asking what about that play arouses them might help you not only understand others, but perhaps discover something new for yourself as well.

Laws of the Land

Play space rules

Each space you go to will have different rules. Some may be similar — but read each waiver, and each set of behavior expectations. What are the rules at this specific party? Are there different rules for different spaces at the event? Especially if it is a legal waiver, you don't want to be held liable for rules you did not actually read. If there is no form to read, you might instead be having a casual conversation with friends or hosts about what is cool to do in their house.

Dungeon rules are there for a reason. They are not random and arbitrary, they are not there only to protect newbies, they are not there to spoil your fun or to piss you off. Don't take the rules personally.

There are many reasons why rules may be in place, and they include but are not limited to:

- **Rules driven by laws.** Sometimes, the rules are about legal boundaries. These include "no prostitution at the party" rules, as well as play-specific ones driven by local legislation. Some health departments have strict admonition against blood drawing, and your simple needle scene could get an entire conference shut down and the hosts heavily fined. Playing fast-and-loose with your own interpretation of rules based on legal issues isn't cool. If the venue may potentially have health inspectors walking through to make sure that no sex is happening on premises, now is a bad time for you to have a few fingers inside someone and then argue later that it was not really sex; such arguments may end in a nonconsensual handcuff scene.

- **Rules driven by insurance coverage.** Public dungeons and events ideally have an insurance policy. In order to keep it in good standing, they may be unable to allow specific types of scenes. This is often the case with erotic strangulation or fire play.

I encourage party hosts to make their statements clear, to write in easy language, and to try to clarify what are often considered "unspoken rules." What you might perceive as common sense may not be that common, or make sense to everyone.

- **Rules driven by safety.** Fire in a space with overhanging draperies is a recipe for potential disaster. Suspension from a point that might look sturdy but is built for hanging plants is, too. You may not know the details of a situation, but arguing your point in the middle of the dungeon in the middle of the party is inappropriate. Hash it out prior to or after the event.

- **Rules driven by past incidents.** An accidental needle-stick to someone's foot as a result of improper disposal might lead to the relegation of temporary piercings to a contained area. Likewise, that weird rule about no hemp rope in the play-space may stem from concerns because someone once had a severe allergic reaction. Regardless, respect the wishes of the space.

- **Rules driven by culture.** Leather culture might have rules on wardrobe appropriateness, while female-dominant-only gatherings might require all men in attendance to bring gifts for the party hostess. Rules may also be driven by the ethnic, socioeconomic and religious culture of a gathering. If something seems odd or you're baffled, it's OK to ask politely what motivated the hosts to establish the particular rule.

- **Rules driven by preference or emotional issues.** Sometimes, people specifically host parties and events so that they can ensure safe space as they see it. If someone has a severe phobia around the sound of whips cracking, they may host a whip-free party. If the host of the party has a fear of clowns, they may have a rule against clowns, mimes, and circus characters at their events. Likewise, a party that insists on a latex-only dress code might be the ultimate fantasy for the host, and departing from that stringent limitation would diminish the effect that they are endeavoring to create.

Types of rules you may encounter

While rules vary from region to region and gathering to gathering, there are some common themes that appear over and over again.

- **Hours.** When does the space open or close? Are there guidelines around noise, or stipulations about how loud you can be at certain hours (the volume has to drop at 1:00AM in consideration of the neighbors)?

Awareness of time limits can help you avoid setting up for that epic scene, then finding out the party is set to close in twenty minutes.

- **Wardrobe.** Many events include dress codes; see Chapter 3 for examples. Some events may be very specific about what you need to wear, while others will list excluded textiles. Wardrobe rules may specify whether you can be nude, wear a g-string, or must remain fully dressed. Keep in mind that there may be legal issues at stake, so keep nipples and genitals covered unless specifically permitted. Parties may also require event badges and wrist bands. It doesn't matter if the green wrist band clashes with your orange PVC dress; in the words of *Project Runway*'s Tim Gunn, "make it work."

- **House safeword.** Some parties have a word like "red" or "safeword" which is considered a safeword for everyone at the party. Bottoms, tops, switches and slaves, ponies and puppies and fetishists alike can use the term to stop the action. House safewords override private and personal safeword systems. Even if you do not personally use safewords, if someone calls a house safeword during a scene, the hosts and venue will still honor it and investigate the situation.

- **Drinking & drugs.** Some venues have bars at the party itself, and others have strong rules that even one drink with dinner beforehand is a serious offense. There are some who find recreational use of mind-altering substances to be an integral part of play, while others are uncomfortable adding any chemicals to the system when play already creates altered states of consciousness. Remember — just because a party is okay with drinking does not mean it is the right choice for you. Know and respect yourself and your limits.

- **Swinging & sex.** Some kink events allow sex, some do not. Of those that do, you will find that some encourage it between established partners, and still others encourage swinging, partner-swapping, orgies and other anonymous or group sexual play. No matter the format, events that allow sex will probably have rules or an established culture around what is appropriate, and what safer sex protocols are expected. Learn as much as you can beforehand, and observe as much as you can when initially exploring the party or event you're attending. For example, some spaces ban sex for sale for legal reasons, ban unprotected sex due to health code

As an alcoholic in recovery, I like to know in advance if the venue allows adult beverages along with their adult activities. While I am not personally perturbed by others consuming alcohol, part of my self-care involves having as much information as possible about the vibe around booze before I arrive.

constraints, or restrict sexual activity from specific rooms (such as the area where food is served). If the party has safer sex rules, follow them. Even if you have been fluid-bonded for 25 years, respect the space; follow the rules or play elsewhere. If a DM brings you safer sex supplies, do not take it as an offense, they are just reinforcing party rules or culture.

- **Recording.** In the era of cell phones, digital cameras, and other personal recording technology, an assumption of "record first, ask later" has taken over much of our culture at large. The exact opposite applies to kink communities, where many venues have very strict limitations restricting recording devices of any kind. Some don't even allow cell phones on site, because most phones these days have cameras. Other venues, like street fairs, are free-range open-air photo opportunities, and people often will take a photo without asking. It is optimal to ask first before recording audio, video, still images... or even transcribing someone's words. Do ask party hosts if any electronic or recording devices are present or permitted. If in doubt, leave your recording devices at home, in your room, locker, car, etc.

With that said, as we progress into the digital age, you will find that fetish balls are not the only events being recorded for posterity. In fact, some events feature staff photographers, are streamed live on the Internet, are simulcast between venues, and more. It is appropriate for venues to inform attendees before they arrive that events are being recorded or are part of a live feed, and to obtain explicit written consent as well as model releases if the footage may be used for commercial purposes. Some parties will provide armbands that identify whether or not participants are willing to be photographed. However, if in doubt, and until you know and trust the venue, protect your identity if concerned... or ask in advance!

- **Have Fun!** Yup, this is on rules sheets too, sometimes. In such cases, it is not just a tongue-in-cheek comment. It may be a request from party hosts to have you leave your drama at the door, or leave the party if you're having a hard night.

Dungeon Dos and Don'ts

Instead of rules, may venues may have party or play space etiquette. These are the do's and don'ts of a specific venue or gathering — some of which are clearly outlined, some of which are considered common sense. Also, know that a party's culture around the rules listed above may be considered etiquette, and thus not written down anywhere.

- **Don't touch.** If it's not yours, don't touch it. This includes:

  - **Toys.** If someone else brought it, or if it belongs to the party hosts/venue, ask before touching it, picking it up, or using it. It may have specific rules, be expensive, or have sentimental value. It is also not yours, so ask.

  - **People.** A slave in collar and chains, a dominant in a pair of sexy boots, or a human pony in its corral have not granted you permission to touch them. Ask them, ask someone who knows them, ask their handler/owner... don't just assume it is okay unless you have been granted explicit permission.

  - **Atmosphere.** Do not attempt to change the lighting or music, or move dungeon furniture. If you would like them adjusted or altered, please talk to a host or DM. The music or piece of equipment may be there for a reason.

  - **Mobility Devices.** Don't "help" move someone's crutches "out of the way" or move their wheelchair for them while they are in it, without explicitly asking first and then waiting for an affirmative response.

  If someone touches your stuff, have compassion the first time. They might be excited, or genuinely clueless. They

> **You don't have to play.** Not everyone plays in dungeons, sexually or with BDSM. It is perfectly okay at most play parties to dress up, show up, watch, and take that energy home. Just because you're not an exhibitionist does not mean you're not a pervert. Don't worry; parties that require all attendees to play or get involved should state this clearly in advance.

probably aren't deliberately trying to piss you off. Calmly explain why the behavior was inappropriate, and give them room to apologize. Compassion, however only needs to go so far – do not tolerate someone taking advantage of you, your partners, your stuff, or your generosity.

- **Don't interrupt.** If anyone or anything seems not-okay, tell a DM or host immediately, identifying your specific question or concern. Interrupting a scene in progress yourself or cutting your way into conversations is rarely appreciated. The play space is not for idle conversation and chit-chat. Nor is it the place to be critiquing or applauding the scene. If you're not in a scene, keep quiet or take it to the social area.

Reach out

If you need assistance, are confused, or are concerned about something, do not be afraid to reach out and ask someone. Whether this is a host, DM, or fellow partygoer, most folks at kink parties are happy to answer questions in the social area, or very quietly and unobtrusively in the dungeon. You might find out that that "edgy" scene is how that couple always plays, that the party is running later tonight, or that in sharing your overall interest you can make new friends.

There may be occasional scenes that openly invite audience interaction, such as cheering on participants at the kinky dodgeball game, or poking fun at the boy in the dunce cap. Even so, be aware of your surroundings. And if you find yourself upset at the level of noise in a space, take your concerns to the DMs, the spotter (ideally all large audience interactive scenes should have a liaison/spotter for the audience), or an audience member, to see if a middle ground can be reached. They are not having fun just to upset you. With some negotiation and compromise, we can often find a middle ground, rather than suppress the joy of others.

Interruptions can also come from crowding a scene. Be aware of your proximity to the scenes of others. Some parties are more crowded than others, but you can try your best. If you are asked to give more room, give it if possible. If you are playing at the crowded party, be thoughtful of others. Extreme screaming, excessive whip cracking, or other continuous jarring noises and visuals that outstrip the general "level" of the party are also forms of inter-scene interruptions. If your play will be loud, hyper-creative, unusual, or potentially a squick, it's best to clear it with the host or DM in advance.

- **Avoid gawking.** Kink parties provide excellent people-watching opportunities, but there is a distinct difference between respectful voyeurism and leering and ogling. The role of the voyeur is incredibly important in our community – without the voyeur, what would become of the exhibitionist? The voyeur lends their energy to the work we do and play in which we engage. They can hold space as witnesses who will remember and retell a scene for us or in our honor, hold an empathetic energy for those experiencing ordeals, or in some cases be the aftercare person for the top or bottom.

  Think of the energy being projected from the scene as a meal being shared between friends. If you have been handed a plate, or there are appetizers set out for the party, feel free to nibble. If you are going over to the main plates and eating handfuls, or reaching across the table to eat off someone else's plate, this is rude. Become aware of your table manners while feasting your eyes on the bounty of kinky delights.

- **Take turns.** A finite amount of equipment is available in play spaces. Thus, keep track of how long you have been on that spanking bench. As the top, rigger, or scene coordinator, remain sufficiently aware of your surroundings to see if anyone else is queued up and waiting for your station. Even in large play spaces, limit your sprawl; it is considered particularly rude to have your stuff laid out all across the adjacent area. If you have an extensive amount of equipment, bring your own "flogger rack" or small folding table – or ask if the party hosts have one you can borrow. Once your scene is done, take the aftercare elsewhere as soon as possible if anyone is waiting for that space.

- **Leave your valuables at home.** Just like at the airport, you are responsible for your own baggage. If you don't need it at the dungeon, don't bring it. Keep your play bag nearby, and don't forget your stuff – though most parties have lost and found areas near registration or in a back closet of some sort, it is best not to get known for being "that person." Keep your equipment simple, and don't lose your wallet because you are high on endorphins from playing.

- **Clean up after yourself.** Your mother is probably not here at the party, and if she is, hopefully she's busy getting busy. It is a good idea to clean up before you play and after you play: the "Leave No

Trace" ethos is an excellent one when navigating kink space. Before you play, locate the cleanup gear and safer sex supplies, wipe down equipment, and put down tarps, towels or disposable chux. For example: if you're doing anything with needles or disposable blades, you'll need to secure a sharps container, move it with gloved hands, renew and refresh the gloves each time you change surfaces and during handling of the container itself. This makes for a whole lotta trash! If you know there will be a lot of disposables in your scene, have an appropriate receptacle nearby for those gloves, lube packets, condom wrappers, etc, etc.

As you play, stay aware of body fluids that need to be contained. Stringently avoid getting anyone's fluids on carpets or furniture – unplanned contact with someone else's bodily runoff is uncool. You might be fluid bonded to your partner, but getting their effluent on your hands and then touching gear, or a door handle, or someone else's hand is a vector for transmitting all kinds of bugs, and the other folks at the party did not consent to that level of intimacy.

After you play, clean up any body fluids that did manage to get outside of containment, and then clean your hands. No one should have to clean up after you. If you are nude and not playing, travel with a towel or sarong to sit on seats. Having your bare butt where other bare butts may then go is poor etiquette.

Be thoughtful of the space and everyone there. Think to yourself, would it be okay if someone did that in my house? Would I appreciate if they asked first? A play space is someone's home, if only for a night – therefore we all try to leave the venue in a condition as good as or better than we found it, and respect the space overall.

By now, you have probably been dreaming up a wide array of things you might want to do in dungeons, sex clubs, temple spaces and more. So let's next look into connecting with our partners (or would-be partners) and manifesting our fancies, whims and deepest desires!

Chapter 9

Wanna Do Some Stuff?
Negotiating For Play

MASTER   SLAVE   PIG   FREEPLAYER
GOD(DESS)   KNIGHT   BRAT   HEDONIST
WHORE   HANDLER   SISSY   PONY   SIR
BUTLER   OTHER   OWNER   MISTRESS   NINJA
GURU   APPRENTICE   SERVANT   SENSUALIST
RHEOSTAT   OBJECT   LORD   TOP   BOTTOM
YES   TOY   HEDONIST   FETISHIST

What sets **BDSM** apart from other forms of sexual interaction is its focus on negotiation and consent. A lot of what we do can look pretty scary, but behind the whips and chains is a mutual desire for pleasure and fulfillment. We get to that fulfillment by plumbing the depths of our desires, coming to terms with our longings, and navigating our way to our fantasies.

The concept of negotiation is one of the things that make kink a radical sexual model. We strive for emotional transparency — clear expression of our needs, wants and desires — rather than expecting our partner to be psychic and "just know what we want." Negotiation can take place before we've even met with a potential partner, during an event as we meet new people and learn new things, or after a scene, based on the inspirations we've received. In fact, negotiation can (and should!) take place before we've interacted with anyone else at all.

Who To Negotiate With

Ourselves

Before we begin to share our desires with anyone else, it is important to consider those desires for ourselves. Ruminate on the following questions, and be honest with yourself about why you want to play with this person, engage in this activity, and do so at this specific time:

- Are you doing this type of play for yourself, or someone else?

- Are you ready for this?

- Do you want to play with this particular person, or simply experience a particular type of play?

- Why do you want to play with this particular person or experience this type of play?

- Why do you want to play now?

- If you want to play with this particular individual, would you be okay with a range of playstyles? How about sitting down for a cup of coffee with them?

- If you want to engage in this specific style of play, how important is your connection with the person playing with you?

- Do you know this person well enough to play with them?

- Do you understand this type of play well enough to engage in it?

For most of us, the answers to all of these questions will shift over time. This is because our desires change over time as we gain experience and learn new things — about ourselves, our play partners, our kinks. Sometimes we want to play simply to experience sensory input. Other times we want the high of a new or exciting physical adventure. Alternately, we might also crave emotional vulnerability and radical connection.

> **Core of Your Kink**
> As you examine your yearnings and negotiate them with yourself, ask yourself if there are any common threads connecting your desires. Do all of your fantasies involve sensuality, connection, or feral energy? Are you hungry for touch, surrender, or control? By becoming aware of the core of your kink, you expand on the possibilities for play, think "outside of the box" and find new territory that will still get your juices flowing.

Self-awareness stands us in good stead when it comes to our negotiations with others. For additional points to ponder for self-evaluation, make sure to look back at Chapter 6 for more questions before you go to an event, which also apply to before you negotiate.

There are many ways to approach this self-exploration. For many it is helpful to ask ourselves these questions in a private journal, or sitting alone and meditating on our thoughts. Other folks are more extroverted in their contemplation. You might consider bouncing some thoughts off a kinky friend or an ally on the Internet who can bring some objectivity. Make it clear that you aren't looking for problem-solving or personal opinions. Letting them know you just need to feel safe and have that unconditional support will create a context wherein you can see how your thoughts resonate.

Partners

When you proceed to negotiating with your partners, consider the specific nature of the partnership in question. Negotiation with a spouse of twenty years will probably look different from negotiating with a play partner who has been an occasional part of your life for a few months. And both of those will look very different than negotiating with someone you've met in the hallway of a kink convention and who happens to pique your interest.

I'm an "Out Loud" processor. I use all manner of social media to communicate my thoughts, and sometimes this "crowd sourcing" is an amazing way to reduce my feelings of alienation. I was VERY shy about confessing my curiosity about pony play, but when I worked up the nerve to share that with a small circle of online friends I found several who were as shy as I was, also looking for support – and tips on buying pony gear.

Not every partner will respond the same way to negotiating, or to incorporating a new form of play. Consider watching a movie together that reflects a facet of your desires (see Appendix 4C) and gauging their reactions, or sending them tantalizing tales that may pique their interest. For some, a direct approach would rock their world. For others, coming on strong would freak them out. There's a big difference between "I have been seriously fantasizing about fisting you!" and "I saw something really sexually intimate online and was curious if I might be able to explore the idea with you."

Friends and allies

It can be very useful to communicate your desires and interests to your friends. They can often provide emotional support, references, and recommendations when you are exploring new territories. If you are doing complex multi-player scenes or ones that may need extra aftercare, your friends can be invaluable. Friends might be willing to

• Participate in a group scene.

• Act as a spotter or backup if you are playing with new folks.

• Provide aftercare.

• Help maintain safe space for big scenes.

• Be a point person for post-scene check-in.

Friends and allies can be there for security, support, or as a sounding board for processing – but only if you ask them, and only once they consent. Surprise brain dumps or unscheduled hours of emotional processing can tax a friendship, so don't assume that your friends are willing to take that responsibility. Kinky sex is about consensual exploration, including how we interact with our allies. Don't take your friends for granted. Do ask for help, do check in while doing so, and do express your gratitude when people are there for you.

Strangers

Every friend was once a stranger. However, just because that person with whom you chatted at last week's munch shares your mummification and caning fetish does not make them your new best friend for life and a perfect match as a play partner.

Here are some suggestions for methods and tools that folks in the kink communities may use when vetting new partners, or playing with people they don't know well.

- Asking them for personal or character references.

- Requesting references from other play partners.

- Verifying the references these people provide.

- Inquiring among your friends about a potential play partner.

- Watching the potential play partner playing with others.

- Meeting in public, in a neutral location, to get to know them a bit before playing.

- Playing in public until you get to know them better.

- Keeping play on a basic level when first playing. (For example, being inescapably bound and gagged means your options for communication and reasserting your control are severely limited.)

- Obtaining a play-partner's legal name and running it through registered sex-offender lists (available online).

- Having a spotter or trusted voyeur who is empowered to intercede if negotiated play does not go as planned.

- Building security systems such as a "safe call" – someone apprised of your date's legal name, address and phone number who will alert authorities if you do not contact them within a certain timeframe. If you have set up a safe call, make sure to follow through — failure to do so may lead to an awkward encounter with law enforcement.

- Building a friendship over time before playing.

No system is perfect. Some of these may make sense for you while others leave you cold. We strongly encourage you to think for yourself about your own concerns, and what approach to personal safety and accountability might be optimal. Entrusting someone with our bodies, hearts and minds is a powerful act, and one that should be taken seriously.

Dominants and tops: these cautions are for you as well. You too can be at risk: a new partner might become obsessive, retroactively revoke consent, experience "buyer's remorse" about a scene days or weeks later, or even become violent during a session. If you've played in private, it is your word against theirs should they experience a change of heart, or should things go off-track. While there are no guarantees, some of these precautions can help to reduce the risks associated with playing with a new partner.

Pay close attention to your gut instincts. Unconscious information that manifests in the form of uncertainty, discomfort, or fear is often the body giving us a signal that we might be better off not engaging with a particular person. You likely have some experience taking care of yourself in the default world; don't leave these skills at the door when you enter the play-space. Regardless of your chosen role, self-care, self-respect, and self-awareness are vital to keeping yourself safe as you learn and grow.

What And Why To Negotiate

When I have negotiated from a place of desperation or emotional hunger, I really wasn't negotiating – which has gotten me in some tight spots. This includes negotiating when depressed, feeling anxious, or having recently ended a relationship.

We each negotiate for different reasons. For some, it is a chance to gain intimacy with a partner by exposing their core desires. Some negotiate in order to maximize the chance that a scene will have a pleasurable, positive outcome for all involved. Some do it to share important information before they play, or to flirt voraciously. There are those who will want to talk about their sexual history as part of the negotiations, while others will not.

Share as much as you can of the truth about your joys, desires, fears, passions, limits, boundaries and capacity as you negotiate. This increases the chance for a mutually pleasurable experience. We advise doing your negotiation from a mutually empowered place, while you are clear-headed. This process lowers the likelihood of later resentment from feeling manipulated during the negotiation process. If you're feeling pressured to say "yes," even though your gut is balking, you cannot protect yourself and your best interests. No matter how you choose to share your truths, you are ultimately responsible for yourself and your journey. Empower yourself to communicate, and you empower yourself for success.

YESes and fantasies

Our YESes are things we long for, strongly desire, and are excited to experience. They are not our "Sure, that would be okay" items – they are the stuff on our "HELL YEAH!" list. If we share our real YESes, we increase our chances of manifesting this joy. If we never share our YESes, we never have the chance to be heard.

Just because you say yes to one type of kink fantasy or desire does not mean that you want to say yes to everything. Sure, you might have a hot abduction fantasy... but that does not mean you want that hot abduction scene served up with a side of stringent bondage and a dollop of deep humiliation. Consider whether your partner shares your YESes and fantasies with you. Listen to what they are actually sharing, and try to avoid layering on your own desires, or reading additional elements into their fantasy without checking in.

Some of our fantasies are best left firmly in the realm of

One of two times I've had a scene seriously derail was when a friend decided to surprise me with an additional element to a scene we'd planned. I was prepared for us to do a pretty heavy humiliation scene – I was not prepared for my friend to add a hardcore interrogation element to the scenario. On top of that, intense physical sensation and a marathon session resulted in my emotionally losing track of myself in the scene, experiencing a difficult mental disconnect, and the scene going far off the track of what we had previously negotiated.

fantasy. Others burn within with a craving for fulfillment. Still other fantasies are ones we wish to revisit again and again, and which never lose their appeal. As you negotiate and share your YESes, remember to share your passion and excitement – even in the midst of nervousness and trepidation – with your partner.

Fantasies and YESes are different things. Sometimes a fantasy is just a fantasy. Just because your partner shares a fantasy does not mean they want to do it. Make sure to actively gain consent before surprising your partner with that gang bang, or showing up at their flat dressed like a clown – they may not have actually wanted it to manifest in reality.

As you ponder your YESes, consider also what you need to succeed. Will your scene be a downer if you are not touched with bare hands by your lover? Would words of praise from this new play partner help you fly? Do you crave detailed feedback after the scene in order to feel secure that it all went well? By being aware of our core needs and sharing them on our YES list, we increase our chances of hitting it out of the park.

Definitions and language

Clarifying our own personal definitions during negotiation can help us avoid misunderstanding: water sports might mean a lively game of "Marco! Polo!" or a hot piss play scene. By being clear about what we mean, and the source of our desires, we can deepen connections and get everyone on the same page.

Some questions and concepts to consider include:

- **What does** that kind of play mean to you?

- **What might** that look like?

- **How should** we address one another in the scene?

- **What words** and phrases turn you on?

- **What kind** of language is a buzzkill?

Our language also affects our longer-term relationships. A word like "slave" might be a highly erotic persona for a single scene, or be a sacred term for a particularly deep intimacy for someone else. Words can also be identical but mean different things in different communities. In BDSM, topping usually means being the one guiding the progress in the scene or encounter, using bondage, discipline, dominance, submission, sadism and masochism. In the gay men's community, topping can refer to the insertive role during anal sex or fisting. If a misunderstanding takes place, it can be dangerous indeed. Hashing these issues out in advance, or discussing them frankly and honestly if they happen to pop up, can help prevent a lot of heartache.

Communication systems

There are various methods of communication available during scene interactions. One of the most basic is, you guessed it, talking. Creating a continuous stream of actively encouraged verbal dialogue during your play is a great way to keep the lines open.

"Oh, yes, that feels great!'

"No, that doesn't feel right, can you do it a little lower?"

"Ow! That sucked, quit it!"

"I love it when you do that for me."

This flavor of active communication assists in actively engaging your partners, and keeping the play connected.

If you're doing a hot role-play scene, sometimes "plain talk" can get in the way of suspending your disbelief. If you want to have the sensation of resisting, and to be ble to shout "No! Stop! I hate you, you sonofabitch!" – then words like "no" and "stop" are no longer useful as deterrents. That's how safewords originated. While safeword systems were born in the desire to maintain the integrity of a role-play scene, they are now often used to manage the ebb and flow of play. With a safeword, the top or bottom or other participant can "check in" with a simple verbal cue that lets participants know that

I was negotiating with a friend who comes from a background in the swing community, and he asked me "What kind of play do you want tonight?" I was puzzled, because I thought we were planning on fucking. I stammered a bit – "I thought you weren't into playing all that much?" We blinked at one another for a moment until we both burst out laughing, realizing that playing for him was fucking, and playing for me meant a kink or BDSM interaction, and was almost always independent of negotiations for sexual intercourse. Ultimately (and fortunately!), we both had the same thing in mind. And the fucking commenced.

something is up. When engaging in the safeword approach, everyone gets one. The top, the bottom — *everyone*.

Safeword systems include:

- **Stop lights.** "Red" generally means stop: it can mean "stop everything, there is a problem," or it can mean "stop the current activity." All players should be clear, in advance, as to what degree of "red" red is for that scene. "Yellow" usually indicates a need to pause and check in, and "green" may signal "go on, gimme more!"

- **Saying the word "safeword."** At larger events, this term is often used as a catch-all safeword, though screaming "red" comes in a close second.

- **Fantasy-specific terms.** Examples include "mercy please" in historical scenes, or "I am unworthy, ma'am," in female dominance scenes. Each is designated in advance and agreed upon by all parties.

- **Unlikely words.** These safewords catch the attention because they're wildly out of place. Examples include "rutabaga," "screwdriver," or calling out your own name. Don't make your safeword so complicated or obscure that you forget it in the heat of the moment.

- **Grunt systems.** When gagged, one stern grunt can mean "yellow" and two or more grunts can mean "red."

- **Dropping an object.** If playing in a scene where the bottom is in bondage, the bottom can hold a physical item such as a ring of keys or a rubber ball that can be dropped if they need a check-in.

- **Squeeze systems.** A top can pause throughout the scene to squeeze the hand of their play partner. If the person doesn't respond when asked to squeeze back, it is a cue to check in.

The challenge with safeword systems is that not everyone has the capacity to speak up when things have gone too far. Some individuals may become non-verbal when they play, and might experience difficulty communicating. If you are one of these people, sharing this fact pre-scene is critical and can allow for the creation of a system that might work for everyone. If you are bottoming, and you are likely to become unable to communicate during a scene, the person topping you has the right to know that so that they can make an informed decision about the risks inherent in scening with a partner who might be unable to "use their words."

Don't say you're okay when you are not. Make sure to use your NOs as well as your YESes.

Another helpful tool is the use of "joywords." Joywords are terms that say "I am in a good place right now, and ending the scene in this moment would feel great!" This is a different philosophical approach than safewords, which are often used to communicate when things have gone too far.

Some employ a "no-safeword" approach to in-scene communication. This method traditionally uses body language and non-verbal signals to create a communication flow. Some forms of no-safeword involve extreme edge play, where the players have negotiated that the top may do as they see fit. This level of intimacy is usually found when players have developed a relationship and established trust with one another, and might not be the best approach when first getting to know a partner or before you have some experience under your belt.

When you're with a new partner, if you're new to playing, or simply new to a specific type of scenario, you may not be aware that you have challenges with a specific type of communication system. Sometimes, there is pressure not to use safewords (or have them), or people may be unaware that when they get into tight bondage that they will end up non-verbal as they slip into "subspace" — this may not come up until it happens for the first time. Frank and detailed discussion of these issues, and then respecting and adhering to agreed-upon systems is vital to maintaining clear consent between parties.

I have heard of a wide variety of hard limits. Standing in a corner, feet, being touched lovingly, birds, soft fur, and spitting are all examples I've seen before. I have learned to thank people for sharing their limits, even if I don't understand them. It helps build trust.

If you notice that you or your partner is regularly using safewords to renegotiate the stated intention of your scenes, take a step back and look what all parties are agreeing to during

In the past, I've fallen under the spell of what I like to call "masochismo" – a stubborn belief that I, as a masochist, must take more and more and more to prove my toughness to myself and to others. This is a potential trap that I have learned to share with my play partners. In the same way I advise them in advance that I often become non-verbal in play, I let them know I will push myself sometimes, and we discuss good boundaries so that neither one of us feels we have gone beyond our intended comfort zones in the heat of the moment.

initial negotiation. This will facilitate the integrity of the scene and the desires of the players to be maintained.

Boundaries and limits

As discussed in Chapter 6, understanding and sharing known and potential physical, emotional and mental limits is very important for pre-event planning. This also applies to our pre-play negotiations. People use varying terms such as hard limits, soft limits and boundaries to describe the frontiers of their play. Ascertaining before play what all these terms mean to you and to your potential play partner can help minimize miscommunications and derailments.

Boundaries give us an idea of where each person's comfort zones lie. Generally, hard limits are things that go against our core values or personal identity, or are outside our capacity. This might also be referred to as a "never" list. Soft limits, on the other hand, are often activities that give us pause, but we might entertain under the right circumstances. Play that we find to be personally edgy might not be on a "hard limit" list, but might well be pushing a particular boundary. It is important to consider possible fallout when negotiating these scenes, and remain vigilant about maintaining your limits.

Even if a limit or boundary seems silly to you, it may be very serious for your partner. For that reason, when someone is sharing their challenges, it is important to come from a place of active listening and compassion. There is a great deal of trust involved in sharing these deep, dark secrets. What is intense is different for every individual.

Types of limits may include:

Privacy
One thing to make sure to negotiate is your privacy. Who can know about your play? Can photos be posted on social networking sites using your legal name, or can even a mention of playing with you never come up, even with your scene name, ever?

* Things that conflict with our morals or values.

The Prime Directive
Amongst many in the kink, leather and BDSM communities, the Prime Directive is a guiding principle in well-balanced power-exchange relationships. It elegantly creates a system designed to keep everyone healthy and facilitate compassionate interactions: **It is the primary responsibility of the slave to protect the master's property at all times, up to and including protecting the property from the master.** This version of the Prime Directive can be modified to suit your personal dynamic. The essence is that your *first* job is to maintain your emotional, physical and spiritual well-being. To be transparent, to speak honestly about where you are, to share when you are struggling: this is how you create and maintain safe space. And, furthermore, *not* sharing your issues is in direct conflict with the best practices for the relationship. Whatever your dynamic, however (or if) you exchange power, this system is a brilliant way to provide a fail-safe when things get rocky, or are in flux.

- Physical limitations or activities that are beyond your performance capacity.

- Psychological triggers or landmines that may "go off" in our psyche.

- Personal squicks or things that make us uncomfortable.

- Ideas we find scary or threatening.

- Risks or concerns that would compromise our relationships.

- Trauma from our past.

- Concerns about physical, mental, emotional or social repercussions.

- Play in which we have engaged repeatedly.

- Play in which we have never engaged.

We strongly recommend against renegotiating limits mid-scene. While limits can change for some folks with time and exposure to new ideas, this is certainly not the case for everyone. Some things will not shift. We are, however, dynamic creatures, so renegotiating limits is worth considering from time to time. Tools like the checklist system presented in Appendix 3 are great for doing just that.

Medical realities and concerns

Do you have allergies, old injuries, asthma or diabetes? Are you on medication? Do you wear glasses, contacts, hearing aids or prosthetics? Are you receiving ongoing mental health treatment or have phobias that might affect the play you are doing? Sharing these details during negotiation can reduce the chance that these challenges will

After testing positive for HSV I and HSV II, I experienced a volley of emotional reactions to the diagnosis. Never having had an outbreak or a cold sore, I was shocked. I dreaded having to tell potential partners about being a carrier for Herpes. I decided to simply incorporate disclosure of my status into larger conversations about the prevalence of STDs, and talk about the statistics around transmission rates. Rather than experiencing rejection or disgust, I found people wanting to discuss their own diagnoses, or get better information about risk abatement.

be triggered during a scene. If you do have medical realities that may affect play, it is also worthwhile to let folks know what to do if these issues come up. Even if you don't see the relevance of a particular medical condition to your scene, share as much information as you can with your partners. That way, if the unexpected does occur, everyone is up to speed on the health conditions of their partner. Tops and dominants, this is important for you too! If, for example, you forget to take your medication and have a blood-sugar drop, the people you're playing with should know that getting you a snack should be a priority.

As un-sexy as it may sound, if sexual contact is on the table, all involved parties *must* discuss safer sex limits. (See Appendix 4E for information on STDs, STIs and safer sex options.) Everyone has their own limits; however, we feel best practices include treating all partners as if they are potentially positive for a sexually transmitted disease. Not everyone will disclose their status, either through deliberate omission or because they simply haven't been tested. Therefore, we suggest defaulting to the highest reasonable level of protection between yourself and your partners.

But You Look Fine

Just because someone's disability is not visible does not mean they do not have a disability. Lupus, fibromyalgia, joint injuries, cognition differences and more can affect how someone plays – or not! Don't make assumptions on whether someone is differently abled in some way, or whether their disability actually affects their ability to play.

Aftercare

What does aftercare look like for you? For some folks, this is hours curled up talking, wrapped in fuzzy blankets, nibbling dark chocolate. For others, it's both parties hopping up, hugging each other, and going their separate ways.

Still others crave being kicked into a dark corner to revel in their abject misery, or being left alone to jerk off.

No two people's approaches to aftercare are identical. Knowing what you are likely to need for yourself is the first step. Finding out what your partner is likely to want immediately afterwards (or a week later, or after six months have elapsed) is important.

For those into intense scenes where re-connecting within the context of the play isn't feasible or desired, I recommend "aftercare buddies." This can be as simple as a friend who will just sit with you and talk for a bit while you get your feet back underneath you, or as intimate as a partner who takes you home for post-play love-making.

Sometimes, poor aftercare can be the tipping point where a wonderful scene slides over into the realm of an unpleasant memory. Sometimes, the top's or dominant's need for aftercare falls by the wayside. It is important to remember that everyone involved in the exchange of energy will have needs which need to be met post-scene.

Will the top want a follow-up phone call the next day? Might the bottom want a check-in later that night at the party, and otherwise to be left alone for the week? Does someone expect to be glued at the hip, to sleep in the same bed, to process verbally for the next four hours after the scene? Perhaps both partners are not into elaborate aftercare.

Some people think creatively about mismatched aftercare needs. If the dominant partner needs cuddles after he's been the bad guy, but their partner has another date, can the aftercare be outsourced to a friend? Others may choose tools like pre-care, where partners cuddle or engage in other activities that are often perceived as aftercare *before* the scene. No matter what shape aftercare may or may not take, it is important to negotiate in advance, and then make certain you follow through.

Setting Play Dates

Making dates to play doesn't have to be an epic production, an elaborate courtship ritual, or a daunting proposition. Sometimes, just asking for time to connect is the best approach. The "wanna do some stuff?" technique (as compared to "do you want to play?") was introduced formally

It is a lot more work to avoid someone who is interested in playing with you than to politely tell them "No." Dodging people in the halls to avoid them asking again is stressful. Don't say "not now" unless you mean "not now."

by long-time kinkster Phillip the Foole. We like it because it leaves so many options available, and can free negotiations from our pre-conceived notions or limited ideas about what "play" might mean.

One of the things that is different between playing at an event as compared to playing at home (or in a hotel, or at the beach, or...) is that many folks choose to set play dates. A play date is a kink-centric tryst, established in advance, where we plan to connect with another individual. We can set play dates before or during an event. We can have them with ourselves, our partners, our play partners, or people that are new to us, depending on our situation and desires.

Think of setting a play date in the same way one might consider setting up any other date. The steps for the initiator of a play might look like this:

- Consider your interest.

- Demonstrate your interest.

- See if they are interested.

- Propose the idea of doing some stuff together.

- Discuss what everyone is interested in doing together.

- Confirm interest and negotiate plans.

- Get together at the pre-arranged time.

- Explore the activities or time together.

Showing interest can take many forms. An email, a note on a social networking site, an in-person conversation, or being introduced by mutual friends are all great ways to initiate interaction. In most cases, there is an opportunity provided to connect first as people, making sure there is in-person chemistry before a more specific proposal of play takes place.

Once a time and location have been set to get together for your play date, it is important to keep that date. What gets in the way of people keeping their dates?

Setting up a play date and then not showing up can really hurt someone's feelings. If you must cancel, please take the time to communicate it compassionately.

- Forgetting an appointment.

- Neglecting to calendar your meeting.

- Double-booking dates.

- Overbooking and creating overlapping play-dates.

- Deciding you aren't in the mood.

- Realizing you simply don't want to have the date.

- Being unsure how to cancel the date.

- Forgetting to cancel a date.

Being a person of integrity in the kink community includes being diligent about keeping, re-scheduling or canceling your play dates. If you have to cancel, do so with grace and clarity. You can offer a counter-proposal of a new time, or a new type of play. Consider telling them why you are cancelling. Letting someone know you have to be up early can ease their mind if they feel as though you're just blowing them off. And if you do find yourself on the receiving end of a decline, consider it a gift. If the other person is tired, unfocused, or just isn't that into you, the scene probably wouldn't have been all that enjoyable anyway. Graciously accepting the decline, whatever the reason, leaves you in a good place to move on and find a new adventure.

Remember – making dates, including play dates, takes practice. Saying no takes practice. And for that matter, saying yes takes practice too! Being polite, civil and compassionate goes a long way.

At the core of negotiation is the desire to have your desires met. As you progress and grow, you'll no doubt find that some negotiations flow trippingly off of the tongue, while others may take years to bear fruit. Optimizing your style and approach, and growing at your own speed and pace, will serve you well as you gain confidence in yourself and in your explorations. Remaining open and flexible, keeping sight of your needs, and maintaining respect for your desires and the desires of others will help you manage and fulfill your innermost fantasies while keeping yourself healthy and safe.

Chapter 10

Even Perverts Get The Blues: Staying Healthy (and Happy) at Events

N O ONE ARRIVES at a kink event, looks around, rubs their hands together and thinks "Right! I'm looking forward to having an emotionally fraught and difficult weekend!" And yet, it happens. Sometimes we get sick, lonely, frustrated, overwhelmed, or hurt. It can feel like emotions are taking us on a rollercoaster ride, and we end up dizzy from the craziness of it all.

Yep... even perverts get the blues. You are not alone. And by knowing in advance that things might not always go smoothly, we can avoid some of the pitfalls that have waylaid those who have already walked this path. Or we may not – but it's worth a try!

There are definitely things we *can* each control:

* Our attitude.

* Our behavior.

* Our responses.

* Our time management skills.

* Our health awareness.

* Our self-care.

And there are things we *cannot* control:

* Other people's attitudes.

* Other people's behaviors.

* Other people's reactions.

* Surprising situations.

* Other people's relationships.

* Encountering things that squick us.

* Activating phobias.

* The conference schedule.

> Grant me the serenity
> to accept the things
> I cannot change;
> courage to change
> the things I can;
> and wisdom to know
> the difference.
> – Reinhold Niebuhr

Look at those for a moment. Being aware of what you can change and what you can't can help you gain perspective and put the brakes on when things feel as though they may be spinning out of control.

Maintaining awareness of what you cannot control gives you room to truly focus on that which you can. You can become aware of managing your needs, wants and desires, and taking care of your physical and mental health. You can give yourself permission to be kind to yourself when you encounter that which you could not control, and you can let go of the belief that you "should" have been able to control that person, place or thing. Forgiving yourself is the first step towards forgiving others, and in turn helping build a great community for us to play in.

Managing Needs, Wants and Desires

As we have been discussing throughout this book, it is important to be aware of your needs, wants and desires. Doing so begins to bring to light our conscious and unconscious expectations, not only of the event, but of our partners, the community, and ourselves.

Is it the Con Or Is It Me?
Are you having a bad week? Taxes getting you down? Dog died? Lost your job? Have a pimple? Maybe it's not the conference, but your underlying concerns distracting you. And you know what? That's okay. Honor your emotions and focus on what you need to do for you. For some that means facing their underlying issues; for others it is about diving fully into the con as a distraction.

Some events do not live up to our expectations. And some events just fail. However, sometimes it's our own attitude and expectations that cloud our own ability to see the forest for the trees. Consider adjusting your expectations to see if you can find some joy available in unexpected ways.

Bored? Make your own fun! Frustrated? Take a break from the event and come back. By taking some personal responsibility, you become more in control of your own destiny.

To set yourself up for success, set your expectations in advance. Murphy's Law can leap into effect at any kink event. By arriving with simple expectations, we have an opportunity to be pleasantly surprised when we get more.

One of the problems we may experience is based in the language we use. When we say "I *will* get flogged in the dungeon," there is no space for other types of fun — so if our partner's shoulder gets hurt or if we are out of energy and want to take a nap, we'll feel like we've failed. Setting an intention that we want to play, connect with our partner(s), or just try something new allows for the flogging to turn into a caning, the kink scene to transform into excellent sex, or our public play to go private... without being let down. Consider for yourself whether planning in advance will help hype your happiness or detract from your delight.

As we mentioned in Chapter 6, pre-negotiating with yourself and your partners can really increase your chances for experiencing event excellence. However, when you are at a con and it sucks, it still just... sucks. You won't like everyone, enjoy everything, or have fun with it all. There is some small comfort knowing that this is one of those Fucking Opportunities for Growth, and remembering that you've acquired new information to help you do it better next time. Going forward, you'll know to tell your companion specifically about your expectations for play, advise your wingman that it frustrates you when you find yourself alone, or remind yourself to pack more toys. But right now you have to deal with... well, right now.

Remind yourself of your intentions! Hidden in there are probably the cores of your needs, wants and desires. Were you here to learn something new, but the classes let you down? Go to the dungeon and absorb a new technique by watching. Were you hoping to meet new people, but the mixers left you underwhelmed? Go volunteer in the hospitality suite and say hello to someone new. Wanted to buy a new toy and nothing caught your attention? Strike up a conversation in the social area with someone who has gear you think looks interesting, and ask them where they got theirs.

Con Drop and Con Crud

Two of the more typical challenges we face attending conferences are known as "con drop" and "con crud." When we're exposed to a weekend of new experiences, high energy, large numbers of people, and intimacy in all forms, and we're pushing our bodies hard, it makes sense that our energy level might drop afterwards (con drop) or that we might get sick (con crud).

It is not unusual to experience sadness, or an abrupt emotional shift, at the end of an event or gathering. Sadness, uncertainty, nervousness and exhaustion are regularly reported forms of con drop — and it does not take a conference to get there. Munches, fetish balls and parties can have a "drop" afterwards as well.

The other regularly reported form of energetic drop is more of a hangover – feeling fuzzy, distracted, or lethargic. This can be a result of experiencing "highs" from adrenaline, endorphins and other body chemicals that have likely been cranked through your system. You were high, and now you are coming down.

If these experiences hit you, try to avoid layering on more judgment; it happens to many of us. And sometimes you won't experience drop at all; you'll roll off of the event feeling fine or even energized and on top of the world. There is nothing wrong with not experiencing a drop of any sort.

Caring for your body

Sometimes, you can't avoid catching "that thing that's going around," or experiencing a feeling of let-down. However, some instances of con drop and con crud can be avoided with some preventive care. Caring for our bodies is profoundly important at events, because the sexual sports we engage in are ones that need us playing at our best. Some basic aspects of self-care can fall by the wayside amidst the intense excitement of experiencing a kink gathering.

Water gets me wet.

Things you just gotta have include:

- **Water.** Many of us become ill or lethargic because we are dehydrated and don't know it. Playing hard produces sweat, which is our bodies losing water. Salivation takes water. Talking takes water. Hotels are closed systems, running on HVAC. These machines pull moisture from the air, resulting in a dry atmosphere within the hotel complex. And don't get us started on the dehydration that happens while flying! Our bodies need fluids. Drinking water or hydrating beverages can seriously boost your overall health. Avoid alcohol, caffeine, and sugary drinks, as they can dehydrate you.

- **Food.** Our bodies are high-performance machines, and deserve the best fuel possible if we expect optimum functionality. This means taking a serious look in advance at where and what you plan to eat at events. Do not pass up a meal for a chance to squeeze in that extra class or scene. It can also be easy to look at the time available or your budget and decide to live off fast food for the weekend. But the shock of greasy food to the system is rarely a perfect choice. Many hotels let you request a fridge in advance, or you can bring your own cooler with your own food.

Consider food that is more than empty calories. If you are bringing potluck items to a party, you can be the one who brings protein, vegetables and other "real" food, not just a bag of chips. For an afternoon snack, a piece of fresh fruit or a cup of yogurt is probably better than an EPIC OMG SIZE SNICKERS. This choice can be tricky, as some events have been known to provision their hospitality suite as cheaply as possible, which often means food with low nutritive value.

Feeling cranky, irritable, short-tempered? When was the last time you ate? If you're playing until 4am, and haven't eaten since 8pm, you have a higher chance of dropping, both during the scene and in the next few days. Many week-long play events that offer meal plans are moving to a four-meal-per-day model for just that reason. No matter how busy you are, having two balanced meals a day is strongly encouraged. It takes fuel to engage at full capacity.

- **Sleep.** No one becomes more rational or coherent when sleep-deprived. Sleep helps us re-invigorate, so that we are not walking around as the restless dead or as manic monsters who want to do it all. Try to schedule a good solid block of sleep time. And it isn't a bad idea to carve out time for a power nap, or just an hour to lie down quietly and indulge in some relaxation.

    Re-invigorating may take other forms as well. Hitting the hotel gym, having a great conversation at 2AM in the lobby, having great sex or a hot, energized scene, taking time to read a chapter of a favorite book – these can all help us re-fuel our spirits.

- **Medication.** If you take medication, bring it with you and take it as prescribed. If you're flying, never check it; always pack it in your carry-on. Call the hotel in advance to request a fridge if your medication must be refrigerated. Find ways to remind yourself to take your meds as you normally would, causing less shock to your system. This includes mental health medication – just because you feel really excellent at an event is not a reason to go off your regimen. Doing so can lead to repercussions that ripple out far beyond the end of the con.

For many, following medical advice also means adhering to a nutritional system. Remember, every restaurant might not have provisions for gluten-free ovo-lacto vegetarians with diverticulitis. Call ahead, ask around, and bring what you need to keep yourself safe and healthy.

> If you're sick, please don't come to the event. I was helping run an event when an attendee showed up on leave from the military, where he was stationed in the Middle East. He was only on leave for two weeks, and so even though he was sick, he came, played with, and made out with everyone he could. By the end of the weekend, almost a quarter of us went home with what we called the "Bahrain Death Flu." We were violently sick for weeks.

- **Sick already?** If you are sick with a communicable illness, please think twice, or four times, before coming to the event. Being ill sets you up for getting even sicker as you stress your body further. It also puts everyone else at the event at risk for getting what you have. If you have something that isn't contagious, consider consulting a physician about what course of action is best for your specific case.

  If you're really sick, contact the event producers to see what their policy is on cancellations due to illness. Those with major illnesses or major life crises will often be able to get a partial refund or credit towards the next event. This is especially true if it means not bringing your contagious bug to the con.

- **Exercise.** BDSM is hard on the body — it is an extreme sport and deserves its own workout regimen. The most common injuries in the kink community are accidental ones — rotator cuffs torn by people throwing floggers, strained muscles from strenuous bondage poses. This means that we must stretch before and after we play, and work our way up to being fit for this play.

  Stretching can take many forms, whether you are a top or bottom. Dancing, yoga, and making out can all help warm up our bodies to make us fit to fuck. Classical stretching can be done as a partnered exercise, or can be done individually. Many of us work full-time jobs in front of computers, and going from that straight into play on Friday night can lead to serious shock to the system.

Beyond stretching, it is important to be fit in general. Every type of body is beautiful, and using that body to its optimum capacity is important. By physically "ramping up" for the big event ahead of time, we are better prepared for the adventure ahead. When we move from a couch potato lifestyle straight into three days of intense whips, chains and six-inch heels, unintended injury is much more likely.

- **Shower.** Getting funky on the dance floor is one thing; being funky from neglected hygiene is not nearly as charming. Showering every day will get your body ready for that sexy encounter, remove some sweat, and prime you for getting your groove on. It can also help you take a break from the conference. Spencer Bergstedt, respected attorney, transgender activist and veteran of many, many conferences, once gave the following bit of advice regarding conferences: "Get your head wet. Once a day." He went on to advise that, at the end of the day, a shower can help you physically relax and symbolically (or even ritually) cleanse yourself, releasing the energy of the day so that you can rest, or energizing you for the day ahead.

- **Listen to your body.** Was that a grumbling belly? Consider feeding it. Was that a twinge in your back? Consider communicating that to your partner. Feeling strange about talking to that person? Your body has a gift of its own wisdom, and listening to all of the messages it is trying to share can help keep us safe, healthy and hale.

Caring for your mind and energy level

Kink events can be emotionally, energetically and mentally challenging, even for the most experienced kinksters. Getting into an upbeat headspace as we prepare for an event is a great way to work out your mind. If we don't approach in a positive mindset, there's a higher chance that we might crash and burn at the con itself. There are things you can do to help you achieve a good mindset from the outset, such as:

- **Doing your homework.** Have you scoured the website and discovered all of the classes and activities available? Perused the program book or pamphlet that was provided when you registered? Having an idea of what to expect can help us get jazzed up about the event.

- **Sex it up.** Looking at porn, having sexy conversations with a partner, or flirtatiously negotiating that hot scene on the way to the con are all fun ideas that can help get you in the mood. If you have the time to have a mini-scene with yourself or someone else before hitting the business of the convention or party, all the better.

- **Unplug.** Getting offline for the weekend by turning off your cell phones, Internet and social media can help as a transition tool for getting into headspace. It can also help prevent yo-yoing each day from the event to the default world and back again. This might not be an option for those with children or jobs that need to contact us, but is a useful tool for many who can step away from the constant stream of virtual input.

If you do find yourself exhausted at the event, be honest with yourself and others about your capacity. This is especially pivotal before trying a new scene for the first time or before engaging with someone new. Pushing yourself past your limits is not only a recipe for health challenges, but mental challenges as well. Resentment, anger, blame, depression and more can breed in an environment of low energy combined with a perceived pressure to perform. By letting yourself and others know that you're just not feeling it, you have an opportunity to address the issues with grace rather than trying to tough through the realities of the situation.

It is also important to schedule downtime with yourself and/or a partner. Time away from the often frenetic energy of the convention – to read a book before bed, go for a walk, go offsite for a meal, etc. – can facilitate post-event reintegration, as we will not have been "on" for so many days straight. Downtime can include a daily debrief with

Sharing my energy level and capacity with my friends and play partners gives them permission to do the same. I've had moments where I turned to my top and said "You know, I'm just too fucking tired for this"... and had them heave a sigh of relief and say "I'm so glad you said something. I'm bloody exhausted too, but I didn't want to let you down." While the epic rope suspension scene didn't happen, a yummy evening of cuddling and conversation did happen, and that brought our relationship to a new level of intimacy.

I travel with a sarong that was gifted to me by friends. It has a lovely depiction of the Hindu god Ganesha on it. I'll hang it up in my hotel room, light a small candle, use the coffee maker to brew up a cup of my favorite tea and within a few minutes, I have my own meditation space.

yourself (through journaling or self-reflection) or quiet time with a partner, so that there is a regular stream of communication in all directions.

When it comes to the large hotel-based event, you're probably going to be staying, where? In a hotel. Your room is your castle, your cave, your Fortress of Solitude. It is important to consider the space you will be in.

- **Can you stay in the "host hotel"?** Yes, there are often adjacent spaces for lodging in the vicinity, but consider the commute. Staying offsite can mean having to leave the party sooner, waking up earlier for classes, having to drive when feeling loopy from playing, or waiting for hotel shuttles. The exception is if you are someone who decompresses while driving or traveling between sites — in which case, get driving!

- **How can you make your space comfortable?** Bring your own music, a few knick-knacks, perhaps your favorite tea from home. These small details will make the generic hotel room feel like your haven from the madness.

- **Do you want an extra bed?** Usually you'll have the option of two queen beds or one king-sized bed. If you don't want to fight over who gets to sleep on the wet spot, or you like having one bed to sleep in and another for spreading out your clothes and sorting out your loot, consider the two-bed approach. If you enjoy sprawling across that vast Cal King, or you might have a few friends over for late-night fun, the larger bed is a great option.

- **Think smart about roommates.** To save money, many folks acquire roommates for events. Consider whether the money is worth the potential stress. Rooming with friends is one thing (though your best friend may not be your best roommate); rooming with strangers can be a gamble. Don't be afraid to interview that potential roomie! Ask what their sleep hours are, if they snore, what their level of tidiness is...and be honest and forthcoming with them about your own answers to these questions. And check references. It might be a good idea to meet them in advance for coffee before you spend the weekend with them, if possible. If you're coming from different cities, make time to chat them up before you wind up shacking up.

- **What is the room "for?"** Is the room for sleeping only, or is it an open drop-in space? Is there time for having sex, primal scream therapy, wank breaks, changing, or spending hours watching television at the end of a day? Can each person request alone time in the room, or is it always communal? This is important to know in advance, in case your body tells you that you need downtime and you find out your roommate has booked a hot gangbang for the same time.

- **Sleeping in your space.** For some, bringing their own pillow is vital for great sleep. For others, it is about listening to your circadian rhythms and going to the party early, sleeping early, and waking early – even if the other perverts are night owls. If you sleep best with your teddy bear, that's okay, Teddy is welcome to come along too.

If you are having an intense emotional crisis and going to your hotel room or taking a few deep breaths isn't cutting it, consider asking to speak with the medical staff for an event, or the producers: find out if there are any crisis counselors on site. For larger events, there might be a handful of folks on-call who have volunteered to help with an understanding ear. The sorts of predicaments that lead people to seek crisis intervention range from viewing things you have no idea how to process that have taken you into a tail-spin, violent relationship encounters, emotional injuries from difficult scenes, extreme depression, and more – each person, each situation, is unique. Don't be afraid to obtain professional medical help if it is warranted: taking care of yourself is the most important thing you can do at any event.

Reframing "Negative" Experiences

From time to time, events just aren't fun, scenes derail, and we get frustrated by the world around us. Perhaps we have run into a former partner, had a difficult epiphany, or have been involved in an accident. The following ideas are tools that your authors have found useful for transforming our attitudes when facing difficult emotional situations.

- **Take a time out.** Often at events, we just need some alone or off-campus. Think of a convention as a university. If we spend all day and night on campus, we can get burned out, sick of the same faces and same food, and frustrated with even the most diverse curriculum. So it is with conferences. Taking a break to re-set can help. Go see other parts of the city you are visiting. Go for a swim, if the hotel has a pool. Take a long shower. Curl up in a local park with a good book. Go out somewhere for dinner. Treat yourself to a massage or other body care. Have a nice dessert.

  Sometimes, the immersion in BDSM itself can overwhelm. Another possibility is to take a mental break from the kink. Schedule a social date with friends. Strike up a conversation about gardening. Taking a breather or reconnecting with the default world can help you ground, so you can return to the convention refreshed and with renewed energy.

- **Use your network.** Whether you came to an event with a friend, partner or loved one, picked up a con buddy, or came on your own, you have a support network. If you came with a friend, consider finding some time and privacy to talk with them about what is up. Or perhaps you need time alone to get your head together; sometimes taking care of yourself is the best way to take care of your relationship at an event. If you're flying solo, pick up a phone, send a text message, find someone with whom you can connect. If your network is not on-site, you can still use them: mention in advance to a best friend or your online social network that you are off to have a big weekend. If you warn them in advance, they'll be less likely to be confused at why you are having a hard time in a fun place. Remember, kink events can be quite the emotional roller coaster ride, and if your network knows that, they can give better support.

- **Do something.** Volunteering is another great way to shake the blues. By helping others, we often help ourselves. Simply *doing* something can re-direct difficult feelings; taking action can help pull us out of a potential spiral, and shake us back into the here and now.

- **Avoid dramatic language.** Sometimes we can get caught up in the passion of our experiences. We end up saying things like "this event is a total failure," "everyone here is so cold and unfriendly," "I am such an idiot for coming." All these are forms of dramatic language. Consider instead "I was hoping to have a more engaging event" or "that encounter left me feeling frustrated." Framing our language in a more positive manner can be an important way to help us avoid diving into dark emotions

- **Process.** Give yourself time to treat yourself with compassion. Sometimes we react to people, places or things very strongly because they've elicited a deep emotional reaction. Sitting and processing – feeling our emotions without judgment – can help get us back on track. Taking time in a quiet space, taking a brisk walk, or kvetching with a friend over dinner can all work to help cough up those emotional hairballs. Consider what works best for you, and what will leave you feeling empowered and stable.

  Journaling, keeping a written record or blogging about your emotional process can be a therapeutic tool for individuals who are having a rough time. This is not be to confused with pouring out toxic feelings – or, worse yet, publicly name-dropping the people we're upset with – to the world at large. Consider maintaining a personal, private journal for working through raw emotions.

  Processing may also take the form of seeing a counseor, therapist, coach or spiritual advisor after the fact. Flotsam and jetsam within our subconscious can rise to consciousness during our explorations in BDSM and the kink community: from childhood programming to assumptions about who we are as people, all sorts of ideas may be challenged. It doesn't even have to be a "big" scene or event to have this happen. Finding a kink-friendly person with whom you can process can be a useful tool for many.

- **Use your safeword.** Sometimes, you just hit a wall. By bowing out of a few elements of the event, you leave breaks in the business so that the hidden treasures of kink events can shine through. That fleeting and beautiful conversation, the chance to watch an amazingly connected and moving scene – these won't happen if you just "give up" on an event. The art of letting go of expectations that everything will be perfect can help avoid emotional crashes.

Got the urge to stay in your room for the rest of weekend watching television and ordering room service...with a play partner or on your own? It's okay. You can also call "yellow" on the event by becoming a wallflower, cutting down your level of involvement, or skipping a party one night. Check your emotional barometer. Is this event good for you? If not, consider opting out.

If you are thinking about leaving an event, carefully weigh the pros and cons. Make sure that you will be leaving in a rational state of mind rather than storming off into the night without telling anyone where you are going. Because yes, sometimes you will feel lonely, angry, or tired of it all. Even in a crowd full of beautiful people doing beautiful things, it can happen. At the end of the day, your primary need is to take care of your own needs.

Above all else, remember two key points:

- **You are responsible for yourself and your own journey.**

- **Be kind to yourself.**

By remembering these two points, you increase your chances of success... even when you get the pervy blues. A positive attitude, attention to self-care, compassion for yourself and others are wonderful ways to take out some "emotional insurance" and help set you up for the big win.

And so, now, you've gotten through the amazing energy of the event: how do you handle re-entry? Coming back to the default world can be challenging. Read on for some help on how to come back from the depths to the surface without getting the bends!

Chapter 11

Transitioning with Grace:
Back In the Default World

THE PARTY IS OVER, everyone has left the munch, and the tear-down crew is packing the hotel dungeon back into the moving van. It's time to wriggle out of that latex, button up the button-down and get back to the office...

But how do you go back into the default world after having seen so many wonderful things and experienced such exceptional energies? The key is an awareness and respect for the transition itself. You must develop tools for facilitating that transition, knowing, identifying and accessing your allies, and remaining true to your authentic self along the way.

Real World? Fantasy World?

The default world is known by many names. Often people refer to it as the "vanilla world." You may also hear it called the "real world."

For some, the default world *is* the "real world." For them, the kink community is a place to escape, to adopt a fantasy persona, to play dress-up and freely inhabit a new and different way of being. For others, though, the world at large is certainly not the real world. For them, the kink community *is* the real world, a place where they do not have to wear the mask of "polite society." This is the place where such people find their chosen family, their tribe, and for them it's the realest place there is. Still others never transition: there is only one world, and they move seamlessly between the kink and default worlds without boundaries.

There is no right way to view the default world. And rest assured, your thoughts will change. Rather than focusing and fretting about managing solid, inviolate barriers, ponder instead what nourishes you. Do you need to connect with this community or your specific tribal group daily? Every few weeks? At a

Running from Obligations

Some folks have been known to enter into the kink community and decide immediately that this will comprise their full-time reality. They burn bridges back in the default world – leave their jobs, abandon families, or ditch their "boring vanilla" friends who would "never understand" this amazing new world they've discovered. If this is you, we suggest taking a long hard look at whether you truly want to join the kink community to the exclusion of everything else, or if you are simply using it as a rationale for abandoning your responsibilities. Ask yourself whether total immersion, to the exclusion of all that came before, may be harming yourself or others. Is this a form of addiction? Does it interfere with your daily life? If you do decide to incorporate kink into your full-time life, it will be more fulfilling and sustainable if you can find your way to doing so from a place of honor, respect and clarity.

monthly SIG meeting? Or only at the big annual con? Do you live and breathe on that kinky social networking site, but really only need to do an in-person event once every few years? Or do you feel no need for a community of kink, and feel happy being at home with your pervy partner and collection of toys?

Transition Tools and Techniques

Whatever your degree of involvement and philosophical approach may be, as of the day this book goes to press there remains a distinct divide between what most of us perceive as the kink community and the world at large. And anytime we move between cultures, as well as physical or emotional experiences, our bodies and spirits need tools for transitioning.

After being humbled by adoration, receiving touch and affection, having deep conversations or experiencing profoundly intense physical sensations, how do we go back to a place that does not always have that same degree of intensity?

"Drop" can come after an event, especially for those who have played hard. This phenomenon may be related to the biological and neurological realities related to the "high" of the kink encounters in which we engage. Or it may be the realization that the default world does not come with a greeter's table, cuddle party or hospitality suite. It may also include having to move back to mundane reality after the protracted time frame in which we unleashed our hidden victim, wicked villain, spirit animal or inner child. Thus, a day or week later, feelings of being tired, drained, sad or depressed can come up. These feelings are normal.

We made suggestions in Chapter 10 about how to reduce the likelihood of event

When I first started attending big kink events, that first day back in the corporate trenches felt very much like leaving the Technicolor Land of Oz for the gray reality of Kansas. I wondered how people lived in this place where relationships weren't explicitly negotiated, where I had to watch my language, where I was not free to be who I was, all of the time. Then I realized that, in my particular situation, I had a great deal more freedom than I originally thought. Eventually, over the course of a decade or so, I found ways to make my living with kink-friendly companies, came out to my family, and learned to kick down the barriers that I felt held me back from manifesting my most authentic self.

drop through preventive care. We can also do work after the fact to help reduce its effects. Being kind to yourself as you transition is thus the first step of transitioning with grace. You may also wish to:

- **Have an exit strategy.** Knowing in advance what your plans will be for entry back into the default world, no matter what they are, can help prevent crashing. If you can look forward to an hour of shiatsu massage, a few hours alone for a good hot bath, or time spent with your primary partner, this anticipation can give you an attainable benchmark and goal, and anchor your process.

- **Take a vacation from your vacation.** If you can, taking a day off after the event to decompress and come back into the default world can ease the burn of re-entry into your atmosphere. It can be rough to go straight back into the office the day after your whole world was shaken up. But even if you can't take the day off, acknowledge that you may need time to transition emotionally and physically. Even if your routine has to remain the same, you can cut yourself some slack.

- **Plan a decompression party.** Set up an after-event group dinner, a small get-together at someone's house, or some other "step down" from the big conference. Even hitting a munch can help you to tag a pleasant "coda" onto the experience.

- **Ritualize your exit.** Gathering a group of friends and removing your event wrist bands at the same time, or at the end of each event always blowing the venue a kiss, can create a consistent way for the unconscious mind to remember that it is over, and that it is okay. Some folks will carry the end of event energy to an "afterglow" party, which might be as simple as gathering at the hotel lounge for a round of beverages and a lingering goodbye.

- **Cherish trinkets and swag.** Holding onto event programs, conference badges, t-shirts, run pins and other swag can help us recall the event fondly days, weeks or months later. The same is true of going back through notes taken in classes.

- **Share your stories.** Whether you post a scene report, chat with a friend, or write a review of your favorite class, sharing your experiences – the highs and the lows – can be a great way to process and decompress.

- **See kinky friends a few days later.** Scheduling your attendance at a local munch, or booking dinner with a friend from the event, can help give you something to look forward to. If the hot new person you met lives across the country, consider booking a phone date for later that week. Either way, connecting with *people* is vital.

- **Get your kink on.** In the days after the event, *play*. Whether you're making love to yourself while recalling that hot scene from the convention, connecting with a partner who did not attend, playing with a lover who was there as well, or hooking up with a new friend from the con, this type of reconnection can help you transfer into the world at large.

- **Actively process your thoughts and feelings.** Whether you work with a counselor, life coach, spiritual leader or mentor, talk therapy can be helpful for some. You might be haunted by the sensation of guilt, or again confronted by your personal programming around kink being "wrong." Seeing a kink-friendly therapist (or other professional) can help us when stuff has been dislodged within our psyche. Please be aware: some therapists still pathologize kink, and may reinforce your fear that what you did was wrong. In Appendix 4B, you can find resources for locating professionals who will respect your kink and BDSM lifestyles.

- **Do that self-care thing.** Eat well, stay hydrated, watch a fun movie, read a good book, or get that long-deserved pedicure. Taking care of your body will help reduce that energetic crash.

> **Taking a Break from Community**
>
> For those of us who have been in the scene for a while, or who have found ourselves overwhelmed by what we have experienced, sometimes taking a break from being immersed in the kink world is healthy. Taking a month, or even a few years, away can help us process, and find our voice or place in the community. Not being part of the community does not mean that we are not kinky. Staying at home to play is OK and a great choice for many folks. It does not mean that the community is not a good thing, or that you need to abandon it altogether. And don't worry: we will still be out there should you choose to return.

- **Plan for the next one!** Figuring out when you can attend your next play party, fetish ball, weekend intensive or con can be a transition tool for some: if you know when your next encounter is due, it can feel less like a loss when you move back to the default world.

Remember, as you change your headspace from an event into the default world, that the chasm is not as large as we think. We can bring the joys, connections, lightness and revelations that we made in the kink world back with us. We are the same people, even if we have had major epiphanies and beautiful revelations. There is no need to lock ourselves away and spiral into a crash. You can do it. And if hiccups come up, remember that you have allies, so leverage them!

I was attending a kinky conference with a bunch of TNG folks. As they ran inside a diner to grab breakfast, I sat outside with our ten roller bags. As they were coming back, a lovely older woman asked me where we were going. I said we were off to a conference where people work on their relationships. She lit up and said that she didn't work on her relationship until twenty years into her forty year marriage, and she was happy we were doing it so young. My friends asked later why I lied to the old lady. I didn't, I said, I was simply speaking her language. Not everyone wants the details, and sharing it all can be too much for a stranger to digest.

Who to Tell, What to Tell

Once we are back in the default world, it can be challenging to find our filters. Who do we tell what about our explorations in BDSM? Chapter 4 presented you with some ideas of what to tell folks as you sail forth into the wild, wonderful adventures in kink. The same ideas apply when we re-integrate: your co-worker does not need to hear the details of your kinky escapades; they are asking if you had a fun weekend as a way to connect with you. And sharing your new-found obsession with spanking may well land you in front of a Human Resources Officer if your co-worker isn't open to sharing your experience. Letting folks know you had fun with friends is just fine.

When folks ask further questions about the answers we give, we each have choices as to how much information is appropriate. Perhaps we will ask, "How much would you like to know?" Perhaps we will choose to share vague details, but not specifics. Perhaps we'll opt out by changing gears, maybe asking folks what *they* did over the weekend. It can be easy to jump to the conclusion that others are prying or trying to judge us, but most often people ask questions out of a sense of curiosity.

If folks do discover the details of our alternative explorations, be prepared for a variety of responses. Some will not care. Others will be taken aback, or even consider what we do as evil, immoral, or wrong. Some might come out of the closet and share their own stories in turn. You can never tell by looking at someone what their response will be. What their responses are about is more often about their journey than ours, but a negative response can still hurt.

Many outsiders' perception of what they think goes on within the kink world is far more exotic than the truth. Their visions are swimming with those sex ninjas and prowling erotic sharks we discussed before. Society loves sensationalism; thus, they may seek out the titillating stories — the proof of their theories — or they may project their fears or desires onto you.

That is not to say that only our non-kink friends, family and coworkers may be the ones to project on us. Our kinky friends may do much the same: expecting us to have a great time and demanding that we share all our stories with them. This can be tricky if we had a tough time at an event, as some kinky folks don't want to hear that we spent the weekend processing our break-up or feeling like a freak among freaks. It can also be challenging if we experienced something beautiful and intimate that we want to keep as "ours" and not expose to the world at large. You may not want to share with anyone in the scene or beyond what you have been up to, keeping it as your own lovely or unlovely secret. Share what feels comfortable, and maintain your boundaries about the rest. Your boundaries around privacy are as sacrosanct as your limits around play, and maintaining them is part of your self-care.

If you are considering divulging the truths of your kinky escapades, ask yourself why. Does this person need to know that fact, or in that level of detail? Are you sharing just to shock someone, to see them rattled or uncomfortable? Is sharing all of those prurient details actually helpful? Are you overexcited? Will you accidentally out someone's identity with your story? Evaluate the context of your sharing, and remember that every single one of us is, in effect, an ambassador for the kink community as a whole — be sure to represent us, and yourself, with dignity and respect.

And if you *don't* decide to share the details, or in fact *any* of the kink? It's totally cool! Bring home funny anecdotes, show your family some pictures of tourist traps, and connect with them at their own level and within your comfort zone.

While your friends, family and coworkers may not need to know about your kink, there is a chance your doctor may need to know. Yes, you always have the choice of simply stating that you sprained your ankle, rather than mentioning you did it by falling off your six-inch stiletto heels. That rotator cuff injury will need different treatment modalities if it is the result of playing tennis than if it is a side effect of strenuous rope bondage. If your doctors don't know, they won't be able to treat you to the best of their abilities. Believe us, they've heard it all, and more. But if you still have concerns, check out Appendix 4D: it contains helpful tips for talking to health care professionals.

The other people with whom we will need to reconnect in the default world are our children. Though some folks choose to be out to their kids, consider again the age-appropriate language to use. Explaining that you had a date weekend is likely more conducive to healthy connections than a more graphic or detailed description. Children will pick up on cues around them, no matter how subtle, and there is no need to hear from the elementary school that little Pat was talking about "flogging" on the playground, or got their hands on your favorite pair of vintage manacles for "Show and Tell." For the most part, kids just want to know that you are healthy and happy, and that they are safe and loved.

> **Big Town, Small Town**
> In cities like San Francisco or New York, it is easy enough to say that you met someone at a party without raising many eyebrows. However, in smaller towns or in areas with a small town mentality, even mentioning that you know someone else can be met with a slew of questions. Where do you know them from? What sort of party? What friends do you have in common? Where did you meet that person? What is their name? Think in advance about what you want to share, what information you need in advance, and how to integrate these new friends into your default world.

Honoring Your Journey

As you find your feet when it comes to the come-down, challenges of identity may rise to the surface. Odysseus had nothing on your journey though these exciting seas of kink and oceans of eroticism! You'll realize so much about who you were, learn how to manifest who you are, and discover how to bring to light the amazing person you are becoming.

However, finding new ways to balance these points of awareness can be disorienting. You may have moments of intense elation, and emotional troughs of profound confusion. You may even feel weird as you examine what you have found out about yourself. It happens to us all.

As you walk this path and engage in your process, you learn awesome stuff about yourself. Even as you plumb the murky depths of your desires, and find the shadow side of yourself, you can become aware that light is the source of any shadow.

And yes, you will change as a result of this process. Change and growth is vital to our development as thinking, creative, loving beings. Discovering, investigating and exploring BDSM, or becoming a part of the kink community, can be a wonderful facet of the shining being that is you.

I have been aware of my bent since 1993, active in the leather and BDSM communities since 1995... and I still hit road bumps, strange hitches, and surreal moments of Zen. I've found myself breaking down laughing in the middle of a scene: when my friend stopped to check in, he asked why I was laughing. "Dude. Here I am, in the basement ballroom of an international hotel chain. I'm standing here butt-ass nekkid, tied to a giant X, being whipped by my friend, and I'm acting like this shit is... *normal!*" I laughed so hard I teared up, and my friend's best efforts to beat the giggles out of me resulted in... you guessed it... more hysterical laughter. Sometimes reality checks restore some balance to my own wonky worldview.

If you're feeling like you are "coming home," take stock in what your new home means to you. If you feel lost, sad or confused, it is up to you, and only you, to decide what steps you take from here. If you want to go to one munch and then go home having met some interesting people – that is your valid choice, your best outcome. If you want to become a performer at fetish balls and build your own dungeon space, so be it – *that* is your valid choice, *your* best outcome.

Be an explorer. Follow your passions. And find a way to honor your journey by journeying your way. You deserve it!

Afterword

Take a breath, get yourself a blanket, grab a glass of water, or go for a brisk walk to shake it all off...

This is your aftercare, of a sort. Feel free to cuddle the book if you'd like!

We've gone a long way and explored a lot since we began our adventure together. We have wandered from the core questions of why you might want to explore kink, debunked some of the myths about the kink communities. Together we have traversed the ranges of the many types of kink events and spelunked the caverns of possible pitfalls. We've negotiated the twisty trails of negotiation, taken the lay of the land of play spaces, broken down the thorny brambles of BDSM, taken soundings on how to connect... and, finally, sailed full circle back to re-discovering ourselves in the default world.

We hope you are wiser for the journey, and that you feel empowered to take the next steps.

Now what? What are those next steps?

Glad you asked!

It's all you, baby. You get to figure out where you want to go from here.

You have the tools to go out into the world, observe the communities available to you, perhaps create your own, and explore. Play. Have fun. Join groups. Run for titles. Become an advocate for your passion. Change the world, one orgasm at a time. And play. And have fun.

Did we mention having fun?

This path is not set in stone. It is ever-changing, and there are always new trails to blaze. And, hopefully, you'll find your own niche, or carve out a new one, and do it all with your own flair, with grace, humor, and compassion, armed with the knowledge of how to do it, while playing well with others.

And as you do so... know you are not alone.

Your Sexual Sherpas,
Lee Harrington and Mollena Williams

Appendix 1

Kink Lingo Glossary

GETTING KINKY FOLKS to agree on anything is a monumental task. In the interest of establishing a common lexicon for the purposes of our book – and being as clear as we can with our language – we present the following definitions for some of the more common terms you'll encounter in your explorations of the kink community. Enjoy!

1950s Household – Slang for a male-dominant, female-submissive power exchange dynamic, often featuring domestic discipline.

24/7 – A form of extended power exchange dynamic.

Aftercare – Post-scene activities or processing. Styles of aftercare vary.

Ageplay – Any role-playing that focuses on or involves age. May include a range from infantilism/adult baby and littles / kidz, to adultz and geriatric roles.

Animal Role-playing – (See also *Furry*) A style of play where individuals dress and/or role-play as animal characters or manifest an animal persona. Common animal roles include dogs/puppies, horses/ponies, cats/kittens, pigs, cows and worms. May include mythical creatures. (aka *human animal, pet play, ponygirl/ponyboy, pony play, puppy play*)

Asexual – A sexual orientation categorized by an absence of sexual interest or sexual attraction to others. May also be considered having no sexual orientation. (aka *nonsexuality*)

Bad Pain – Intense physical sensation outside the desires of the participants.

Barebacking – Unprotected penile penetration. This is edge play. Please note that persons engaging in barebacking should be aware of the risks involved. Please see *Appendix 4* for STI/STD information.

BDSM – An acronym used to stand for Bondage/Discipline, Dominance/ Submission, Sadism/Masochism and Slavery/Mastery. This acronym is sometimes used to refer to the kink communities as a whole or any kink activities in general.

Bisexual – (See also *Pansexual, Queer*) A sexual orientation categorized by an interest or sexual attraction to both men and women.

Black Sheets Party – An orgy for individuals who engage in kinky sex.

Blood Play – Activities involving the deliberate drawing of blood. This may include temporary piercing, cutting, suturing, medical staples, or intense whipping. Often considered edge play. Please note that persons engaging in blood play should be aware of the health risks involved and take appropriate precautions. (aka *blood sports*)

Body Modification – Any practice that is intended to modify or change the appearance of the body, often permanently. This may include piercing, tattooing, branding, scarification and waist training/extreme corsetry.

Boi/Boy – A term used within the LGBT and kink communities to refer to a sexual and/or gender identity.

Bondage – (See also *Mental Bondage*) Any practice that involves the application of physical restraint. This may include total restraint, partial restraint or decorative restraint. Materials include rope, metal, cling wrap, fabric, leather, latex, and more.

Bootblack – An individual who enjoys giving leather care and boot care as service or as a leather fetishist.

Bottom – An individual who cedes a degree of control by becoming the recipient of physical sensation in a scene. (aka *bottoming*)

Boundaries – (See also *Hard Limits, Soft Limits*) Personal guidelines that outline a person's desires and comfort zones.

Breath Play – Activities involving the restriction or control of respiration. Some types of breath play are considered edge play. Please note that persons engaging in breath play should be aware of the health risks involved and take appropriate precautions. (aka *asphyxiation, asphyxiaphilia, breath control*)

Calling Cards – A card used as a social networking tool for introductions and providing contact information. (aka *slut cards, trick cards*)

Capitalization – The practice of identifying roles through upper and lower case writing, popularized online (e.g. "Mistress Molly and slave sally invite you to O/our play party"). Only used in select segments of the kink population, and dismissed by others.

CBT - (See also *Genitorture*) An acronym for Cock and Ball Torment.

Chastity - The practice of orgasm denial and erotic sexual restriction. This may include the use of locking devices, chastity belts, or genital piercings. (aka *tease and denial*)

Cherry Popping - Originally referenced concerning the "loss" of virginity, in the kink communities this term is used to celebrate having explored a kink activity for the first time.

Classes - Learning opportunities within the kink communities on topics ranging from relationships to sexual and play techniques.

Co-bottom - The practice of two or more individuals bottoming together in a scene (aka *co-bottoming*)

Co-top - The practice of two or more individuals working together to "run" a scene. (aka *co-domming, co-topping*)

Collar - (1) A garment or item that fastens around or frames the neck. (2) Any item signifying identity, submission, surrender, or ownership.

Collared - (See also *Contract, D/S, M/S, Power Exchange*) The state of an individual engaged in a committed power exchange relationship, often signified by a ceremony of some kind. Variations include temporary collars, play collars, training collars, and collars of consideration, the last of which is used in select segments of the kink population, and dismissed by others. (aka *owned*)

Colors - The identifying insignia for a BDSM, leather or kink club, group or organization.

Compersion - The feeling of pleasure when a loved one feels pleasure, often from an outside source. (aka *frubble*)

Con - A large gathering of individuals who share a common interest. In the kink community, this is often slang for a conference, convention, or other longer event that has a specific kink theme or special interest.

Con Crud - Slang for being ill or having a cold, often in reference to something acquired at an event.

Con Drop - (See also *Drop*) Post-event blues.

Consensual non-consent - (See also *Rape Fantasy*) A scene or dynamic in which consent has been granted to "violate" specific boundaries. Often considered edge play. Please note that persons engaging in consensual non-consent should be aware of the risks involved and take appropriate precautions.

Contract - (See also *Collared, M/S, Power Exchange*) A negotiated agreement between individuals involved in a power exchange dynamic. Contracts may be as simple as a verbal agreement, or as complex as a lengthy written document. (aka *formalized agreement, slave contract, temporary contract, verbal contract*)

Corporal Punishment - Activities involving punitive physical discipline.

Cross-dressing - Sexual arousal or gratification from wearing clothing appropriate for the opposite sex.

Cruising - The act of walking, driving, visiting bars, socializing at an event, or looking on the Internet in search of a sexual partner, often of an anonymous, casual and one-time variety.

Cuckoldry - The practice in which an individual experiences sexual gratification through their partner having intercourse with other people. This may include an aspect of humiliation. (aka *cuckold, bull, cuckoldress*)

D/S - (See also *Power Exchange*) An erotic play or relationship style that focuses on power exchange. (aka *d/s, D/s, Dominance/Submission*)

Daddy/Dad - A term used within the LGBT and kink communities to refer to a sexual and/or gender identity.

Default World - A slang term for the broader society outside the kink community. (aka *vanilla, world at large*)

Diminutive - A form of address denoting smallness, familiarity, affection, lesser stature or triviality.

Discipline - Psychological restraint, supported by rules and enforceable by punishment, designed to control behaviors.

DM - An acronym for Dungeon Monitor. Someone who is empowered to facilitate the party, event or dungeon experience of others. Their roles may include safety, ambiance, medical assistance, and labor. (aka *event assistant, party monitor, PM, safety monitor, SM, venue facilitator*)

Dominance - The act of asserting control.

Dominant - (1) adj. The quality of asserting authority or influence. (2) noun. An individual who exercises control in a power exchange dynamic. (aka *Dom, Domme*)

Dominatrix - A female dominant.

Drop - A physical and emotional post-scene reaction. This can be characterized by feelings of loss, sadness, anxiety or regret. (aka *bottom drop, con drop, dom drop, sub drop, top drop*)

Dungeon - A space where BDSM encounters take place. (aka *play space*)

Edge play - (1) A type of play that pushes personal boundaries or limits. "Edge play is wherever your edge is." (2) A BDSM activity that involves a higher degree of physical or psychological risk. This list includes fire play, gun play, consensual non-consent, breath play, blood play, and ball busting. Many forms of edge play are banned or limited in public (and private) play spaces.

Electrical Play - Activities involving the use of electrical discharge. This may include the use of shock collars, tasers, stun guns, electric fly swatters, violet wands, TENS units, or e-stim devices. Some forms of electrical play are considered edge play. Please note that persons engaging in electrical play should be aware of the risks involved and take appropriate precautions.

EMT Shears - A type of scissors used by paramedics and other emergency medical personnel to quickly and safely cut clothing from injured people. Often used in BDSM play to rapidly remove a person from bondage in the event of an emergency. (aka *bandage scissors*)

Endorphin Rush - A term for the "high" resulting from physical and emotional stimuli. Endorphin is a generic word for a morphine-like substance originating from within the body, produced under duress or physical stress. Endorphins can also be produced through exercise, excitement, pain, orgasm, and consumption of spicy food.

Exhibitionism - The compulsion, desire or fetish to expose oneself to others. This may include physical, mental or emotional exposure. (aka *exhibitionist*)

Exploratorium - A gathering of kinky people that offers the opportunity to experience a variety of techniques. (aka *sampler, tastings*)

Female Supremacy – A kink lifestyle that asserts that women are by nature dominant over men. (aka *gynarchy*)

Fetish - (See also *Paraphilia*) A sexual arousal resulting from specific objects, situations, or individuals. (aka *fetishism, a kink*)

Fetish Ball - A kink-themed event featuring performances and a high fetish dress code. (aka *kinky ball, fetish gala*)

Fetish Night - A kink-themed party event, often in a night club. (aka *club night*)

Fire Play - Activities involving the deliberate use of fire on or around the body. This may include fire cupping, flash cotton, cell popping, branding, torches, or fire flogging. Often considered edge play. Please note that persons engaging in fire play should be aware of the risks involved and take appropriate precautions.

Flagging - (See also *Hanky Code*) The use of props, symbols or tools to denote role, orientation, identity or sexual interest. Examples may include bandannas, handcuffs, keys and more (see *Appendix 2* for further examples of flagging).

Flogger - A multi-tailed impact tool, often made of leather. (aka *cat-of-nine-tails, flail, scourge*)

Fluid Bonding - Unprotected sex or fluid exchange in established relationships. This is often entered into once medical advice has been sought, STI statuses are known, and agreements have been made concerning safer sex practices outside the relationship(s).

Fisting - A sexual activity of inserting a lubricated hand into the vagina or rectum. (aka *handballing*)

Frenzy - Obsessive interest in experiencing everything kinky, sometimes sacrificing common sense or safety.

Furry - (See also *Animal Role-playing*) A style of play where individuals dress and/or role-play as anthropomorphic animal characters. (aka *fursuiter, furvert*)

Genitorture - The torment or torture of the genital region. (aka *ball busting, CBT, cock and ball torment, cunt torture*)

Girl/Grrl - A term used within the LGBT and kink communities to refer to a sexual and/or gender identity.

Good Pain - Intense physical sensation desired by the participants.

Gorean - (See also *Kajira*) A style of power exchange based on the Gor erotic novels of John Norman, predominantly featuring male dominance and female submission.

Gun Play – Activities involving the concept or use of actual or simulated firearms. This may include the mindfuck of guns being involved, use of toy guns, pieces of disassembled guns, permanently disabled guns or empty firearms. Most forms of gun play are considered edge play. Please note that persons engaging in gun play should be aware of the risks involved and take appropriate precautions.

Hanky Code – (See also *Flagging*) Flagging colored bandannas or handkerchiefs to denote role, orientation, identity or sexual interest. (see *Appendix 2* for the breakdown of the Hanky Code)

Hard Limits – (See also *Boundaries, Soft Limits*) Scenes or activities that are forbidden as non-negotiable, usually because they are contrary to core values, identity or capacity.

Harem – A group of submissive individuals or slaves serving one or more dominant individuals.

Heterosexual – A sexual orientation categorized by an interest or attraction to individuals of the opposite sex or gender.

Historical Role-playing – A style of play where individuals dress and/or role-play as characters from other time periods, or manifest a persona from another era. Common historical roles include serf, geisha, concubine, odalisque/sex slave, butler, maid, lord, lady, royalty, and military roles. May include fantastical characters.

Homosexual – A sexual orientation categorized by an interest or attraction to individuals of the same sex or gender.

Honorific – A form of address denoting superiority, deferral, respect, or higher status.

House – A group of individuals who have chosen to create a leather family of choice. (aka *household, leather house, leather family*)

House Party – A kinky gathering in a private residence.

Impact Play – Any practice that involves physically striking the body. Tools may include bare hands, fists, belts, birches, canes, paddles, whips and more.

Infantilism – (See also *Ageplay*) A consenting adult taking on the role of an adult baby or small child. This type of play may involve parent/child or babysitter/child dynamics.

Invasion - An orchestrated gathering of a kinky special interest group at a larger event. (aka *takeover*)

Joyword - (See also *Safeword*) A communication tool used to manage the flow of the scene. Often used as a means to indicate that now would be the best time to wind down.

Kajira - (See also *Gorean*) A woman who identifies as a slave in Gorean roles. A male kajira is known as a *kajirus.*

Kink - The great big world of sexual adventure including but not limited to voyeurism, exhibitionism, fetishism, fantasy role-playing, cross-dressing, power exchange, swinging, leather identity, erotic restraint, consensual non-monogamy, "naughty sex" and BDSM between consenting adults. In short, the realm of sexuality perceived to be outside the mainstream.

Kinkster - An individual who engages in voyeurism, exhibitionism, fetishism, fantasy role-playing, cross-dressing, power exchange, swinging, leather identity, erotic restraint, consensual non-monogamy, "naughty sex" and/or BDSM between consenting adults.

Kinky - An identity or description of societally non-normative sexual expression.

Knife Play - Activities involving the deliberate use of a blade. This may include sensation play, temperature play, cutting, or scarification. Often considered edge play. Please note that persons engaging in knife play should be aware of the health risks involved and take appropriate precautions.

KOBRAS - An acronym for Kinky Old Bastards (or Broads) Really Are Sexy. A group which caters to older people involved in BDSM, typically ages 50+.

Land Mine - (See also *Squick, Trigger*) A negative or unwanted trigger.

LDR - An acronym used to stand for Long Distance Relationship.

Leather - (1) A material made from the tanned hides of animals. (2) (See also *Old Guard*) A subculture that traces its origin back to gay male leather and kink of the mid-20th century. (3) A personal identity based on the constructs of the leather sub-culture.

Limit - (See also *Boundaries, Hard Limit, Soft Limit*) Personal guidelines that outline what is outside an individual's comfort zone.

LTR - An acronym used to stand for Long Term Relationship.

Masochism - The act of receiving intense sensation, pain or suffering for sexual, sensual, or emotional gratification.

Masochist - An individual who experiences sexual, sensual, or emotional gratification from the act of receiving intense sensation, pain or suffering.

Master - (1) An individual who practices consensual ownership or possession of another human within the structure of a power exchange dynamic. An individual may identify as a master regardless of relationship status. (2) An individual who demonstrates proficiency and skill in a particular play style, tool or form of kink expression.

Mental Bondage - (See also *Bondage*) Any practice that involves psychological or emotional control of the body. This may include verbal commands, self-restraint, or mental conditioning.

Mentor - (See also *Protector*) An individual who is more experienced or more knowledgeable in a field, who is helping a less experienced or less knowledgeable person.

Metamour - Slang for the partner of a partner, or lover of a lover, popularized in the polyamory community.

Military Role-playing - A style of play where individuals dress and/or role-play using uniforms, hierarchy, protocol or military-style settings. Common types of military play include interrogation, boot camp, prisoner of war, and take-downs.

Mindfuck - A technique for psychological play that utilizes misdirection to intensify or enhance a perceived experience.

Mistress - An individual who practices consensual ownership or possession of another human within the structure of a power exchange dynamic. An individual may identify as a mistress regardless of relationship status.

Monoamory - The desire, practice or acceptance of having one emotionally intimate relationship at a time. Monoamory does not necessarily preclude the possibility of outside connections.

Monogamy - The practice of knowingly and voluntarily engaging in one relationship.

Mommy/Mom - A term used within the LGBT and kink communities to refer to a sexual and/or gender identity.

M/S – (See also *Power Exchange*) An erotic play or relationship style that focuses on ownership or possession within a power exchange dynamic. (aka *m/s, M/s, mastery/slavery, ownership/slavery*)

Munch – An informal gathering for people involved with or interested in kink, usually in a public venue. Originally referred to as a Burger Munch. (*birds of a feather, coffee, happy hour, liquid munch, meet-up, round-up, salon, wet munch*)

Negotiation – (1) The act or process of negotiating. (2) Mutual discussion of and arrangement for the terms of an interaction or relationship.

Non-monogamy – The practice of knowingly and voluntarily engaging in multiple relationships. (aka *consensual non-monogamy, open relationship, polyamory, swinging* – see *Appendix 4*)

NRE – An acronym used to stand for New Relationship Energy. NRE is a state of mind experienced at the beginning of a relationship, often involving heightened emotional and sexual receptivity and excitement.

Old Guard – (See also *Leather*) A term used to refer to a previous generation of leather folk. Sometimes used to refer to codified identity, ideas or principals associated with mid 20th century gay men's leather groups.

Orgy – A sexual encounter involving four or more people. May also refer to a gathering of swingers.

Orientation Violation – A form of consensual non-consent in which an individual is "forced" to engage sensually or sexually with someone outside their stated sexual orientation. (aka *cross-orientation play, forced bisexuality, forced heterosexuality, forced homosexuality*)

Outing – The non-consensual disclosure of someone's sexual or cultural affiliations, status, identity, or activities.

Pansexual – (See also *Bisexual, Queer*) A sexual orientation categorized by an interest or attraction to individuals of any sex or gender.

Paraphilia – (See also *Fetish*) A biomedical term used to describe sexual arousal resulting from specific objects, situations, or individuals that may cause distress or serious problems for the paraphiliac or persons associated with them.

Pegging – Slang for sexual play where a female wears a strap-on and fucks a male.

Pervert – A reclaimed term used by many individuals in the kink community to identify themselves.

Pick-Up Play - Scenes or play of a spontaneous or casual nature.

Play - (1) (See also *Work*) The actions and interactions within a scene. This term is often used in the kink communities. (2) Sexual interaction between two or more individuals. This term has been adopted by some in the swinger or anonymous sex communities.

Play Date - A pre-agreed time to connect with another individual, usually for the purpose of exploring kink together or having a scene.

Play Party - (See also *House Party*) A kink, leather or BDSM event where space is created so that participants have the opportunity to engage in scenes. (aka *dungeon party, dungeon event, house party, private party*)

Polyamory - The desire, practice or acceptance of having more than one intimate relationship at a time, with the consent of all parties involved.

Psychological Play - Activities that focus on mental or emotional techniques or interaction. This may include playing with fear, terror, intimacy, vulnerability, taboos, humiliation, objectification and mindfucks. Often considered edge play. Please note that persons engaging in psychological play should be aware of the risks involved and take appropriate precautions.

Power Exchange - (See also *D/S, M/S*) An interpersonal association in which the participants mutually consent to assume or yield authority.

Professional Dominant - An individual who earns money by dominating or topping their clients (aka *dominatrix, pro dom, pro domme, professional master*)

Professional Submissive - An individual who earns money by bottoming or submitting to their clients. (aka *pro sub*)

Protector - (See also *Mentor*) An individual who is more experienced or more knowledgeable in the scene, who acts as a buffer for less experienced or knowledgeable individual as that person develops their confidence or experience level. Protectors are often aligned within the identity of an individual seeking protection (e.g. an experienced submissive "protecting" a less experienced submissive, or a house "protecting" a novice member of the community).

Protocol - A code of behavior that delineates expectations. Protocols may be used within a community or power exchange dynamic to standardize etiquette.

Queer - (1) An umbrella term for individuals operating outside of or beyond social/societal constructs of behavior, gender, identity or sexuality. (2) (See also *Pansexual*) A sexual orientation categorized by an interest or attraction to individuals, unfettered by gender identities or labels.

RACK - An acronym for Risk Aware Consensual Kink.

Rape Fantasy - (See also *Consensual Nonconsent*) A form of consensual non-consent that explores rape and ravishment role-playing.

Rocky Road - Slang for an individual who has both "vanilla" sexual desires and kink predilections.

Sacred Kink - Kink activities or expression which explore the connection between kink and spirit, energy, and/or a higher power (aka *erotomancy, sado-shamanism*)

Sacred Sex - Sexual activities or expression which explore the connection between sex and spirit, energy, and/or a higher power.

Sadism - The act of providing intense sensation, pain or suffering for sexual, sensual, or emotional gratification.

Sadist - An individual who experiences sexual, sensual, or emotional gratification from the act of providing intense sensation, pain or suffering.

Safe Call - A safety technique used with a scene partner where an individual shares information about the scene (location, planned activities, general information about the people involved) with an unbiased outside individual and specifies a check-in time. If there is no check-in at the agreed upon time, permission is given to release information to a predetermined authority. (aka *silent alarm*)

Safer Sex - Tools and techniques for reducing the potential transmission of sexually transmitted diseases and infections. (See Appendix 4)

Safeword - A communication tool used for managing the flow of a scene. Often used as a means to indicate that there is a problem or may soon be a problem. Common versions include the stoplight system (red meaning stop, yellow meaning pause, and green meaning go) or simply saying "safeword" to end. (aka *safe signal*)

Scat - Activities involving fecal material. This may include enema release, "messy" anal sex, rimming, ass to mouth, feces on the body, or fecal consumption. Considered edge play. Please note that persons engaging in scat play should be aware of the health risks involved and take appropriate precautions. (aka *coprophilia, brown shower*)

Scene - (1) An umbrella term for the kink community as a whole. (e.g. "We are part of the scene.") (2) (aka *scenario, session*). A kink encounter that has a delineated beginning, middle, and end. (e.g. "They had a scene.")

Scene Name - A pseudonym used to maintain the anonymity of an individual, or to delineate between one's kink and default world experiences.

Sensation Play - Activities that focus on a wide range of physical or sensory techniques or interactions. This includes exploring touch, sight, scent, taste, sound, or the deprivation of input to those senses.

Service - The process of providing assistance, engaging in helpful activities, or facilitating experiences.

Session - See *Scene*.

Shibari - (See also *Bondage*) A westernized version of Japanese rope bondage, also known as *kinbaku*.

Sissy - An individual (often male-bodied) who engages in stereotypical "feminine" activities or behaviors (e.g. doing household chores, putting on makeup). Sissy Maids fetishize the uniforms and mannerisms of female household servants.

Slave - An individual who practices consensual servitude to another human within the structure of a power exchange dynamic. An individual may identify as a Slave regardless of relationship status.

Soft Limits - (See also *Boundaries, Hard Limits*) Scenes or activities that are potentially negotiable, but usually require very detailed negotiation and /or a higher degree of intimacy between the involved parties.

Space - An altered state of consciousness, often as a result of fully engaging in one's kink desires or activities. This can be characterized by euphoria, disorientation, hyper-sensitivity, disassociation, reduction of communication skills, hyper-focus, or primal energy. (aka *bottomspace, domspace, headspace, ropespace, subspace, topspace*)

Spanko - Slang for an individual with a spanking fetish.

Squick - (See also *Land Mine, Trigger*) The sense of repulsion from encountering a specific concept, situation, or type of play.

SSC - An acronym for Safe, Sane and Consensual.

STD, STI - Acronyms for Sexually Transmitted Disease and Sexually Transmitted Infection.

Submission - The act of ceding control.

Submissive - (1) adj. The quality of ceding authority or influence. (2) noun. An individual who surrenders control in a power exchange dynamic. (aka *sub*)

Subdrop - See *Drop*.

Subspace - See *Space*.

Swapping - Slang from the swinger community for a couple who consensually engage in trading sexual partners with another couple.

Swinging - The activity or lifestyle in which individuals or couples consensually trade or engage with others. Styles of swinging vary and may include gang bangs, orgies, group sex, swapping or cuckoldry.

Switch - (1) An individual who enjoys playing in the role of both top and bottom. (ex. "They are a switch") (2) The act of moving from "top" to "bottom" in the course of a scene or encounter. (ex. "They switched mid-scene") (3) An individual who explores fluidity within power dynamics. (ex. "They switch within their relationship")

Taken In Hand - A style of monogamous heterosexual marriage based on the concept of male dominance and female submission.

Tease and Denial - (See also *Chastity*) A sexual activity in which erotic satisfaction is deliberately thwarted in order to maintain sexual tension.

TNG - An acronym for The Next Generation. A group or organization which caters to younger people involved in BDSM, typically ages 18-35.

Tools - The items used to create an effect within a scene. This word is often considered more formal in its approach that using the term "toys."

Top - An individual who controls the action of and is the provider of physical for sensation in a scene. (aka *topping*)

Top Drop - see *Drop*.

Top Space – see *Space*.

Total Power Exchange – A form of extended power exchange dynamic. (aka *TPE*)

Toys – The items used to create an effect within a scene.

Training – The process of formally providing and reinforcing structure, discipline and/or goals within the context of a consensual power exchange dynamic.

Trigger – (See also *Landmine, Squick*) A strong physiological or psychological reaction caused by a specific concept, situation or type of play.

Troll – Slang term in the kink and alternative sexuality populations for individuals who post online or come into groups with the intention of causing maximum disruption or getting maximum attention.

Unicorn – Slang term in kink and alterative sexuality populations for a type of individual currently seen as rare and/or highly desirable.

Vanilla – Slang for individuals who are not kink-identified, not actively engaged in BDSM activities, or not part of the kink lifestyle. May refer to non-kink activities. This term is sometimes used in a derogatory fashion.

Voyeurism – The compulsion, desire or fetish to view others. This may include physical exposure or mental and emotional observation. (aka *voyeur*)

Warmup – The practice of gradually escalating the intensity of a scene. Warmup may include both physical and mental adjustment to the session.

Water Sports – Activities involving the deliberate incorporating of urine. This may include peeing on oneself, being urinated on by others, group urination, or the drinking of urine. Water sports are often considered edge play. Please note that persons engaging in water sports should be aware of the health risks involved and take appropriate precautions. (*golden showers, piss play, yellow hanky*)

Wax Play – Activities involving the deliberate application of hot wax to the body. This may include paraffin dips, soy massage candles, hot dripping wax, wax removal, or depilatory waxing. Considered by some to be a form of fire play.

WIITWD – An acronym for "What It Is That We Do." A euphemism for any form of kinky activity or alternative sexuality.

Work – (See also *Play*) The actions and interactions within a scene. This word is considered more formal in its approach than the term "play."

YMMV – An acronym for Your Mileage May Vary.

Appendix 2

Kink Flags and Symbols

Better Know Your Hanky Code

The Hanky Code (aka flagging) is a great way to pick up play, flirt, get to know people and cruise your fellow kinksters. Widely used in the 1970s as a system in the gay men's community to meet folks and show what you are into without risking open discussion in places where the activities were taboo, nowadays flagging is a great tool for perverts of all flavors, and is common throughout many kink communities. Keys can also be worn on the appropriate side to show top (left) or bottom (right).

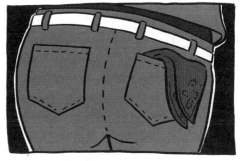

Though some of the colors are agreed upon universally (yellow, black, red and brown, for example), the other colors, especially some of the more obscure ones, get debated. Below is an easy list to start with — but if you're unsure what someone is flagging — ask! You might think they are flagging Tan (cigars) but it turns out they think it's Beige (rimming)- and that could end up with everyone feeling a bit awkward. Wearing a hanky does not necessarily mean you are game to play with anyone into that activity — it's a way to start the conversation and get the ball rolling.

Are you into lots of stuff? Versatile? Switch? Consider changing out your hankies every once in a while to show what mood you are in *right now* instead of flagging fifty things at once... though multiple flagging is a choice too. Items in parentheses below show common secondary interpretations.

In some regions, a bandanna or hanky in a back pocket or tied on the body may also be a way to signal gang involvement. Think smart about whether boldly flagging in your area is appropriate, or if something more subtle might be a better choice.

Left	Color	Right
SM Top (Heavy SM Top)	**Black**	SM Bottom (Heavy SM Bottom)
Fister (Fist)	**Red**	Fistee (Fist Recipient)
Piss Top	**Yellow**	Piss Bottom
Bondage Top	**Grey**	Bondage Bottom
Wants Oral Sex (Suck Me)	**Light Blue**	Gives Oral Sex (Mouth)
Sex Top (Fucker or Anal)	**Navy Blue**	Sex Bottom (Fuckee or Anal)
Safer Sex Top (Fucker)	**B&W Checker Print**	Safer Sex Bottom (Holes)
Piercer	**Purple**	Piercee
Daddy	**Hunter Green**	Likes Daddies (Daddy's Boy)
Uniform Wearer	**Olive Green**	Likes Uniforms
Mommy	**Mint Green**	Likes Mommies
Gives CBT	**Teal**	CBT Bottom
Spanking Top (Spanker)	**Fuchsia**	Spanking Bottom (Spankee)
Tit Torturer	**Dark Pink**	Tits to be Tortured
Scat Top	**Brown**	Scat Bottom
Anything, Anytime, Anywhere (Truly Anything Top)	**Orange**	No Thanks (Truly Anything Bottom — *HUGE regional difference*)
BBW Chaser/Bear Chaser	**Apricot**	BBW/Bear
Does Drag	**Lavender**	Wants a Drag Queen/ King
Celebrity/Star/ Titleholder	**Silver Lamé**	Star Fucker/Groupie
Works Out	**Gold Lamé**	Likes Muscles
Top	**Keys**	Bottom

Flags

Leather Pride: The Leather Pride Flag was designed by Tony DeBlase in 1989, and was first presented at the International Mr. Leather event in Chicago, Illinois, that year. The nine horizontal stripes alternate black and royal blue, with a central white stripe, and a large red heart in the upper left quadrant. It has been adopted by the broader BDSM and kink communities as a flag for alternative sexual practice and lifestyles. Sub-sections of the leather and BDSM communities have modified this flag to make it their own. For example:

BDSM Pride: Red and white Triskeli symbol centered over the field of stripes.

Puppy Pride: Bone in red on the center, or a red dog paw print in the top left corner, instead of a heart in the top left.

Canadian Kink: Red maple leaf replacing the heart.

Australian Kink: Southern Cross stars in white on top of Leather Pride flag.

Bootblack: Black boot print on flag, or black boot shape on center of flag, with or without heart in corner, or red boot on the center with no heart.

... and more! In general, red, black, blue and white are considered the Leather/BDSM/Kink Pride colors, and appear in multiple formats on jewelry, clothing, flags, and similar items.

Leather Boy/Boi: The leather boy pride flag was created by Keith P, and debuted at Mid-Atlantic Leather in 1998. It was based on the leather pride flag, with the same number of stripes, but they are diagonal from left to right. Dark green replaces the blue of the leather pride flag, representing the hanky code color for daddy/boy. The heart is moved to the right corner to represent where "a boy's heart is."

Leather Girl/Grrl: The leather girl pride flag was created by sheryl (American Leatherwoman 2003) with significant assistance from jp, Toss Inc, and girl nancy. It was unveiled at the Ms. San Diego Leather Contest in 2003. It is inspired by the leather boy pride flag, turned to be tall rather than wide, with pink replacing the green, representing the culturally standardized color for "girl."

Pony Pride: The pony pride flag was created by Carrie (aka Mystic Storm) in 2007, and was first presented at the Florida Fetish Weekend that year. The flag features a black field (leather community ties), a white bar (inner spirit), a blue line (excellence, and a nod to denim and cowboys/girls), a green circle (grass and environment), and horseshoes (unification of all ponies).

Littles and Adult Baby Pride: This flag was designed to help age play practitioners recognize each other, and to create solidarity amongst adult babies, age roleplayers and littles. It features a blue and pink background, with a red and white striped heart at the center. Another variation on the flag features three colors of blue and three colors of pink stripes, with a large diaper pin, on a white background, to specify pride in adult baby activities and identity. This second flag debuted at Stockholm Pride in 2005 and was designed by David.

Rubber Pride. Used as a symbol of latex and rubber fetishism pride and desire, the image was designed in 1994 by Peter Tolos and Scott Moats. The flag features black (representing lust and the look of black shiny rubber), red (for passion), and yellow (for drive and intensity). The chevron is "kinked" at an angle to specifically express kinkiness.

 **Ownership Pride:** Designed in the United Kingdom in 2006, this flag was introduced by Tanos as part of the Ownership Icons project (see *Ownership Icons* on p. 258). The black and white striped field represents the clear distinction between owners and property, as well as the bars of a cage. The foreground features a red shield with a thick white circle, representing the collar, as well as owned submissives and slaves.

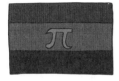 **Polyamory Pride:** Designed by Jim Evans, the poly pride flag consists of blue, red, black and black stripes and the Greek symbol *pi* in gold at the center. Each represents desires of this consensual non-monogamy community — blue for openness and honesty, red for love and passion, and black for solidarity. Pi is used to represent the first letter of polyamory.

 **LGBT Pride:** The Rainbow Flag was designed by San Francisco artist Gilbert Baker in 1978, and has become the icon for lesbian, gay, bisexual and trans-gender (LGBT) pride and diversity. Shown with six colors, the colors (from top to bottom) are red (life), orange (healing), yellow (sunlight), green (nature), blue (harmony), and purple/violet (spirit). When the flag first came out it also featured the colors pink (sex) and turquoise (art/magic). The flag represents the diversity of the LGBT population, but also refers to the song *Over the Rainbow*, considered an allegory of gay coming out.

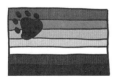 **Bear Pride:** The International Bear Brotherhood Flag was designed by Craig Byrnes in 1995. Its colors denote human hair colors — brown, red, blonde, light blonde/peach, white, gray, and black, and features a black bear paw in the upper left quadrant. The bear community champions size acceptance for gay men, and an appreciation of a fur-covered or rustically macho aesthetic.

Transgender Pride: Designed by Monica Helms (a transgender woman) in 1999, the flag consists of five horizontal stripes: two light blue, two pink, and one white in the center.

Bisexual Pride: This flag in deep pink (representing same gender attraction), royal blue (representing opposite gender attraction) and lavender (attraction across the gender spectrum) was designed by Michael Page in 1998.

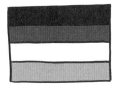

Asexual Pride: Black, grey, white and purple adorn the asexual pride flag. In 2011, the flag was carried by asexual contingents of pride parades in San Francisco, London, Stockholm, and Toronto.

Symbols

Triskelion (or Triskele): a three-armed symbol used to represent BDSM and kink pride. The three segments are often believed to stand for bondage and discipline, dominance and submission, and sadism and masochism respectively, though other interpretations abound.

Pink/Black Triangles: Originally used in WW2 Nazi Germany to identify gay and lesbian prisoners, these symbols have been reclaimed as representations of gay and lesbian pride.

Labrys: This double-headed axe, whose iconography originated in Crete, represents lesbian and/or feminist pride. It can also be used to symbolize matriarchal or female power.

Kef (Gor): The Gorean symbol for a Kajira or female slave, based on the work of fiction author John Norman.

Marque: Based in the works of fiction author Jacqueline Carey, the Marque is a sign of slavery, submission, sacred whoredom or sexual empowerment. In the novels, each tattooed marque is unique and designed for the individual wearing it.

Infinity Heart: The infinity heart is a polyamorous pride symbol where an infinity symbol in blue is interlaced with a blue heart.

Gender Symbols

Female: Based on the planet symbol for Venus, this symbol can represent female, woman, or feminine energy. Two female symbols interlinked has been used to reference lesbian, dyke or female/female sexuality.

Male: Based on the planet symbol for Mars, this symbol can represent male, man, or masculine energy. Two male symbols interlinked has been used to reference gay, fag or male/male sexuality.

Transgender: There are three common variations on the transgender symbol. The first is a combination of the male and female symbols. The second combines both symbols and adds this third hybrid symbol, often depicted within a triangle. The third is based on the planet symbol for Mercury, and can represent transgender, transsexual, genderqueer, or genderqueer energy – though it is less commonly used than the first two. All three have also been used to represent a variety of identities under the trans, transgender, transsexual, genderqueer, and queer identities umbrella.

Ownership Icons

	No Gender Shown	Female	Male	Transgender
Master/Mistress				
Owned Slave/ Property				
Unowned Slave/ Property				

Designed by Tanos in 2006, the Ownership Icons flag the identities of individuals who have power exchange dynamics or desires. The shield represents a master or head of household. On the inside a simplified gender symbol can be placed, or a head of household might place their own household or personal icon instead.

For slaves, submissives and property, there are two types of symbols. The thick, closed circle is for owned slaves, submissives or property, representing the closed or locked collar. The second, a broken square consisting of four corners and four gaps, is for unowned slaves, submissives or property. This second symbol represents the unlocked or open cage, which suggests that the bearer, seeking enslavement, may seem free, but is already in a cage waiting to find connections that will fulfill their needs or desires.

Barcode – Slave registry: Created by the Slave registry website, it is a user specific UPC geared and designed for slaves to register themselves.

Items/Clothing/Props

The following items can be used to flag an interest or involvement in kink:

Handcuffs

Collar

Muir cap (aka cover)

o-ring (aka slave ring)

Other items that might be used for flagging are:

Cock ring worn on a leather jacket (worn on the left to represent sexual top, right to represent sexual bottom)

Diaper pin (worn on a shirt to represent interest in adult baby or diaper lover interactions)

Gorean Slave Silks (specific colors of attire that denote a slave's function, rank, house affiliation or calling).

Appendix 3

Negotiation Tools

On the following pages you will find three different versions of a negotiation questionnaire, known as the "Playcard," "Questionnaire" and "Checklist and Extended Questionnaire." These can be used in a variety of different ways, including:

- Self-examination

- Flirtation

- Filling out and sharing with a partner

- Negotiating with others once each partner has done the form independently

- Working through the form with your partner

- Conversation starter

- Daydreaming

- Being inspired by the wide variety of human desire out there!

You can do them with a specific partner in mind, or thinking in general about your desires. You can do them once, or reassess your desires periodically as a way to examine how your desires shift. And of course, you can use it to play kinky "never have I ever" or "truth or dare."

Before We Play
Playcard

Name/Scene Name:

Want To Do Some Stuff?
☐ Yes   ☐ Maybe   ☐ Not Today   ☐ No, Thanks

© Lee Harrington and Mollena Williams — *Playing Well With Others*. Permission from authors is given to photocopy this questionnaire only for personal use.

Before We Play Questionnaire

This questionnaire is intended to generate discussion and facilitate negotiation with a particular individual, or individuals. It is most useful when you think of what your desires are for this particular interaction rather than encompassing the full spectrum of your desires. Feel free to choose multiple responses, or to write in your own answers!

Name/Scene Name:

Safeword (or plain language only):

Check all that apply:
Top ☐   Bottom ☐   Switch ☐   Dominant ☐   Submissive ☐

Other Orientations/Identities:

Are bruises/marks acceptable?

Medical, Physical or Emotional Concerns to be Aware Of (allergies, injuries, asthma, diabetes, phobias):

Medical, Physical or Emotional Limits and Boundaries (no go zones):

Is sexual play OK? If yes, what are your safer sex practices?

Pain/Sensation Play I Enjoy Receiving ☐   Giving ☐:

Erotic Restraint I Enjoy Receiving ☐   Giving ☐:

Sexual Activities I Enjoy Receiving ☐   Giving ☐:

Fetishes I Enjoy:

RolePlaying I Enjoy:

Anything not on this list that we should talk about?

© Lee Harrington and Mollena Williams – *Playing Well With Others*. Permission from authors is given to photocopy this questionnaire only for personal use.

Before we Play Checklist and Extended Questionnaire

Fill out the form alone, then compare notes afterwards; or fill out the form together... be warned, you may get different answers if you do. This questionnaire is meant to generate discussion, not to be the end of the talk. Feel free to write in notes under answers, choose all that apply, choose none, or make up your own answers. Enjoy!

Name/Scene Name:

How would you like to be addressed during scene? (Name, Honorific, Diminutive)

Safeword(s) (or plain language only):

Are you (check all that apply)...
Gender:
Female ☐   Male ☐   Transgendered ☐   Intersex ☐
Two-Spirit ☐   Bigender ☐   Male-to-Female (MtF) ☐
Female-to-Male (FtM) ☐   Crossdresser ☐   Genderfluid ☐
Gender Neutral ☐   Transsexual ☐   Genderqueer ☐
Butch ☐   Femme ☐   Transvestite ☐   Non-Gendered ☐
Man ☐   Woman ☐   Womyn ☐   Trans ☐
Gender Non-Conforming ☐   Third Gendered ☐   Androgynous ☐
Cisgendered ☐   Boi ☐   Grrl ☐   Boy ☐   Girl ☐
Pangender ☐   Other _____

Sexual Orientation:
Heterosexual ☐   Heteroflexible ☐   BiSensual ☐   BiCurious ☐
BiSexual ☐   Omnisexual ☐   Pansexual ☐   Questioning ☐
Straight ☐   Homosexual ☐   Homoflexible ☐   Gay ☐   Lesbian ☐
Queer ☐   Fluid ☐   Asexual ☐   Anything Goes ☐   Dyke ☐
Fag ☐   Androphile ☐   Gynephile ☐   Demisexual ☐   Asexual ☐
Abstinent ☐   Other _____

© Lee Harrington and Mollena Williams – *Playing Well With Others*. Permission from authors is given to photocopy this questionnaire only for personal use.

Relationship Status/Identity:

Monogamous ☐   Sexually Monogamous ☐
Emotionally Monogamous ☐   Socially Monogamous ☐
Polyamorous ☐   Polygamous ☐   Polyandrous ☐
Polyfuckery ☐   Swinger ☐   Open Relationship ☐   Player ☐
Ethical Slut ☐   Unattached ☐   Single ☐   Married ☐
Divorced ☐   Engaged ☐   Widow/Widower ☐   Partnered ☐
Lover ☐   Fuck Buddy ☐   Dating ☐   In a Leather Family ☐
Member of a House ☐   Group Marriage ☐   Complex ☐
Collared ☐   Owned ☐   Available ☐   Attached ☐   Unavailable ☐
Tonight Only ☐   Polyfidelity ☐   Domestic Partnership ☐
Monoamorous ☐   Polysexual ☐   Polyflexible ☐   Monoflexible ☐
Promiscuous ☐   Free Love ☐   Celibate ☐
Other _____

Role Orientation/Identity (for Roleplaying only, see Roleplaying section of Activities):

Master ☐   Slave ☐   Guru ☐   Acolyte ☐   Mistress ☐
Property ☐   Dominant (partner) ☐   Submissive (partner) ☐
Owner ☐   Object ☐   Handler ☐   Pet ☐   Brat ☐
Freeplayer ☐   Daddy ☐   Boy ☐   Boi ☐   Mentor ☐
Apprentice ☐   Mommy ☐   Girl ☐   Grrl ☐   Trainer ☐
Trainee ☐   Sir ☐   Servant ☐   Ma'am ☐   Butler ☐
Top ☐   Bottom ☐   Switch ☐   Sadist ☐   Masochist ☐
Sensualist ☐   Hedonist ☐   Whore ☐   Slut ☐   Pig ☐
Toy ☐   Baby ☐   Sissy ☐   God(dess) ☐   Knight ☐   King ☐   Queen ☐   Serf ☐   Brother ☐   Sister ☐   Protector ☐
Protected ☐   Other _____

Who can know about your kinky sex life?
☐ Only my partner(s) may know
☐ A few trusted friends only
☐ People can know, but only under my "scene name"
☐ People in the Scene know
☐ Anyone but my family/coworkers
☐ Anyone can know

© Lee Harrington and Mollena Williams – *Playing Well With Others*. Permission from authors is given to photocopy this questionnaire only for personal use.

Who can be part of your kink play?

☐ Only by myself
☐ Just me and my partner(s)
☐ Threesomes
☐ Pre-approved people only
☐ I enjoy swinging
☐ I only partner swap
☐ Small groups
☐ Many more

Are bruises/marks acceptable?

☐ I can be black and blue head to toe
☐ Please no marks that cannot be covered by pants and a turtleneck
☐ Must hide beneath t-shirt and shorts
☐ Must hide beneath bra and underwear
☐ Can last for weeks
☐ Must be gone in a few hours
☐ No marks at all

What you NEED to get out of this scene to be happy:

What you WANT to get out of this scene to be happy:

Medical, physical or emotional factors to be aware of (allergies, injuries, asthma, diabetes, glasses/contacts, hearing aids, menstruation, joint challenges, surgeries, ongoing treatments, mental health, phobias)

Supplements, medication (prescription and over-the-counter), and substances you are currently taking

Medical, physical or emotional limits and boundaries (no-go zones)

Is sexual play ok? What does sexual play look like to you? What are your safer sex practices?

© Lee Harrington and Mollena Williams – *Playing Well With Others*. Permission from authors is given to photocopy this questionnaire only for personal use.

Activities

In this list of potential activities, know that not everything is listed- it's amazing how fertile the human imagination is! If you want to do it, and it's not on the list, just write it in. Please fill out each category in three ways: (1) have you done it before, (2) thoughts on top/giving and (3) thoughts on bottom/receiving.

Key code:

3	Oh gods Please YES! NOW! More!
2	I really would/do enjoy this activity
1	This could be ok
0	I have no interest in this
NO	hard limit, please do not push me on it, I will tell you if this ever changes
?	I have no idea what this means
*	I am embarrassed to discuss this, but am interested

Sensation	Done? Y/N	Top/ Giving	Bottom/ Receiving
Abrasion			
Biting			
Body Painting			
Branding			
Breast Torment			
Breath Control			
Caning			
Cock and Ball Torment (CBT)			
Clips and Clamps			
Cupping/Suction			
Cutting			
Electricity (TENS, Violet Wand)			
Fire Play			
Firm Touch			

© Lee Harrington and Mollena Williams – *Playing Well With Others*. Permission from authors is given to photocopy this questionnaire only for personal use.

Sensation	Done? Y/N	Top/ Giving	Bottom/ Receiving
Floggers			
Hair Pulling			
Hook Pull/Suspension			
Ice			
Kissing – Body			
Kissing – Lips			
Knife Play			
Leather Belt Beatings			
Massage			
Oils/Lotions			
Paddles			
Permanent Piercing			
Pinching			
Punching			
Riding Crops			
Single Tail Whips			
Slapping			
Soft Touch			
Spanking			
Temporary Piercing			
Tickling			
Wax			
Other_____			
Other_____			
Other_____			

© Lee Harrington and Mollena Williams – *Playing Well With Others*. Permission from authors is given to photocopy this questionnaire only for personal use.

Bondage and Erotic Restraint	Done? Y/N	Top/ Giving	Bottom/ Receiving
Arm Binders			
Blindfolds			
Bondage Furniture			
Breast Bondage			
Cages			
Casts			
Chain			
Clothing Bondage			
Collars			
Encasement			
Facial Bondage			
Gags			
Genital Bondage			
Hair Bondage			
Handcuffs			
Heavy Metal Bondage			
Holding/Pinning			
Hoods			
Leashes			
Needle Bondage			
Overnight Bondage			
Plastic Wrap / Cling Film			
Rope – Japanese			
Rope – Suspension			
Rope – Western			
Rubber Bondage			

© Lee Harrington and Mollena Williams – *Playing Well With Others*. Permission from authors is given to photocopy this questionnaire only for personal use.

Bondage and Erotic Restraint	Done? Y/N	Top/ Giving	Bottom/ Receiving
Sensory Deprivation			
Slings			
Stocks			
Strait Jackets			
Suspension Cuffs			
Wrist Cuffs			
Other_____			
Other_____			
Other_____			

Sexual Activities	Done? Y/N	Top/ Giving	Bottom/ Receiving
Anal Sex			
Anal Fisting			
Analingus			
Body Worship			
Bukkake			
Butt Plugs/Toys			
Cock Worship			
Cunnilingus			
Cunt Worship			
Dildos			
Dirty Talk			
Double Penetration			
Fellatio			
Finger Fucking			
Forced Orgasm			
Fucking Machines			

© Lee Harrington and Mollena Williams – *Playing Well With Others*. Permission from authors is given to photocopy this questionnaire only for personal use.

Sexual Activities	Done? Y/N	Top/ Giving	Bottom/ Receiving
Gang Bang			
Genital Stimulation			
Group Sex			
Masturbation – Mutual			
Masturbation – Others			
Masturbation – Self			
Nipple Play			
Online/Virtual Sex			
Orgasm Control			
Phone Sex			
Public Sex			
Rough Sex			
Sacred Sex			
Sexting (Sexual Text Messages)			
Strap-ons			
Tantra			
Threesomes			
Triple Penetration			
Urethral Play			
Vaginal Fisting			
Vaginal Sex			
Vibrators			
Other_____			
Other_____			
Other_____			

© Lee Harrington and Mollena Williams – *Playing Well With Others*. Permission from authors is given to photocopy this questionnaire only for personal use.

Fetishes	Done? Y/N	Top/ Giving	Bottom/ Receiving
Anime/Cartoons			
Amputees			
Armpits			
BBW/BHM/Bears			
Blood			
Body Hair			
Body Modification			
Boots			
Chastity Devices			
Corsets			
Cross-dressing			
Crying/Dacryphilia			
Cuckolding			
Denim			
Diapers			
Enemas			
Embarrassment			
Exhibitionism			
Feet			
Filthy/Dirty			
Financial Domination			
Food Fetish			
Fur			
Fursuits/Mascots			
Hair			
High Heels			
Humiliation			
Hypnosis			

© Lee Harrington and Mollena Williams – *Playing Well With Others*. Permission from authors is given to photocopy this questionnaire only for personal use.

Fetishes	Done? Y/N	Top/ Giving	Bottom/ Receiving
Intelligence/Nerds			
Jock Straps			
Lace			
Lactation			
Lap Dancing			
Latex			
Leather			
Masks			
Medical			
Menstruation			
Nylons/Pantyhose/Stockings			
Outdoor Scenes			
Photography			
Porn – Making			
Porn – Watching			
Pregnancy			
PVC			
Scat			
Scents/Odor			
Shaving			
Silk			
Tattoos			
Underwear			
Uniforms			
Vomiting (Roman Showers)			
Voyeurism			
Water (hot tub, pool, shower)			

© Lee Harrington and Mollena Williams – *Playing Well With Others*. Permission from authors is given to photocopy this questionnaire only for personal use.

Watersports (Piss Play)			
Weight Gain/Loss			
Wet & Messy			
Wrestling			
Other_____			
Other_____			
Other_____			

Role-Playing	Done? Y/N	Top/ Giving	Bottom/ Receiving
1950s Household			
Abandonment			
Abduction			
Adult Baby			
Age Play			
Amazon			
Amputation			
Boss/Employee			
Bratting			
Cannibalism			
Clowns			
Contracts			
Cowboy/Western			
Doctor/Nurse			
Female Supremacy			
Following Orders			
Formal Protocols			
Gender Transformation			
Gor			
Harem			

© Lee Harrington and Mollena Williams – *Playing Well With Others*. Permission from authors is given to photocopy this questionnaire only for personal use.

Role-Playing	Done? Y/N	Top/ Giving	Bottom/ Receiving
Human Doll			
Human Furniture			
Human Sex Toy			
Interrogation			
Kitten/Cat			
Medical Fantasy			
Medieval			
Military			
Objectification			
Orientation Violation (Forced Bi)			
Ownership			
Parent/Child			
Pig/Hog			
Pony/Horse			
Posture Training			
Prostitution			
Punishment			
Puppy/Dog			
Race-based Themes			
Rape Fantasy			
Religious			
Resistance			
Science-Fiction			
Sissy			
Slavery			
Snuff Fantasy			
Sports Theme			
Steampunk			

© Lee Harrington and Mollena Williams – *Playing Well With Others*. Permission from authors is given to photocopy this questionnaire only for personal use.

Role-Playing	Done? Y/N	Top/ Giving	Bottom/ Receiving
Teacher/Student			
Vampire			
Verbal Humiliation			
Victorian/Edwardian			
Waitress			
Worm/Bug			
Other_____			
Other_____			
Other_____			

D/S and Power Exchange	Done? Y/N	Top/ Giving	Bottom/ Receiving
1950s Household			
24/7			
Bathroom Restrictions			
Collars			
Contracts			
Earned Leather			
Female Supremacy			
Financial Control			
Following Orders			
Food Restrictions			
Formal Protocols			
Gor			
Internal Enslavement			
Leather Family			
Leather Household			
Male Supremacy			
Marks of Ownership			

© Lee Harrington and Mollena Williams – *Playing Well With Others*. Permission from authors is given to photocopy this questionnaire only for personal use.

D/S and Power Exchange	Done? Y/N	Top/ Giving	Bottom/ Receiving
Multi-Dominant Household			
Multi-Slave Household			
Ownership			
Powerful Slavery			
Service			
Short-term Contracts			
Slave Registration			
Slavery			
Social Restrictions			
Spiritual M/S			
Taken In Hand			
Total Power Exchange			
Victorian/Edwardian			
Other_____			
Other_____			
Other_____			

Anything not on these lists that you would like to talk about?

© Lee Harrington and Mollena Williams – *Playing Well With Others*. Permission from authors is given to photocopy this questionnaire only for personal use.

Appendix 4

Further Resources

4A: Non-Fiction Books

The following list is a selection of available texts on SM, kink, power exchange, sexuality, leather, polyamory, relationships and more. It is not a comprehensive list; such an undertaking would be maddening, as new books come out all the time.

Some of these have stood the test of time, while others are included to feature authors who have shaped the face of public kink. They range from books in the 1980s to the 2010s, to also provide a snapshot of our cultural history and evolution. We have not included any kink technique books, as there are so many and they are beyond the range of this book. Included are sexuality and relationship awareness books beyond the scope of kink, because we believe they present skills that help facilitate communication of our physical and emotional needs, wants and desires.

SM, kink, power exchange and leather

Ask the Man Who Owns Him: The real lives of gay Masters and slaves, by david stein. Perfectbound Press, 2009.

Coming to Power: Writing and Graphics on Lesbian S/M, by Samois. Alyson Books, 2nd revised edition, 1982.

Deviations: A Gayle Rubin Reader, by Gayle Rubin. Duke University Press, 2011.

Different Loving: The World of Sexual Dominance and Submission, by Gloria and William Brame. Villard Books, 1996.

Erotic Slavehood: A Miss Abernathy Omnibus, by Christina Abernathy. Greenery Press, 2007.

How to be Kinky: A Beginner's Guide to BDSM, by Morpheous. Green Candy Press, 2008.

Leatherfolk: Radical Sex, People, Politics, and Practice, by Mark Thompson. Daedalus Publishing, 2004.

Leatherman's Handbook II, by Larry Townsend. BookSurge Publishing, 2007.

Leathersex: A Guide for the Curious Outsider and the Serious Player, by Joseph Bean. Daedalus Publishing, 1994.

The Mistress Manual: The Good Girl's Guide to Female Dominance, by Mistress Lorelei. Greenery Press, 2000.

The New Bottoming Book, by Dossie Easton and Janet W. Hardy. Greenery Press, 2001.

The New Topping Book, by Dossie Easton and Janet W. Hardy. Greenery Press, 2003.

Sacred Kink: The Eightfold Paths Of BDSM And Beyond by Lee Harrington. Mystic Productions Press, 2009.

Screw the Roses, Send Me the Thorns: The Romance and Sexual Sorcery of Sadomasochism, by Phillip Miller and Molly Devon. Mystic Rose Books, 1995.

The Second Coming: A Leatherdyke Reader, by Pat Califia and Robin Sweeney. Alyson Books, 2000.

Sensuous Magic: A Guide to S/M for Adventurous Couples, by Patrick Califia. Cleis Press, 2nd edition. 2002.

The Sexually Dominant Woman: A Workbook for Nervous Beginners, by Lady Green. Greenery Press, 1998.

SlaveCraft: Roadmaps for Erotic Servitude – Principles, Skills and Tools, by Guy Baldwin. Daedalus Publishing, 2002.

SM 101: A Realistic Approach, by Jay Wiseman. Greenery Press, 1998.

Ties That Bind: The SM/Leather/Fetish Erotic Style: Issues, Commentaries and Advice, by Guy Baldwin. Daedalus Publishing, 2nd edition,1993.

The Toybag Guide to Playing With Taboo, by Mollena Williams. Greenery Press, 2010.

To Love, to Obey, to Serve: Diary of an Old Guard Slave, by V.M. Johnson. Mystic Rose Books, 1999.

Urban Aboriginals, by Geoff Mains. Daedalus Publishing, 20th anniversary edition, 2002.

When Someone You Love is Kinky, by Dossie Easton and Catherine A. Liszt. Greenery Press, 2000.

Sex, Relationships, and Polyamory

Big Big Love, Revised: A Sex and Relationships Guide for People of Size (and Those Who Love Them), by Hanne Blank. Celestial Arts, Revised edition, 2011.

(While this book is geared towards teens, we believe it has pertinent information for adults as well.) *Changing Bodies, Changing Lives: Expanded Third Edition: A Book for Teens on Sex and Relationships*, by Ruth Bell. Three Rivers Press, 3rd edition, 1998.

The Ethical Slut: A Practical Guide to Polyamory, Open Relationships & Other Adventures, by Dossie Easton and Janet W. Hardy. Celestial Arts, 2009.

Exhibitionism for the Shy: Show Off, Dress Up and Talk Hot!, by Carol Queen. Down There Press, Revised edition, 2009.

(While this book is geared towards teens, we believe it has pertinent information for adults as well.) *The Guy Book: An Owner's Manual (Maintenance, Safety, and Operating Instructions for Teens)* by Mavis Jukes. Crown Books, 2002.

Health Care Without Shame: A Handbook for the Sexually Diverse and Their Caregivers, by Dr. Charles Moser. Greenery Press, 1999.

Intellectual Foreplay: A Book of Questions for Lovers and Lovers-to-Be, by Eve and Steve Eschner Hogan. Hunter House, 2000.

The Multi-Orgasmic Couple: Sexual Secrets Every Couple Should Know, by Mantak Chia, et al. HarperOne, 2002.

My Gender Workbook: How to Become a Real Man, a Real Woman, the Real You, or Something Else Entirely, by Kate Bornstein. Routledge, 1997.

Nina Hartley's Guide to Total Sex, by Nina Hartley. Avery Trade, 2006.

Nonviolent Communication: A Language of Life, by Marshall B. Rosenberg, Ph.D. Puddledancer Press, 2nd edition, 2003.

Opening Up: A Guide to Creating and Sustaining Open Relationships, by Tristan Taormino. Cleis Press, 2008.

Our Bodies, Ourselves, by Boston Women's Health Book Collective and Judy Norsigian. Touchstone, 40th anniversary edition, 2011.

Pagan Polyamory: Becoming a Tribe of Hearts, by Raven Kaldera. Llewellyn Publications, 2005.

Partners in Power: Living in Kinky Relationships, by Jack Rinella. Greenery Press, 2003.

Radical Ecstasy: SM Journeys In Transcendence, by Dossie Easton and Janet W. Hardy. Greenery Press, 2004.

Sex for One: The Joy of Selfloving, by Betty Dodson. Three Rivers Press, 1996.

Swinging for Beginners: An Introduction to the Lifestyle, by Kaye Bellemeade. New Tradition Books, 2003.

The Ultimate Guide to Kink: BDSM, Role Play and the Erotic Edge, by Tristan Taormino. Cleis Press, 2012.

Urban Tantra: Sacred Sex for the Twenty-First Century, by Barbara Carrellas. Celestial Arts, 2007.

Wild Side Sex: The Book of Kink: Educational, Sensual, and Entertaining Essays, by Midori. Daedalus Publishing, 2005.

4B. Websites and Social Media

As the Internet and other forms of media are changing all the time, the following is not a comprehensive list. Use your search engines, and remember the information in Chapter 5 for managing your virtual self, before venturing out onto the kinky Internet!

- ### AltSex specific social media and connection sites
  Alt.com
  Bondage.com
  CollarMe.com
  DarkSide.se
  FetLife.com
  FetishMen.net
  KinkCulture.com
  PolyMatchmaker.com
  Recon.com
  SwingLifestyle.com

- ### Dating/hookup sites that have a visible kink presence
  AdultFriendFinder.com
  CraigsList.com – Personals Section
  Grindr.com
  ManHunt.com
  OKCupid.com
  PlentyOfFish.com

- ### Finding Kink Events
  The BDSM Events Page – TheBDSMEventsPage.com
  Caryl's Page – DrkDesyre.com
  Fetlife – FetLife.com
  Leatherati – Leatherati.com
  MALL directory on Fetlife – FetLife.com/groups/28108
  Swinger Lifestyle – SwingerLifestyle.com

- ### Kink and AltSex Information
  BDSM Information:
  Fetlife – FetLife.com
  Myths Debunked – BDSMDebunkingTheMyths.com

Robert Bienvenu – SexResearch.us

Women's History in SF – TheExiles.org/history

Leather History and Resources

Carter/Johnson Leather Library – LeatherLibrary.org

Colors of Leather, Leather History Page – ColorsOfLeather.com

Gay Leather Fetish History – CuirMale.nl

Leather and Roses – LeatherNRoses.com

Leather Archives and Museum – LeatherArchives.org

Leather Clubs – LeatherClubs.net

Masters and Slaves Together – MaST.net

Women's Leather History Project – LeatherArchives.org/wlhp

Polyamory, Swinging and Open Relationships:

Anita Wagner's Practical Polyamory – PracticalPolyamory.com

Liberated Christian's History of Swinging – LibChrist.com/swing/
 began.html

Loving More Magazine and Conference – LoveMore.com

Open Relationships Resources – LifeOnTheSwingset.com

Swinger Lifestyle – SwingerLifestyle.com

Tristan Taormino's Polyamory Resources – OpeningUp.net

• Kink and AltSex Podcasts

The Big Little Podcast – BigLittlePodcast.com

The Dark Side – TheDarkSidePodcast.podbean.com

Dart's Domain – DartsDomain.com

Erotic Awakening (featuring Lee and Mollena) – EroticAwakening.com

Fetish Flame (archive) – FetishFlame.com

Freedom of Fetish – FreedomOfFetish.com

Kink Academy – KinkAcademy.com

Kink On Tap – KinkOnTap.com

Masocast – Masocast.com

The Midwest Teen Sex Show – MidwestTeenSexShow.com

Open Source Sex with Violet Blue – VioletBlue.libsyn.com

Polyamory Weekly – PolyWeekly.com

Rev. Mel – TalkingSexRadio.com

Rope Cast – RopeCast.net

The Young and Kinky Podcast (archive) – YoundAndKinky.
 blogspot.com

Kink and AltSex Blogrolls and Blogs

Lee Harrington – PassionAndSoul.com

Mollena Williams – Mollena.com

Sex Carnival Blogroll – TheSexCarnival.com

Top Sex Bloggers – BetweenMySheets.com

AAG Blog – AAGBlog.com

Barking Shaman, Wintersong Tashlin – BarkingShaman.com/blog

Could Be Dangerous... – DangerousLilly.com

Diary of a Kinky Librarian – DiaryOfAKinkyLibrarian.com

Exploring Intimacy, Dr. Ruth Neustifter – ExploringIntimacy.com

Jiz Lee – JizLee.com

Leatherati Blog – Leatherati.com/leatherati_issues

Purveyor Of Pleasure, Scarlet Lotus – OfPleasure.com

Race Bannon – Bannon.com

Raven Kaldera – PaganBDSM.org

Reid About Sex, Reid Mihalko – ReidAboutSex.com

Say Nine – Say-Nine.com

SexGenderBody – SexGenderBody.com

Sex Is Magazine – EdenFantasys.com/sexis

Shanna Katz – ShannaKatz.com

The Spanking Writers – SpankingWriters.com

Tony Buff – TonyBuff.com

Violet Blue – TinyNibbles.com

Other Useful Resources

BDSM Library (erotica) – BDSMLibrary.com

Center for Sex and Culture – SexAndCulture.org

The Center for Sex Positive Culture – SexPositiveCulture.org

The Center for Sexual Pleasure and Health – TheCSPH.org

Erotic Heritage Museum – EroticHeritageMuseumLasVegas.com

Jane's Guide Reviews – JanesGuide.com

Judgement Free Heathcare Project – JFHCP.org

Kink Aware Professionals – NCSFreedom.org/resources/kink-
aware-professionals-directory/kap-directory-homepage.html

The Kinsey Institute – KinseyInstitute.org

Literotica (erotica) – Literotica.com

Museum of Sex – MuseumOfSex.com

National Coalition For Sexual Freedom – NCSFreedom.org

San Francisco Sex Information – SFSI.org
Scarlet Teen – ScarletTeen.com
Sexuality.org – Sexuality.org
UrbanDictionary.com
Woodhull Sexual Freedom Alliance – WoodhullAlliance.org

4C: Sources of Kinky Inspiration

The kink community is based on consciously exploring sexual and personal fantasy in a consensual group setting. We each come with our own influences that have inspired us, and will invariably shape the nature of the communities we build. This section explores the inspirations that have titillated us for generations.

These inspirations are often not reflective of communities or reality in most cases, as movies, television and books regularly tantalize by pathologizing kink. However, getting these notions out into the world does let the average person know that they are not alone. It also ignites desires, and creates a common language for sharing our passions with one another.

These examples cover a wide historical span, from a variety of orientations and interests, and are great conversation starters if you have seen or read them. They are also a fantastic tool for dropping hints to see if someone might be kinky, depending on what their reactions are to mentioning some of these points of inspiration.

- **Fiction Books.** The following selection of fiction books are ones that have touched the authors or their varied social networks in the kink communities in a distinct way. Though works of fiction, they have transformed the private and public landscapes of sexual exploration. Though many readers may know many of these books as movies, they are listed here due to being in written form first.

    Anonymous — *The Way of a Man with a Maid* (1908)

    Antoniou, Laura — The *Marketplace* Series (1993-1995), *The Academy* (2000)

    Atwood, Margaret — *The Handmaid's Tale* (1985)

    Brite, Poppy Z. — *Lost Souls* (1992), *Drawing Blood* (1993)

    Bronte, Charlotté — *Jane Eyre* (1847)

    Califia, Pat — *Macho Sluts* (1988), *Doing It For Daddy* (1994), *Bitch Goddess* anthology (editor, 1998), *Boy In The Middle* (2005)

    Carey, Jacqueline — *Kushiel's Legacy* Series (2001-2008)

    de Sade, The Marquis — *120 Days of Sodom* (1785), *Justine* (1787)

    de Saint-Exupéry, Antonie — *Le Petit Prince* (1943)

    Reage, Pauline — *The Story of O* (1954)

Golden, Arthur – *Memoirs of a Geisha* (1997)

Hamilton, Laura K. – *Anita Blake: Vampire Hunter* series (1993-2011)

Heinlein, Robert – *Stranger in a Strange Land* (1961), *Time Enough For Love* (1973)

Herbert, Frank –The *Dune* Series (1965-2009)

James, E.L. – *Fifty Shades of Grey* trilogy (2011-2012)

Kessel, Joseph – *Belle de Jour* (1928)

McNeill, Elizabeth – *Nine and a Half Weeks: A memoir of a love affair* (1978)

Multiple Authors – *One Thousand and One Arabian Nights* (10th Century-19th Century)

Nabokov, Vladimir – *Lolita* (1955)

Nin, Anaïs – *Delta of Venus* (written 1940s, published 1978)

Nitobe, Inazo – *Bushido, the Soul of Japan* (1900)

Norman, John – *Gor* Series (1966-2012)

Preston, John –*Mr. Benson* (1979)

Rice, Anne – the *Sleeping Beauty* trilogy (1983-1985), *Exit to Eden* (1985), *Interview with a Vampire* chronicles (1976-2003)

Shakespeare, William – *Taming of the Shrew* (1591)

Tan, Cecilia – *Telepaths Don't Need Safewords* (1992)

Von Sacher-Masoch, Leopold – *Venus In Furs* (1870)

Williams, Margery (with Nicholson, William) – *Velveteen Rabbit* (1922)

In addition, fiction that has been inspirational to the community can be found in historical periodicals (such as *The Pearl*), historical treatises on real non-consensual chattel slavery (such as *Incidents in the Life of a Slave Girl* by Harriet Jacobs), adult magazines (such as *Penthouse Forum*), plus slash fiction and fanfiction.

- **Movies.** Movies that involve sadomasochistic, fetish, swinger, and erotic themes are far too numerous to mention. The following movies, though, have had an indelible impact on public kink cultures and have effects which are still discernible today:

8mm (1999)

Ai no Corrida (aka *In the Realm of the Senses*), 1976

Barbarella (1968)

Black Snake Moan (2006)

Blue Velvet (1986)

Body of Evidence (1993)

The Book of Revelation (2006)

Bound (1996)

Boxing Helena (1993)

Bram Stoker's Dracula (1992)

Caligula (1979)

Cat People (1992)

The Cell (2000)

A Clockwork Orange (1962)

Closet Land (1991)

Crash (1996)

Crimes of Passion (1984)

Eyes Wide Shut (1999)

Hana to Hebi (aka *Flower and Snake*), 1974

Harold and Maude (1974)

Hellraiser (1987)

The Hunger (1983)

Il Portiere di Notte (aka *The Night Porter*), 1974)

Ilsa, She Wolf of the SS (1975)

Labyrinth (1986)

Legend (1985)

The Notorious Bettie Page (2005)

Original Sin (2001)

Pet (2008)

The Pillow Book (1996)

Preaching To The Perverted (1997)

Pro Urodov I Lyudey (aka Of Freaks and Men) 1998

Pulp Fiction (1994)

The Rocky Horror Picture Show (1975)

The Secretary (2002)

Seksmisja (aka Sexmission, 1984)

Seven (1995)

Shortbus (2006)

Star Wars: Episode VI – Return of the Jedi (1983)
Ultimo Tango a Parigi (aka *Last Tango in Paris*), 1972
Vamp (1986)
Videodrome (1983)
Wolfen (1981)

In addition, many genres of movies explore kink, BDSM, swinger and alternative sexuality themes. Western, swashbuckler and spy films (especially the James Bond franchise) show wardrobe, bondage and SM themes that have sparked the first kink fantasies for many. Various science fiction films have given permission to explore sexual and gender diversity through the permission of it being "alien," while vampire, werewolf and other fantastical films show the appetites of the "other" or "monster." Finally we have the wide range of adult and pornographic films that have been released in the past 100 years, which have often held kink themes.

- ## Television
  Alias (2001-2006)
  The Avengers (1961-1969)
  Batman original (1966-1968)
  Big Love (2006-2011)
  Buffy The Vampire Slayer (1997-2003)
  CSI (2000-)
  Dexter (2006-)
  I Dream of Jeannie (1965-1970)
  Firefly (2002-2003)
  Law & Order (1990-)
  Looney Tunes (1936-)
  National Geographic: Taboo (2002-2010)
  The New Adventures of Wonder Woman (1975-1979)
  The Prisoner (1967-1968)
  Star Trek franchise (1966-)
  True Blood (2008-)
  Xena: Warrior Princess (1995-2001)

- ## Other Media
  The following media have been pioneers of kinky erotica, roots of inspiration, or are kink-inspired artists who have captured the imagination both inside and outside the kink community.

Artists: Annie Sprinkle, Bishop, Bizarre Magazine, Bunny Yaeger, Fakir Musafar, Charles Gatewood, House of Gord, Irving Klaw, John Willie, Michael Manning, R. Crumb, Randall Housk, Robert Mapplethorpe, Steve Diet Goedde, Tom of Finland

Comics: *Batman, From Hell, Heavy Metal, Superman, Wonder Woman*

Hentai/Adult Comics: *Bondage Faeries, Cool Devices, La Blue Girl, Omaha the Cat Dancer, Tramps Like Us, Xxxenophile*

Magazines: *National Geographic, Penthouse: Variations, Screw*

Music Industry: Britney Spears, Eurythmics, Frankie Goes to Hollywood, Lady Gaga, Leonard Cohen, Lucille Bogan, Ma Rainey, Madonna, Prince, Rihanna, Velvet Underground, The Wet Spots

4D: Out To Your Doctor?: Talking To Health Care Professionals by Barak, RN

So there you are, in the semi-private exam room at your doctor's office. The nurse has taken your vitals, asked some general questions, and, before leaving the room, directed you to get into a gown. You have removed your clothing and have fitted the stylish blue plaid garment as well as possible. The rough material slides over your front, and you get a sore twinge from those nipple clamps you were wearing last night.

The door opens, and as the doctor walks in you blanch, recalling the purple mosaic of bruises that were reflected in the mirror this morning. What do you say? Do you tell the truth? How do you handle it? What is the doctor going to think? Will they turn you in? Will they throw you out?

I have been in health care, as a paramedic and a Registered Nurse (RN), for more than twenty years. I have worked in home health, in doctors' offices, in psychiatric centers, on hospital floors, and, for the past decade, at several busy emergency rooms. Over the course of my career, I have seen almost everything. Really.

So what do you say when you have those beautiful marks all over your back? I encourage honesty. If you are hurt, or there is something wrong, be frank and honest about it; don't try to make something up that "might" fit what happened.

Let's say you had a shoulder injury during a rope scene. There are certain things you might leave out, but make sure you don't leave anything out that contributed to the injury. For instance, while kinksters may love the terms "tied up and fucked," "BDSM," "rape scene," etc., there's no reason to try and play "Shock the Doc." In situations like this, discretion is the better part of valor. Take time and amend possible inflammatory terms. Health Care Providers (HCPs) are usually fine with the terms "kinky sex," "I like it a little rough," and "creative sexual expression."

Depending on what you were actually doing, you may not have to get into that discussion at all. For instance, if you were doing suspension bondage, you might just let them know you were "experimenting with rope," and "were being held off the ground by rope around your arm, shoulder, etc..." when you felt XYZ... or however it happened. Meaning, you don't have to get into *why* you were suspended, other than you were playing around with rope.

You should always be honest about *how* it happened, but there is really no reason to get into the *why* most of the time. Just know that even if you are completely honest, you may get a visit from the friendly facility social worker. They may verify that everything is on the up and up, that your participation is consensual, and there is no abuse going on. However, if the HCP feels as though you are hiding something, deliberately baiting them, or trying to get a reaction, it may cause them take further steps, and look much more closely at you and your explanations. If you set off their red flags, there is a good chance your adventure will turn into much more of an inquiry – one that could involve people with different-looking uniforms and badges.

Speaking of which: if you are worried about being turned in, or your information being shared, let me introduce you to something called the Health Insurance Portability and Accountability Act (HIPAA) of 1996. If you read through this act, you will find that a doctor, nurse or other HCP can only release records or information that is specific to you, or could identify you in any way, if it pertains directly to your care or billing. The HIPAA laws prevent HCPs from disclosing information, even to your immediate family. If this info in shared in any other way, that is illegal and prosecutable, a very serious infraction in the medical field.

This law essentially covers doctor/patient confidentiality rules; however, you may want to be aware of a couple of loopholes. If a doctor or other HCP feels that the patient is in some form of danger – if they think you are being threatened, abused, harmed, etc. – they are mandated reporters, who must legally disclose pertinent information to law enforcement investigators. Remember, this is for your protection.

If the reason you are at the doctor has nothing to do with the bruises on your ass and thighs, just smile knowingly and say, "it's consensual, I like it rough." Then bring them back to the subject at hand, like your sore throat and cough. If they bring you back to it, just be factual and direct. Take a "nothing to see here" attitude.

If you are with your partner, make sure both of you are on the same page, and don't become resentful if the practitioners separate you. They just want to make sure this is not domestic violence. So smile a lot, and make sure you both have the exact same story. One of the best approaches is the one where you shyly admit you like being tied up, and your partner was trying to accommodate you.

Should you come out to your doctor? In the end, that's up to you. However, we HCPs have seen a lot and are very adept at understanding the way the human body looks, acts, and works. We are also aware of the mechanics of damage, trauma and wounds. I can assure you that handprints don't look like something accidental. Whip, flogger and cane marks also appear quite deliberate. Your best bet is to be honest and straightforward.

If you can't or won't come out to your HCP? Then either make sure you don't have marks, don't get injured, or just find another HCP you *are* willing to share with. It's your health and your choice.

Sincerely,

Barak, RN

© Barak 2011

4E: Understanding STDs and STIs: Sexual Expression and Infection Control
By Scotty Thomson

Humans take risks: driving in cars, flying in airplanes, sharing our secret desires with new partners. Many risks we accept, others we ignore. As we explore the depth and breadth of sexual expression, sexually transmitted infections are nearly impossible to ignore.

Half of all sexually active people will contract an STI by the time they are 25.[1] As we learn new ways to express our sexuality, and meet new, exciting folks with whom we want to express ourselves, we will be well served to develop skills and strategies for keeping ourselves healthy. The first step is to know what's out there and where it hides.

Along your adventurous path you may come across blood, semen, mucosal membrane/vaginal secretions and ejaculate, breast milk, saliva, urine and feces – sometimes on their own, sometimes in various combinations. These are the bodily fluids that can carry and spread infection and disease.

Blood: Human Immunodeficiency Virus (HIV), Hepatitis A, B and C Virus

Semen: HIV, Hepatitis B, Chlamydia, Gonorrhea

Mucous Membrane/Vaginal Secretions: HIV, Hepatitis B, Chlamydia, Gonorrhea, NonGonococcal Urethritis/NGU, Syphilis, Trichomoniasis

Saliva: May contain blood or mucous membrane secretions

Urine: Pissing on unbroken skin carries no known risk. Internal watersports carry a theoretical risk of HBV transmission, though as of publication date, there have never been documented cases of HBV transmission through urine.

Feces: Hepatitis A and E, E.coli, Influenza, Polio – feces may contain blood, or semen after unprotected anal sex

You will also encounter **Skin**, and lots of it. Skin-to-skin contact with an infected partner can transmit the following: Herpes Simplex Virus Types 1 and 2, Human Papillomavirus – HPV, Molluscum Contagiosum, Scabies, Pubic Lice.

Particularly at big events, you will also encounter the most common STI: Rhinovirus – the common cold.

---

1   Alan Guttmacher Institute. (1994). *Sex and America's Teenagers.* New York: Alan Guttmacher Institute.

This is a lot to remember. For many folks it is easier to just remember to avoid direct contact with blood, cum, cunt juice, piss, shit, urethral openings, pussies, and assholes. Easier still is to just focus on what barriers you can use to block direct contact. The precautions available vary based on the types of contact you are having:

Fisting and fucking: Use a barrier: latex or nitrile gloves for fisting, latex or polyisoprene condoms, or a female/bottom condom for fucking. Avoid friction that can cause bleeding by using plenty of lube – non-oil-based lube is needed for latex, and non-petroleum-based for vaginas.

Rimming: Licking the asshole can spread scat, STIs and STDs, so if you do it, use some plastic wrap, a dental dam, a condom or a glove cut in half.

Oral sex: Many studies have proven the risk of transmitting STIs through oral sex. Herpes, Gonorrhea and Syphilis can all be easily transmitted through oral. We know that HIV, Hepatitis B, HPV and Chlamydia can be transmitted orally as well. So use condoms, dental dams, plastic wrap or cut a glove open.

Insertion: If it – finger, dildo, nightstick – is going in a hole (such as a mouth, ass, or cunt), put a condom or a glove on it.

Before you use any furniture for play, clean it with an EPA-approved disinfectant, checking to be sure you know how long the disinfectant has to remain on the surface to be effective – some take as long as two minutes.

This all sounds pretty simple, and I bet this isn't the first time you have heard about STIs and condoms. Well, it *is* simple, but it isn't easy. It can be made easy, though, if you practice.

Chances are, you've practiced many different skills that you take with you into the play space. You may have even asked someone to teach you a thing or two, and tried many different tools to find the ones that you like. Take this same approach with condoms and other barriers.

Bring condoms into the light of day. Take them out of the package and unroll one. There are many different shapes, sizes and fits, thicknesses and textures. Experiment. Try masturbating with a condom on. See how the texture of gloves changes the way your fingers feel on your clit, or how you can use the condom to create extra friction on the head of your cock. Now, try it with a glove and some more lube. Nitrile gloves can be great sensation toys. Try making a dental dam out of a glove. Practice. Ask a friend or partner to practice with you. Then take the next step.

Set up a scene that will focus on experimentation with barriers. Try different gloves for sensation or rough body play. Spanking with gloves is a lot of fun. How can you incorporate condoms into humiliation play? Make your safer sex tools a part of your scene and a part of your play. Bring an assortment of condoms and share what you learned about them in a medical scene.

Speaking of medical play: GET TESTED. Many folks think that an annual exam or routine physical will include STI testing. Well, it may not, even if your provider knows you are sexually active. Many health care providers do not do STI testing unless you ask. And even if you do ask to be tested for everything, you may end up with just getting screened for Gonorrhea and Chlamydia. Look up the CDC recommendations for testing and go to your appointment prepared with a list of the tests you want done. Keep in mind that many people may think that they have had a complete STI screening and have no idea that STI testing is not typically included in yearly exams.

Dedicated exclusivity is another very simple way to control infections. Fluid bonding – exchanging fluids with only one partner after complete STI testing and satisfying all window periods – is a perfectly viable strategy. Keep in mind that it is, however, a strategy that relies on trust and open, honest communication, and should not be entered into lightly.

Dedicated tools are another option. Bring your own insertables and don't share. If you are flogging or whipping to blood, dedicate the tools to that partner or use replaceable crackers on your singletails. Either way, limiting a tool's or your own exposure to only one person's bodily fluids greatly reduces your risks and helps to control infection.

Now, about this Rhinovirus: the most effective thing you can do to help prevent the spread of infection is to *wash your hands*. Wash before and after every scene. And if you feel like you have a cold or the flu, stay home and take care of yourself. There will be other dates and other parties. We have a responsibility to ourselves and our community to stay healthy. So please, don't bring your Rhinovirus and Influenza into the dungeon.

There is nothing fun about sexually transmitted infections. At the very least, you will be spending time at the doctor's office and having difficult conversations with partners rather than having fun. It does not take much to protect yourself. Find barriers you like and use them. Get a cigarette case and turn it into your safer sex kit. Be creative. With a little planning and a little practice you can spend more time in the play space, and less time at the clinic.

General STI information from American Social Health Association and Center for Disease Control websites: www.ashastd.org, www.cdc.gov/std/. CDC testing guidelines as listed on ASHA page: www.ashastd.org/std-sti/get-tested/testing-recommendations.html.

4F: Sex, Gender, Identity, Orientation and Behavior
By Aiden Fyre and Lee Harrington

More complex than "is it a boy or a girl," the concepts of identity and behavior within sex, gender, and orientation are deeply entrenched in social and cultural norms. Although these genders are often viewed as a binary, they actually exist along a continuum with far more potential for flexibility than media and cultural messages would have us believe. In order to delve into gender and sexuality, we must first examine terminology.

Sex refers to the biological characteristics that define humans as female or male. Assigned at birth, *sex* is determined by chromosomes (XX or XY), dominant hormones (estrogen/progesterone or testosterone), as well as internal and external genitalia (vulva, vagina, and clitoris, or penis and testicles).

However, even in nature, nothing is absolute. The umbrella term *intersex* refers to a spectrum of conditions involving anomalies of the sex chromosomes, gonads, reproductive ducts, and/or genitalia. Intersex persons have anatomy or physiology, often present at birth, that differs from the societal expectations of male and female. Additionally, sex can be altered medically with hormones, or surgically with reconstruction (SRS, or Sex Reassignment Surgery).

Unlike sex that can be objectively measured or observed, *gender* is a subjective set of social, psychological, and emotional traits that classify an individual as feminine, masculine, or androgynous. *Gender* dictates the economic, social, and cultural attributes and opportunities associated with being female or male, as well as the societal expectations for gender expression and role. Despite many misconceptions, gender expression, roles, and societal expectations are *not* universal; most people are a blend of stereotypically masculine and feminine traits.

- **Gender attribution** or **assumed gender** is the gender and corresponding pronoun assigned to a person based on gender expression; however, a person's outwardly perceived *gender identity* may differ from their internal self-definition. A person may identify as man or woman, a combination of the two, neither of the two, butch, femme, third-gender, two-spirit, transgender, genderqueer, or a multitude of other possibilities.

  Singular pronouns in English are gendered, i.e. He/His/Him and She/Hers/Her; therefore, people identifying outside of the binary of man and woman may use gender-neutral pronouns such as Ze/Hir, They/Them/Theirs, and Yo.

- **Sexual orientation** refers to the inner feeling of who a person is attracted or "oriented" to sexually, erotically, and emotionally. A person's *sexual identity* refers to a person's internal sexual orientation identity, which may include labels such as straight, gay, lesbian, bisexual, bicurious, queer, questioning, asexual, omnisexual, pansexual, and more. While *sexual identity* is how people define themselves, *sexual behavior* refers to what a person actually does, e.g. MSM – men who have sex with men. While sexual orientation, identity, and behavior often correspond, there are some for whom the labels are not fully accurate, such as men on the "down low" who secretly have sex with men while publicly maintaining a straight identity. Regardless of how a person self-identifies, gender identity and sexual orientation are separate concepts; thus, a person who transitions from female-to-male or male-to-female may or may not identify as heterosexual.

- Many individuals have sex, gender, gender expression, and assumed gender which are in congruence with societal expectations; these individuals are sometimes referred to as **cisgendered**. However, some **transgender** individuals choose to transition socially, legally, medically, and/or surgically to have their identity and bodies present a more congruent expression, while still others choose to "play" with gender by trying on different expressions and manifesting a variety of gender expressions. Gender expression and assumed gender are unreliable indicators of a person's physical body and how they choose to engage with it.

Individuals may or may not choose to disclose their sexual journey and/or body experience with others unless it is pertinent to their relationship. The basic rules of etiquette apply to all people – although it is okay to respectfully ask a person how they identity and what their preferred pronoun is, it is rude to ask a person what their genitals look like.

- **Kink** may also be an orientation, identity, or behavior in and of itself. Thus, someone may identify as vanilla (identity), yet still engage in bondage, flogging, and/or cross-dressing (behavior). Some individuals for whom kink is an orientation may choose someone kinky of a different gender than they might otherwise be attracted to over someone of their preferred gender who is not kinky (e.g., a gay leatherman choosing to playing with a lesbian leatherwoman rather than a vanilla gay man).

Each individual we encounter has lived their own life journey and thus may use a wide variety of terminology to express their experience. One person may use the same word to explain their orientation that another may use to express their identity. Behaviors, orientations, identities, and expressions often shift over the course of a lifetime. While some may stumble on these changes by happenstance, others deliberately try out different behaviors, orientations, identities, and/or expressions for an evening, a week, or a year, and some choose fluidity as a way of life. These shifts are indicative of an individual's desires and personal journey along the natural continuum of the human sexual experience.

4G: Relationships Beyond Labels: Some Terminology You May Encounter, and What It May (Or May Not) Mean
By Dossie Easton and Janet W. Hardy

As you explore the world of public sexual adventuring – parties, conferences, munches, gatherings, rituals, potlucks and all the rest of it – you may be doing some cruising or flirting. Thus, it behooves you to be aware of what kinds of agreements the people you're coming on to may have made about their existing relationships, and how those agreements may affect what you'd like to do with those people.

But before we start defining terms, let's start with a big caveat. A lot of the discourse in the world of alternative relationships these days seems to have to do with describing what you *are:* you're polyamorous, or you're in an open relationship, or you're an ethical slut (thank you), or you're a swinger. In the BDSM world, the analogous conversation has to do with whether you're a top or a dominant or a master or a mistress, a bottom or a submissive or a slave. In the greater world, people say they're gay or straight or bi. The definitions of all these terms vary from year to year and from community to community. Even more important, we find this sort of conversation is pretty limiting in the greater world of what people actually feel like doing at any particular time.

Furthermore, relying solely on labels can lead to grave misunderstandings. If you have heard, for instance, that a "true" slave never says no, and a "true" master never gets fucked, you may disappoint or even enrage a lot of potentially fabulous playmates. One-word labels don't really work – rather, we advocate that you insist on being truly yourself and thus free to follow your desires wherever (within the limits of safety and consent) they may lead you.

So we recommend talking about what you like to *do:* "My current relationship(s) are shaped like X, and have Y agreements, and I'm looking for someone with whom to do Z" seems to us to be a far more descriptive and less restrictive jumping-off point. We find that focusing on verbs rather than nouns is a great deal more flexible and less open to misinterpretation, and has the added advantage of not leaving you stuck with an identity that might not correspond what you're in the mood for right now, with that gorgeous creature who's looking at you and waiting for you to propose something that will make you both very happy tonight.

And even if that gorgeous creature has not read this Appendix and insists on talking about what he or she is ("I'm a polyfidelitous switchable omnisexual female-identified ponyboy with fetishes for Tootsie Pops and ballerina flats; and you?"), we strongly suggest that your next question should be the most useful query that any cruiser can use: "Can you tell me more about what that means to you?" Because "polyfidelitous," just to pick the first of that amazing word salad of identities, may mean that your intended may only have one particular kind of sex, say penis-vagina intercourse, with their spousal circle, or it may mean that they don't even kiss anyone with whom they do not share a household and a wedding ring.

In fact, the moral to this entire article is: You Gotta Ask. Let us say it again for emphasis: You Gotta Ask.

Given those parameters, here are some of the ways that you may hear others describing their relationships and agreements.

- **Celibacy** may mean that the individual is avoiding romantic commitments, or that they are not having sex (which may include some but not all of what you think of as "sex"), or even that they don't masturbate. It may or may not mean that they are still doing non-genital BDSM.

- **Monogamy** can mean that the couple keeps some kinds of sex for one another but engages in other kinds outside their relationship, or it may mean that all forms of sexual expression can occur only between the two primary partners. You may encounter folks with agreements that include sexual monogamy but BDSM polyamory, in which case you would be well advised to spend some time finding out what this particular couple has negotiated as "sex." (Is cock and ball torture or cunt torture sex? How about playing with insertable toys? Welts on the behind? Etc., etc.)

- **Polyamory** can mean almost any relationship style besides strictest monogamy (and some relationships that look monogamous to you may feel polyamorous to the people in them, or vice versa). Some people use "polyamory" to talk about long-term multipartner relationships, but many people use it in other ways too. It is absolutely possible to be single and polyamorous; all that means is that you're committed to honestly disclosing your nonmonogamous state to all your partners and potential partners.

- **Polyfidelity** is polyamory-plus – an agreement in which some or all forms of sexual expression are restricted to a closed circle of ongoing partners, like monogamy but with more than two people.

- **Fluid-bonding** is a safer-sex strategy in which two (or, sometimes, more) lovers, who have been tested and are aware of whatever STDs they may or may not be carrying, decide to have unprotected sex only with each other, and to use barrier protection with any outside partners. It is not a measure of intimacy or affection – if you get fluid-bonded with twelve people whom you really, really love, and they are fluid bonded to twelve more people, the purpose, which is to protect your own and your partners' health while making room for some intimate genital contact, will be defeated.

- **Open relationships** often refer to a couple whose agreements allow one or both of them to connect romantically and/or sexually with others – maybe together as a team, or maybe separately.

- **Swinging** refers to folks who connect with other people recreationally, without the expectation of an ongoing romantic or domestic connection. Such liaisons may take place at parties given for the purpose, or privately, through personal ads and other such connectors. Many but not all swing environments are unwelcoming to gay or bisexual men, and a few feel the same way about gay or bisexual women. Transgendered people may be welcome, or may be admitted only on a "don't ask, don't tell" basis.

- **Pansexual** and **omnisexual** refer to an environment or party space in which all genders and orientations are welcome: same-sex, opposite-sex, and all variations in between.

- Folks in a **lifestyle D/S relationship** may or may not have agreements about the submissive partner needing to get the dominant partner's permission before engaging with a new person. It's prudent to assume that someone wearing a collar or other symbol of ownership will need to seek such permission before engaging with you – but, as always, You Gotta Ask.

One final piece of advice. Knowing your own desires and agreements, and being able to articulate them, is your single most important BDSM skill.

You may be able to split a rose petal with your singletail, but in terms of your own happiness, the happiness of your partners, and the success of the events you attend, self-knowledge and the willingness to share your truth generously are the best qualities you can possibly offer.

Have fun and play safe!

4H: SM vs. Abuse
by Jay Wiseman

excerpted from SM 101: A Realistic Introduction

SM play differs from abuse in many of the same ways that a judo match differs from a mugging. Consider the differences:

1. SM play is always consensual.[2] Abuse is not.

2. SM players plan their activities to minimize the risks to one another's physical and emotional well-being. Abusers do not.

3. SM play is negotiated and agreed to ahead of time. Abuse is not.

4. SM play can enhance the relationship between the players. Abuse cannot.

5. SM play can be done in the presence of supportive others — even at parties given for this purpose. Abuse needs isolation and secrecy.

6. SM play has responsible, agreed-upon rules. Abuse lacks such rules.

7. SM play may be requested, and even eagerly desired, by the submissive. Nobody overtly asks for abuse — although self-destructive people may sometimes attempt to provoke it.

8. SM is done for the consensual erotic pleasure and/or personal growth of both or all participants. Abuse is not.

9. SM play can be stopped in an instant, at any time, and for any reason when the submissive uses a safeword. The victim cannot stop their abuser in that way.

10. In SM play, the dominant always keeps their emotions under control. An abuser's emotions are out of control.

11. After SM play, the submissive often feels grateful toward the dominant. A victim never feels grateful for abuse.

For additional help contact the National Domestic Violence Hotline at (800) 799-SAFE (799-7233).

---

2   I use the consent definition formulated by therapist and SM educator Dossie Easton: "An active collaboration for the benefit, well-being, and pleasure of all persons concerned."

41: Is it a Cult?: The Advanced Bonewits' Cult Danger Evaluation Frame (version 2.6)

Copyright © 1979, 2008 c.e., Isaac Bonewits
Reproduced with the permission of Phaedre Bonewits

Introduction. In 1979 Isaac Bonewits constructed an evaluation tool for examining the differences between cults, and groups that happened to have an unusual minority belief system that many found "shocking" in their time. The "ABCDEF" (because evaluating these groups should be elementary), provides a useful tool for prospective members and current members of a given group, but also for the friends and loved ones of members and prospective members. In cult situations it is important to have a relatively simple way to evaluate how dangerous or harmless a given group is liable to be, without either subjecting ourselves to its "power" or judging it solely on theological or ideological grounds.

Though the ABCDEF was designed to examine spiritual, sacred and religious groups, each of the concepts apply within kink, sexual, and sensual groups as well. Instead of offering the secrets of divine wisdom, perhaps a group claims to have ancient sexual secrets that are only available to initiates, for example. It may help individuals in our community to determine just how coercive or dangerous a given group is liable to be, in comparison with other groups, to the physical and mental health of its members and of other people subject to its influence. This is not to infer that BDSM groups are cults in any way, shape or form. However, the tool provides a useful mirror into the world of kink and can be translated into the world of sexuality accordingly.

As a general rule, the higher the numerical total from a given group, the more carefully you should consider how appropriate it might be to be involved with such a group. Though it is obvious that many of the scales in the frame are subjective, it is still possible to make practical judgments using it, at least of the "is this group more dubious than that one?" sort. This requires that numbers are assigned based on actual behaviors of a group, rather than the sexy (or banal) propaganda a kink group may have to lure in potential members. As this can be difficult to do without becoming involved to some degree, consider this an awareness tool as you explore a specific group.

In parts of the world of kink, the following tool is a list of things to be sought out, for example by parts of the master/slave or sacred sexuality populations. If you are part of a population that prizes many of these eighteen traits, do not be surprised if others in the world at large consider you to be part of a cult or potentially harmful influence. At the end of the day, though, we each must make our own choices about what is healthy for our lives and lifestyles.

For further information and translations in other languages, visit www.neopagan.net/ABCDEF.html.

Factors: 1 2 3 4 5 6 7 8 9 10
Low ⟵―――――――――――――――――――⟶ High

- **Internal Control:** Level of internal political and social power exercised by leader(s) over members; lack of clearly defined organizational rights for members.

- **External Control:** Level of external political and social influence desired or obtained; emphasis on directing members' external political and social behavior.

- **Wisdom/Knowledge:** Claimed by leader(s); amount of infallibility declared or implied about decisions or doctrinal/scriptural interpretations; number and degree of unverified and/or unverifiable credentials claimed.

- **Wisdom/Knowledge Credited to Leader(s) By Members:** Level of trust in decisions or doctrinal/scriptural interpretations made by leader(s); amount of hostility by members towards internal or external critics and/or towards verification efforts.

- **Dogma:** Rigidity of reality concepts taught; amount of doctrinal inflexibility or "fundamentalism;" hostility towards relativism and situationalism.

- **Recruiting:** Emphasis put on attracting new members; amount of proselytizing; requirement for all members to bring in new ones.

- **Front Groups:** Number of subsidiary groups using different names from that of main group, especially when connections are hidden.

- **Wealth:** Amount of money and/or property desired or obtained by group; emphasis on members' donations; economic lifestyle of leader(s) compared to ordinary members.

- **Sexual Manipulation of Members** by leader(s) of groups; amount of control exercised over sexuality of members in terms of sexual orientation, behavior, and/or choice of partners.

- **Sexual Favoritism:** Advancement or preferential treatment dependent upon sexual activity with the leader(s).

- **Censorship:** Level of control over members' access to outside opinions on group, its doctrines or leader(s).

- **Isolation:** Level of effort to keep members from communicating with non-members, including family, friends and lovers.

- **Dropout Control:** Intensity of efforts directed at preventing or returning dropouts to the fold.

- **Violence:** Level of approval by leader(s) or group members when violence is used or encouraged, either against other group members or against the world at large.

- **Paranoia:** Level of fear concerning real or imagined enemies; exaggeration of perceived power of opponents; prevalence of conspiracy theories.

- **Grimness:** Level of disapproval concerning jokes about the group, its doctrines or its leader(s).

- **Surrender of Will:** Level of emphasis on members not having to be responsible for personal decisions; degree of individual disempowerment created by the group, its doctrines or its leader(s).

- **Hypocrisy:** Level of approval for actions which the group officially considers immoral or unethical, when done by or for the group, its doctrines or leader(s); willingness to violate the group's declared principles for political, psychological, social, economic, military, or other gain.

Copyright © 1979, 2008 c.e., Isaac Bonewits

4J: Pocket Reference to Dealing With Law Enforcement

Provided by the National Coalition for Sexual Freedom Law Enforcement Outreach Program, www.ncsfreedom.org

- ### In dealing with officers ...

  DO stay calm.

  DO be respectful, polite and courteous.

  DO use your common sense.

  DON'T have a "bad attitude."

- ### Statements and Communication ...

  You have the right not to make statements.

  You have the right not to incriminate yourself.

  Be honest in whatever you decide to say.

  Use simple language – clear and easy to understand.

- ### Entry to your property ...

  You do not have to allow a "consent search" or a "voluntary entry."

  Attempt to handle it outside/at the door.

  If the officer demands to enter, voice your objection and stand aside.

- ### Miscellaneous ...

  Volunteer for your partner to talk to the police.

  Transport toys in a secure location and in trunk of the vehicle. Do not consent to a search.

  Keep in mind those things that demonstrate that consensual SM is different from abuse.

  If you are arrested, do NOT make any statements, and ask for an attorney.

Thanks/Acknowledgments

THIS IS THE BOOK we wished we had when we began our own forays from private kinky sex to public playful and profound perversion.

It ate up our life for a year. Well before that, the seed had been planted and germinated for quite some time. LqqkOut was around to brainstorm with Lee a few years back on the idea, and Lee blames his friends for saying that yes, it would be a good idea. Mollena joined the project with brilliant ideas all her own... and here we are.

Mad props to the kink communities who invited us out to create, educate, celebrate and fornicate with them, from Sydney to San Francisco, Baltimore to Berlin, Göthenburg to Pittsburgh, Boston to Austin, London to Long Island, Christchurch to Columbus, Maui to Milwaukee... you opened up your pervy playgrounds, mini munches, boisterous ballrooms, frenetic fetish balls, beautiful bathhouses, fun floor parties, hidden haunts, kinky cafes, delightful dojos, kinky campgrounds and delicious, down-n-dingy dungeons to this pair of proud perverts, and we can't thank you enough. It's been a wild ride thus far, and we are so proud to consider this community our home.

This book would not be what is without the talented kd diamond. Her artwork brought this project to life with a sense of humor, and we cannot thank her enough for putting up with our "art direction." kd, you are a delight.

To flesh out the book, we decided to call on the insight and skills of an amazing team of appendix contributors. Aiden Fyre, Barak RN, Dossie Easton, Janet Hardy, Jay Wiseman, Leigha Fleming (NCSFreedom.Org) and Scotty Thomson all wrote insightful words on their respective fields, for which we are grateful. Deepest gratitude to our copy editor, Lillian Pike, for her assistance. Special thanks go out to Phaedra Bonewits, who generously gave us permission to use the work of Isaac Bonewits. Isaac, you are missed.

Along the way we got feedback from a bundle of folks, a bunch of readers, and accepted the critique of some amazing allies and associates. Your guidance has helped make this project what it is. Thank you.

We of course have to send a big shout-out to Janet Hardy and Aaron Silverman at Greenery Press! When sent a book concept and sample writing, they believed in the dream... and even gave us some flexibility to follow that dream to its conclusion. Thank you so much for guiding us through our first collaborative book project, and giving us a firm hand when we needed it in turn.

From Lee:

To my partner in passion and adventure, Aiden, thank you for putting up with long and crazy hours, time away, and for all of your loving. You are a blessing for all that you are.

To my parents, for believing I should follow my dreams, no matter where they end up taking me.

To my tribe(s) at large — hugs for taking the time to share your stories, filling out surveys, replying to tweets, making me baked goods, sending me support texts, cuddling at conferences, and commenting in my journals throughout the process, even before the book was a book project. I cherish the whole lot of you.

From Mollena:

To Mom, for squeezing me out in the summer of '69 and subsequently supporting this crazy, kinky kid.

To my Dad, for giving me the gift of travel in my youth and insatiable curiosity about everything.

Thank you to my many circles of friends: theater people, perverts, leatherfolk, storytellers, geeks & nerds, and artists across all media. You keep me alive & sober. Special props to Laura Antoniou & Karen Taylor, the most amazing mal'akh a Negress could possibly want.

To my Demon, Bubbles and my Higher Power... Jai Ganesha! Thank you for pushing me to the edge and bringing me back. Over and over again.

And of course this book goes out to all of you who taught us that playing well with others is so, very, worth it.

With love, so much love...

Your Sexual Sherpas,

Lee Harrington and Mollena Williams
New York City 2012

Lee Harrington is an internationally known spiritual and erotic educator, gender explorer, eclectic artist and award-winning author and editor on human sexuality and sacred experience. He has been an academic and an adult film performer, is a kink/bondage expert, and has been blogging about sex and spirituality since 1998. Read more about Lee at **passionandsoul.com.**

Mollena (Mo) Williams is a native New Yorker, performer, actor, award-winning writer and BDSM educator. She is International Ms. Leather 2010 and Ms. SF Leather 2009. Consciously kinky since 1993 and active in leather and BDSM since 1996, she travels extensively, speaking on topics including kink, BDSM, power exchange relationships and negotiating it all safely. Read more about Mollena at The Perverted Negress, **Mollena.com.**

GENERAL SEXUALITY

DIY Porn Handbook: A How-To Guide to Documenting Our Own Sexual Revolution
Madison Young $16.95

The Explorer's Guide to Planet Orgasm: for every body
Annie Sprinkle with Beth Stephens $13.95

A Hand in the Bush: The Fine Art of Vaginal Fisting
Deborah Addington $13.95

The Jealousy Workbook: Exercises and Insights for Managing Open Relationships
Kathy Labriola $19.95

Love In Abundance: A Counselor's Advice on Open Relationships
Kathy Labriola $15.95

Miss Vera's Cross-Gender Fun for All
Veronica Vera $14.95

Tricks... To Please a Man
Tricks... To Please a Woman
Jay Wiseman . . . . $13.95 ea.

When Someone You Love Is Kinky
Dossie Easton & Catherine A. Liszt . . . $15.95

BDSM/KINK

The Artisan's Book of Fetishcraft: Patterns and Instructions for Creating Professional Fetishwear, Restraints & Equipment
John Huxley $27.95

Conquer Me: girl-to-girl wisdom about fulfilling your submissive desires
Kacie Cunningham $13.95

Jay Wiseman's Erotic Bondage Handbook
Jay Wiseman $16.95

Miss Vera's Cross Gender Fun for All
Dr. Veronica Vera $14.95

Family Jewels: A Guide to Male Genital Play and Torment
Hardy Haberman $12.95

Flogging
Joseph Bean $11.95

The Human Pony: A Guide for Owners, Trainers and Admirers
Rebecca Wilcox $27.95

Intimate Invasions: The Ins and Outs of Erotic Enema Play
M.R. Strict $13.95

The Mistress Manual: The Good Girl's Guide to Female Dominance
Mistress Lorelei Powers $16.95

The (New and Improved) Loving Dominant
John Warren $16.95

The New Bottoming Book
The New Topping Book
Dossie Easton & Janet W. Hardy . . . $14.95 ea.

Play Piercing
Deborah Addington $13.95

Radical Ecstasy: SM Journeys to Transcendence
Dossie Easton & Janet W. Hardy $16.95

The Seductive Art of Japanese Bondage
Midori, photographs by Craig Morey . . $27.95

The Sexually Dominant Woman: A Workbook for Nervous Beginners
Lady Green $11.95

SM 101: A Realistic Introduction
Jay Wiseman $24.95

Spanking for Lovers
Janet W. Hardy $15.95

TOYBAG GUIDES:
A Workshop In A Book $9.95 each

Age Play, by Lee "Bridgett" Harrington

Basic Rope Bondage, by Jay Wiseman

Chastity Play, by Miss Simone

Clips and Clamps, by Jack Rinella

Dungeon Emergencies & Supplies, by Jay Wiseman

Hot Wax and Temperature Play, by Spectrum

Playing With Taboo, by Mollena Williams

Greenery Press books are available from your favorite on-line or brick-and-mortar bookstore or erotic boutique. If you are having trouble locating the book you want, please contact us at 541-683-0961. These and other Greenery Press books are also available in ebook format from all major ebook retailers.